This *Penguin Brigade Training Log* belongs to:

Name: _____

Address: _____

Email: _____

Phone: _____

LOG PERIOD   START: _____   END: _____

THE PENGUIN BRIGADE

TRAINING LOG

SECOND EDITION

John "The Penguin" Bingham

and

Coach Jenny Hadfield, M.A., C.P.T.

BREAKAWAY BOOKS
HALCOTTSVILLE, NY
2003

ISBN: 1-891369-38-5
Library of Congress Control Number: 20031002251

Published by:
Breakaway Books
P.O. Box 24
Halcottsville, NY 12438
www.breakawaybooks.com

Visit the Penguin's website:
www.johnbingham.com

Visit Jenny Hadfield's sites:
wwwjennyhadfield.com
and
www.ChicagoEnduranceSports.com

INTRODUCTION

Since its humble beginning of eighteen people training to run the 1996 Marine Corps Marathon to its current incalculable numbers, The Penguin Brigade has remained a curious and powerful force in what has now been clearly defined as a Second Running Boom. With their trademark Pink Hats—a tradition started by Marine Colonel Ken Meyers—and their devotion to each other (the Brigade motto is "Penguins don't leave Penguins on the course") The Penguin Brigade has touched the hearts and minds of an entire generation of athletes.

The Penguin Brigade Training Log Second Edition holds true to the traditions of the past while making way for the traditions of the future. Unlike many log books on the shelves, this one is written by you, for you, and is ultimately your own book about you. With each entry you are writing your own athletic biography.

The log helps you track your progress, exercise sessions and food choices. It is a comprehensive tool that guides you in establishing realistic goals, planning and tracking your training and celebrating your progress. Week by week, the log will motivate you to get in your workouts, encourage smart training and guide you to make healthier food choices.

The Penguin Brigade Training Log also includes a special place to **record your race experiences**, a **Penguin Pace Chart** to check your pace and a way to monitor your intensity with the **i-Rate**™ system.

The i-Rate™ scale helps you rank the effort of each of your workouts. The goal of the i-Rate™ scale is to help you learn to discriminate among your daily workouts. We've given you some general guidelines to help get you started, but in time you will develop your own, highly personal, i-Rate™ scale.

Keeping a log is very personal. There are plenty of places to **track lots of information about your training and fuel.** The key is to record the information you think is important. The best way to improve your training is to monitor your progress and plan realistic workouts and goals. A well-documented log will keep you honest and allow you keep checks and balances of your fitness and fuel activity.

The Penguin Brigade Training Log guides you in monitoring **distance, time, heart rate, and perceived exertion, weight, sleep hours, weather and mood.** All of these have a direct role in helping or hurting your performance. Keeping track of this information will motivate you to modify behaviors and notice trends. More importantly, logging will guide you to making healthy choices and optimal training and racing strategies.

There is room to plan your daily workouts with **"Today's Goal"** and maintain focus on short-term goals with the **"Goals for the Week"** section.

And finally, you'll notice a new voice, that of Coach Jenny Hadfield. Jenny has been a head coach with the Leukemia and Lymphoma Society's Team in Training for five years and is co-owner of Chicago Endurance Sports, the city's most comprehensive long distance training program. She is a professional writer and adventure racer and is the person who has coached me through the best athletic seasons of my life.

This logbook is dedicated to the members of the Penguin Brigade, old and new, who have taken on the challenge of changing their lives and helping others to change theirs.

To you, the reader, welcome to the Penguin Brigade. We're glad you're here, and whatever your starting date is, and what ever your athletic goals are, we hope that the next twelve months are the most exciting, satisfying, and productive year you've ever had.

—John "The Penguin" Bingham and Coach Jenny Hadfield

NOTE: This log book is undated, so you can use it in any year. The monthly essays are related to the months of the year, though you can start anytime and anywhere you like. Following each of these essays are four weeks, each spanning a Monday to a Sunday, of log pages. To catch up periodically with the real-world calendar, after every third month we throw in a fifth week (and a bonus *six* weeks after December's essay) so you have a total of fifty-three weeks for the year.

WHY KEEP TRACK?

Monitoring your workouts provides a great source of motivation. It feels rewarding to log your activity after a workout especially after major accomplishments like races, personal records or new distances. It is a place to keep a personal journal of your activity. A safe place to celebrate YOU!

HOW TO USE THE LOG

The Penguin Brigade Training Log is easy to use. In just a few steps you will be on your way to planning and tracking your journey.

1. Just in case, complete the personal information and date in the front of the log.

2. Familiarize yourself with the entire log. There is lots of motivational and useful information like the Penguin Pace Chart, a place to set short and long term goals and a place to keep track of your races! Check it out and use it as a training tool.

3. Open to the first week and notice the information that can be tracked. Begin to complete the information that is important to you.

4. Keep track of mileage totals for the week and year-to-date. Be cautious to train smart. It can be tempting to fill the log and make it look impressive. Stick to a realistic and smart training regimen.

BEFORE YOU BEGIN TO TRAIN

Regardless of the shape you're in before you start an exercise regimen it is advisable to note advice from the American College of Sports Medicine:

At or above the age of 35 years of age, it is necessary for

individuals to have a medical examination and a maximal exercise test before beginning a vigorous exercise program. At any age, the information gathered from an exercise test may be useful to establish an effective and safe exercise prescription. Maximal testing done for men at age 40 or above or women age 50 or older, even when no symptoms or risk factors are present, should be performed with physician supervision.

WHY DO I NEED TO MONITOR INTENSITY?

There is one rule that applies to all athletes of all levels at all times. Simply put: EFFORT IS EQUAL, PACE IS PERSONAL. What that means is that at a given level of effort, whatever that is, your pace, my pace, and the pace of a world-class athlete will be different. You'd think that this would be easy to grasp, but it is one of the *most* misunderstood aspects of training. You don't go faster by just trying harder. You get faster by training your body to move faster at the same level of effort. This is true for you, the elite athlete, and me.

Learning to measure your level of effort is key to short term and long-term improvement. If you don't find a way to know how hard your working at a given pace, you'll never be able to tell if your training is doing you any good. There are two ways to measure effort. The most precise is by wearing a heart rate monitor. These monitors will provide instant and accurate feedback and are invaluable if you understand how to use them and what the data means. The second way is to monitor your perceived effort, or what we call the i-Rate Scale™.

Using the i-Rate Scale™ is easy to learn and it guides you in learning how to listen to your body. Familiarize yourself with the 1-10 scale. Then assign a numeric value or adjective that best defines what it feels like during your workouts.

Listen to your breathing: are you gasping for air? If so, you would label that a 10 on the i-Rate Scale™, and would want to slow down. Are you able to sing a song? Then you might label this a 3-4 and may need to pick it up a little. Use the "talk test" as a guide. If you can hold a conversation you are in the "aerobic" (with oxygen) zone between 5-7. If you are unable to talk you are most likely at or beyond your anaerobic (without oxygen) threshold and in the 8-9 zone. If you are ready to just slug anybody that says anything to you this is the "bite me" zone or otherwise known as a 10 on the i-Rate Scale™.

Focus on how your body feels and how hard or easy you are working.

Use the i-Rate™ for every workout. Learn to feel your effort. Even if you have no idea at first, write something down. Make a guess if you have to. But monitor your effort. In time, you'll get better.

i-RATE™ SCALE

0 At rest.

1

2 Very, very, easy. Almost moving backwards.

3

4 Easy effort. Can sing the entire "Star Spangled Banner."

5

6 Moderate effort. Can Sing "Row, Row, Row Your Boat" but with breaths in between.

7

8 Comfortably hard effort.

9

10 Very, very heavy. Almost maximum effort

The key to maintaining an active and healthy lifestyle involves both exercise and nutrition. If one or both are out of balance, your wheel won't roll efficiently. For this reason is the Fuel Log was incorporated. It provides a guide for eating a well balanced diet and monitoring daily food choices.

On a daily basis, simply check off servings of water, veggies, fruits, grains and protein. It subtly reminds you to limit your intake of fat, empty carbohydrates and alcohol. Use the Fuel Log to balance your diet, lose weight or improve your performance by including high nutrient foods.

WHAT IS A SERVING SIZE?

Water: 8 ounces Recommended Daily Servings: 6-8

Fruits: Recommended Daily Servings: 2-4
Serving is 1 medium apple, orange, or banana. 3/4 cup juice: 1/2 cup diced fruit, 1/4 cup dried fruit.

Veggies: Recommended Daily Servings: 3-5
1 cup raw, leafy vegetables; 1/2 cup chopped raw or cooked veggies; or 3/4 cup vegetable juice

Whole Grains: Recommended Daily Servings: 6-11
1 slice bread; 1/2 bun;bagel or English muffin; 1 ounce dry ready to eat cereal; 1/2 cup cooked cereal, rice or pasta.

Protein: Recommended Daily Servings: 6 oz.
Cooked lean beef, pork, lamb, veal, poultry or fish the size of deck of cards; 1/2 cup cooked beans, 1 egg, 2 tbs. peanut butter, 4 ounces tofu (2 ounces extra firm) 1/4cup nuts or seeds = 1 ounce of meat.

Limit your consumption of high fat foods and "empty" carbohydrates like fries, chips and pie. The nutrient value is very low and the caloric value very high. Fatty foods dramatically increase your calorie intake with very little quantity of food. You are paying for a Cadillac but driving a Pinto. Fill up on high quality foods like fruits, veggies and lean meats.

Limit your consumption of alcoholic beverages. This is an easy way to reduce your caloric intake during the week. Alcohol provides *no* nutrient value and it helps you keep those extra pounds you want to lose. Often tracking your intake will allow you to look at how much and how often you are consuming. From there you can modify your consumption and track your results.

WHERE DO YOU SEE YOURSELF ONE YEAR FROM NOW?

Setting realistic goals is the foundation of a healthy and successful exercise program. Whether you are training to complete and marathon or aiming for a regular exercise regimen the first step is to develop your game plan. Focus on what you want long term, one or more years from now. And then work back and set several short-term goals to get you there. Setting shorter, more digestible goals gives your program focus, purpose and reward.

Set them so you can reach them, that is, realistic for where you are now and where you can go. If you are a new runner or walker and want to compete in a race, the race is the long-term goal while getting in twelve workouts in one month is a short-term goal. If you are trying to improve your performance in a marathon, the marathon is the long-term goal, while completing several "practice" races along the way is a good short-term goal strategy. Goals are important, they will guide and motivate your journey and make it meaningful.

Think about what you want to achieve. It doesn't have to be going to the moon. It could be as simple as getting in shape. But define the goal and be specific so you can qualify it and know if you are there. (i.e. To get in shape by the end of the year and complete my first half marathon.) Here's a sample:

My Long Term Plan (goals):
1) Run-walk the Chicago Distance Classic 20K on August 3.
2) Lose 20 pounds slowly and healthfully by monitoring my food choices, eating balanced meals and controlling portions.

How I am going to get there — Short-term goals:
1) Develop a buddy system with John and train three times per week.
2) Sign up for and participate in the Shamrock Shuffle 8K March 23.
3) Monitor and track my fuel choices every day. One day at a time I will consume the minimum recommended servings of water, fruits, and veggies.
4) I will limit my sweets or sugar consumption to three treats per week.
5) I will not eat after 8 P.M. every night.

PLAN YOUR PATH TO REACHING YOUR LONG-TERM GOALS:

_____

_____

_____

_____

_____

_____

_____

How will you get there? Write down a few specific check-points (short-term goals) to reach along the way.

_____

_____

_____

_____

_____

_____

_____

_____

_____

NOTES TO MYSELF

THIS IS A GREAT PLACE TO WRITE DOWN NOTES ON
TRAINING, RACING, AND LIVING.

THE PENGUIN'S TOP TEN TIPS

1. Size matters, at least when in comes to shoes.
I'd worn size 8 1/2 shoes since I was 17 years old. So at age 42, when I went to buy my first pair of running shoes, I bought—you guessed it—size 8 1/2. I didn't even bother to try them on, I was so sure they would fit. And they did fit. Sorta. I thought that running shoes should hug my feet, make my toes feel "snug," and be laced up so tight that they nearly cut off my circulation. I didn't lose all of my toenails before I figured it out, but almost. **Buy shoes that fit, without even looking at the size on the manufacturer's label.**

2. Clothes make the man.
I thought that I could just dig out some of my old T-shirts and sweatpants and start running. I thought that all the technical "stuff" that real runners wear was only for the fast runners. I was wrong. The reason why those runners wear technical clothing is the same reason that I finally did. Performance. Fabrics that wick moisture are cooler in the summer and warmer in the winter. **You don't have to carry the weight of your own perspiration on your favorite cotton T-shirt anymore** .

3. Three steps forward, two steps back.
I thought that I would continue to get better and better. I thought my progress would be linear. For a while, it worked that way, although considering where I started that shouldn't be a surprise. For several months I got faster with nearly every run. Then the progress suddenly stopped. **Long term improvement is a constant cycle of getting faster, hitting a plateau, slipping backwards, regrouping, and then getting faster again.**

4. Talk is cheap.

When I first started, I spent more time planning my runs than actually running. I also spent a lot of time talking about running, and not nearly enough time running. I thought that knowing about running was the same as being able to run. I thought that being able to using a phrase like anaerobic threshold in a sentence was as good as experiencing it. **Once you start training more and talking less, your running improves.**

5. Garbage in, garbage out.

I had no idea how food worked once it was inside my body. I understood how it made me feel when I ate it, but knew nothing about how food functions. I didn't understand the correlation between what I was asking my body to process and what I was asking my body to perform. As I began to view food as fuel rather than as comfort or recreation, I discovered that the foods I wanted and the foods I needed were almost always the same. **That doesn't mean you can't give in to an occasional craving, but don't ignore the effect that food has on your performance.**

6. Sometimes, less is more.

I never considered myself the sharpest knife in the drawer. I knew there were people smarter, better educated, and more talented that I in my profession. But I also knew that I had the capacity to outwork anybody I had ever met. I took that attitude into my running. When I read that one day of speed work was good, I thought that three days would be better. If everyone else increased their mileage by 10% per week, then I'd increase mine by 20%. **Improvement comes at the point of balance between effort and recovery.**

7. There are no secrets.

I was sure that there were hidden 'truths' about running that would make me faster sooner. I read everything I could find, trying to uncover those hidden truths. After a while I discovered that most of what I needed to learn I was going to have to find out on my own, with my own two feet.

Training for a long distance race is sometimes a frustrating process of trial and error. **If there are any secrets, you are going to have to find them on the roads, not in books.**

8. My body, my self.

In the early stages I waited for the magic transformation of my body into the body of a runner. I expected my legs to get longer and leaner, my muscles to become tight and sinewy, and all my joints to work exactly like they were supposed to. There may be less of it now, but it is still basically the same body I had when I started running. **It turns out tha t you have to learn how to train with the body you have.**

9. Being a runner is a process, not a destination.

I was convinced that I could get into shape and stay there. I thought that once I had achieved a certain speed or distance, I could relax and enjoy the view. But, there is always something new to learn, some new distance to try, or some new pace to struggle toward. **Running is a constant process of assessing and evaluating where you've been, where you are, and where you want to be.**

10. Races are celebrations.

I've always been a big motorsports fan. I've attended hundreds of races. They were battlegrounds. But runners are different. Once I overcame my fear, I raced nearly every weekend. I couldn't wait to line up with friends and find out what their best was on that day, and to show them MY best at the same time. **Despite the competition between individuals, there is still an overwhelming sense of shared achievement at races.**

RACE CELEBRATION!

Make memories. Whether you reach your goal or come in a little short, there is always something to learn from every experience. Use these pages to log your race progress. Some day you'll look back at your log, realize your accomplishments, and revel in just how far you've come.

Race or event: _____

Date:_____

Notes:_____

_____

_____

Race or event: _____

Date:_____

Notes:_____

_____

_____

Race or event: _____

Date:_____

Notes:_____

_____

_____

Race or event: _____

Date:_____

Notes:_____

_____

_____

Race or event: _____

Date:_____

Notes:_____

_____

_____

Race or event: _____

Date:_____

Notes:_____

_____

_____

Race or event: _____

Date:_____

Notes:_____

_____

_____

Race or event: _____

Date:_____

Notes:_____

_____

_____

Race or event: _____

Date:_____

Notes:_____

_____

_____

Race or event: _____

Date:_____

Notes:_____

_____

_____

Race or event: _____

Date:_____

Notes:_____

_____

_____

Race or event: _____

Date:_____

Notes:_____

_____

_____

Race or event: _____

Date:_____

Notes:_____

_____

_____

Race or event: _____

Date:_____

Notes:_____

_____

_____

Race or event: _____

Date:_____

Notes:_____

_____

_____

Race or event: _____

Date:_____

Notes:_____

_____

_____

PENGUIN PACE CHART

PACE (minutes per mile)	5K (3.107 miles)	5 Miles	10K (6.214 miles)	10 Miles	1/2 Marathon (13.109 miles)	15 Miles	20 Miles	Marathon (26.219 miles)
6:00	18:39	30:00	37:17	1:00:00	1:18:39	1:30:00	2:00:00	2:37:19
6:30	20:12	32:30	40:23	1:05:00	1:25:13	1:37:30	2:10:00	2:50:25
7:00	21:45	35:00	43:30	1:10:00	1:31:46	1:45:00	2:20:00	3:03:32
7:30	23:18	37:30	46:36	1:15:00	1:38:19	1:52:30	2:30:00	3:16:39
8:00	24:51	40:00	49:43	1:20:00	1:44:52	2:00:00	2:40:00	3:29:45
8:30	26:25	42:30	52:49	1:25:00	1:51:26	2:07:30	2:50:00	3:42:52
9:00	27:58	45:00	55:56	1:30:00	1:57:59	2:15:00	3:00:00	3:55:58
9:30	29:31	47:30	59:02	1:35:00	2:04:32	2:22:30	3:10:00	4:09:05
10:00	31:04	50:00	1:02:08	1:40:00	2:11:05	2:30:00	3:20:00	4:22:11
10:30	32:37	52:30	1:05:15	1:45:00	2:17:39	2:37:30	3:30:00	4:35:18
11:00	34:11	55:00	1:08:21	1:50:00	2:24:12	2:45:00	3:40:00	4:48:25
11:30	35:44	57:30	1:11:28	1:55:00	2:30:45	2:52:30	3:50:00	5:01:31
12:00	37:17	1:00:00	1:14:34	2:00:00	2:37:18	3:00:00	4:00:00	5:15:37
12:30	38:50	1:02:30	1:17:41	2:05:00	2:43:52	3:07:30	4:10:00	5:27:44
13:00	40:23	1:05:00	1:20:47	2:10:00	2:50:25	3:15:00	4:20:00	5:40:51
13:30	41:57	1:07:30	1:23:53	2:15:00	2:56:58	3:22:30	4:30:00	5:53:57
14:00	43:30	1:10:00	1:27:00	2:20:00	3:03:32	3:30:00	4:40:00	6:07:04
14:30	45:03	1:12:30	1:30:06	2:25:00	3:10:05	3:37:30	4:50:00	6:20:10
15:00	46:36	1:15:00	1:33:13	2:30:00	3:16:38	3:45:00	5:00:00	6:33:17
15:30	48:09	1:17:30	1:36:18	2:35:00	3:23:03	3:52:30	5:10:00	6:46:24
16:00	49:43	1:20:00	1:39:26	2:40:00	3:29:45	4:00:00	5:20:00	6:59:31
16:30	51:16	1:22:30	1:42:33	2:45:00	3:36:18	4:07:30	5:30:00	7:12:38
17:00	52:50	1:25:00	1:45:39	2:50:00	3:42:52	4:15:00	5:40:00	7:25:44
17:30	54:23	1:27:30	1:48:46	2:55:00	3:49:25	4:22:30	5:50:00	7:38:51
18:00	55:56	1:30:00	1:51:52	3:00:00	3:55:58	4:30:00	6:00:00	7:51:57
18:30	57:29	1:32:30	1:54:59	3:05:00	4:02:32	4:37:30	6:10:00	8:05:03
19:00	59:03	1:35:00	1:58:05	3:10:00	4:09:05	4:45:00	6:20:00	8:18:10
19:30	1:00:36	1:37:30	2:01:12	3:15:00	4:15:38	4:52:30	6:30:00	8:31:16
20:00	1:02:09	1:40:00	2:04:18	3:20:00	4:22:11	5:00:00	6:40:00	8:44:23

JANUARY

NEW YEAR, NEW YOU

It happens every year. Millions of people decide that THIS year will be different. This year they will start an exercise program and stick with it. This year they won't get impatient with their progress and quit. This year they are going to win the battle against inactivity and weight gain. And every year they fall victim to their own unrealistic expectations and unrealistic goals and quit before the first bud of Springtime.

The quitter's program goes something like this: Day One, get all fired up, slap on the gear, hurry out of the house and exercise to the point of exhaustion (which doesn't take all that long). Day Two, achy but still all fired up, gently put on the gear, walk slowly out of the house, and exercise to the point of exhaustion (which takes even less time than Day One).

Day Three, sorta fired up, painfully put on the gear, limp out of the house, and exercise to the point of exhaustion (which on Day Three takes almost exactly forty seconds). Day Four, not at ALL fired up, stare at the gear, limp around inside the house because you're too exhausted to exercise. Day Five, Quit and convince yourself that you'll never get fit.

How do I know? I did it myself at least ten times over the course of my life. Each time I tried I'd get a little more desperate. Each time I tried I'd get a little more panicked because I was afraid it was going to be the last time. And each time I failed because I was getting older but not any smarter.

If this is your first attempt at getting up, getting out, and getting going let me welcome you to the club of active, healthy, adult-onset athletes. Everything you ever dreamed was true about athletes . . . that they are happier . . . that their lives are richer and fuller . . . that their days are filled with the satisfaction of honest effort . . . is true. It's all true. And it's all available to you if you'll just take your time.

Contrary to the popular myth, athletes are not born, they're made. They're made over time. They're made through the repeated cycle of stress and recovery of muscle. They're made through pushing the limits of their bodies and minds.

Athletes are forged in the furnace of effort. And you are just as capable of finding that level of honest effort which brings you the greatest satisfaction as any other athlete.

Have been running since May 1st

MONDAY / Date: 7-31-06
Training notes:

Didn't run on drive home from
C.A

FUEL LOG

WATER: 6-8 × 8 OZ.	FRUITS: 2-4	VEGGIES: 3-5	WHOLE GRAIN SERVINGS: 6-11	PROTEIN: 4-6 OZ.	LIMIT FAT?	ALCOHOLIC BEVERAGES?	LIMIT "EMPTY" CARBS?
☐☐☐☐ ☐☐☐☐	☐☐ ☐☐	☐☐ ☐☐	☐☐☐☐ ☐☐☐☐ ☐☐☐	☐☐☐ ☐☐☐	Y N	Y N	Y N

Distance:
Time:
Heart Rate:
i-Rate (1-10):
X-Training:
Sleep Hours:
Weight:
Mood: ☺ ☺ ☹ Other

WEATHER:
SUN WIND
RAIN CLOUDY
SNOW
TEMP: _____

TUESDAY / Date: 8-1-06
Training notes:

Ran went stopping. Def. harder than
running in CA.

FUEL LOG

WATER: 6-8 × 8 OZ.	FRUITS: 2-4	VEGGIES: 3-5	WHOLE GRAIN SERVINGS: 6-11	PROTEIN: 4-6 OZ.	LIMIT FAT?	ALCOHOLIC BEVERAGES?	LIMIT "EMPTY" CARBS?
☐☐☐☐ ☐☐☐☐	☐☐ ☐☐	☐☐ ☐☐	☐☐☐☐ ☐☐☐☐ ☐☐☐	☐☐☐ ☐☐☐	Y N	Y N	Y N

Today's goal:
run 3.8 miles w/out
stopping

Distance: 3.8
Time: 38:26
Heart Rate:
i-Rate (1-10):
X-Training:
Sleep Hours:
Weight:
Mood: ☺ ⊗ ☹ Other

WEATHER:
SUN WIND
RAIN CLOUDY
SNOW
TEMP: _____

WEDNESDAY / Date: 8-2-06
Training notes:

Tired think I slept too long

FUEL LOG

WATER: 6-8 × 8 OZ.	FRUITS: 2-4	VEGGIES: 3-5	WHOLE GRAIN SERVINGS: 6-11	PROTEIN: 4-6 OZ.	LIMIT FAT?	ALCOHOLIC BEVERAGES?	LIMIT "EMPTY" CARBS?
☐☐☐☐ ☐☐☐☐	☒☒ ☐☐	☐☐ ☐☐	☐☐☐☐ ☐☐☐☐ ☐☐☐	☒☐☐ ☐☐☐	Y N	Y N	Y N

Today's goal:
Did 100 push-ups +
sit-up in between break

Distance:
Time:
Heart Rate:
i-Rate (1-10):
X-Training:
Sleep Hours:
Weight:
Mood: ☺ ⊗ ☹ Other

WEATHER:
SUN WIND
RAIN CLOUDY
SNOW
TEMP: _____

THURSDAY / Date: 8-3-06
Training notes:

Ran 5.6 miles. I felt great, but my
feet hurt really bad. I run after work
bc I didn't wake it during the
morning too tired.

FUEL LOG

WATER: 6-8 × 8 OZ.	FRUITS: 2-4	VEGGIES: 3-5	WHOLE GRAIN SERVINGS: 6-11	PROTEIN: 4-6 OZ.	LIMIT FAT?	ALCOHOLIC BEVERAGES?	LIMIT "EMPTY" CARBS?
☐☐☐☐ ☐☐☐☐	☒☒ ☐☐	☐☐ ☐☐	☐☐☐☐ ☐☐☐☐ ☐☐☐	☐☐☐ ☐☐☐	Y N	Y Ⓝ	Y N

Today's goal: run 5.2 w/out
walking.

Distance: 5.6
Time: 55:18
Heart Rate:
i-Rate (1-10):
X-Training:
Sleep Hours: 8
Weight: 129.6
Mood: ☺ ⊗ ☹ Other

WEATHER:
SUN WIND
RAIN CLOUDY
SNOW
TEMP: _____

FRIDAY / Date: 8-4-0u

Today's goal: Push-ups 100

Training notes: Did 90.

FUEL LOG

WATER: 6-8 × 8 OZ.	FRUITS: 2-4	VEGGIES: 3-5	WHOLE GRAIN SERVINGS: 6-11	PROTEIN: 4-6 OZ.	LIMIT FAT?	ALCOHOLIC BEVERAGES?	LIMIT "EMPTY" CARBS?
☐☐☐☐ ☐☐☐☐	☐☐ ☐☐	☐☐ ☐	☐☐☐☐☐ ☐☐☐☐☐☐	☐☐☐ ☐☐☐	Y N	Y N	Y N

WEATHER: SUN WIND RAIN CLOUDY SNOW TEMP: ____

Distance:
Time:
Heart Rate:
i-Rate (1-10):
X-Training:
Sleep Hours:
Weight:
Mood: ☺ ☺ ☹ Other

SATURDAY / Date: 8-5-0u

Today's goal:

Training notes: Road bike for 16.5 miles. It felt good.

FUEL LOG

WATER: 6-8 × 8 OZ.	FRUITS: 2-4	VEGGIES: 3-5	WHOLE GRAIN SERVINGS: 6-11	PROTEIN: 4-6 OZ.	LIMIT FAT?	ALCOHOLIC BEVERAGES?	LIMIT "EMPTY" CARBS?
☐☐☐☐	☐☐ ☐☐	☐☐ ☐	☐☐☐☐☐ ☐☐☐☐☐☐	☐☐☐ ☐☐☐	Y N	Y N	Y N

WEATHER: SUN WIND RAIN CLOUDY SNOW TEMP: ____

Distance: 16.5
Time: 12 pm
Heart Rate:
i-Rate (1-10):
X-Training:
Sleep Hours: 6
Weight: 129, 2
Mood: ☺ ☺ ☹ Other

SUNDAY / Date:

Today's goal: Day off

Training notes:

FUEL LOG

WATER: 6-8 × 8 OZ.	FRUITS: 2-4	VEGGIES: 3-5	WHOLE GRAIN SERVINGS: 6-11	PROTEIN: 4-6 OZ.	LIMIT FAT?	ALCOHOLIC BEVERAGES?	LIMIT "EMPTY" CARBS?
☐☐☐☐	☐☐ ☐☐	☐☐ ☐	☐☐☐☐☐ ☐☐☐☐☐☐	☐☐☐ ☐☐☐	Y N	Y N	Y N

WEATHER: SUN WIND RAIN CLOUDY SNOW TEMP: ____

Distance:
Time:
Heart Rate:
i-Rate (1-10):
X-Training:
Sleep Hours:
Weight:
Mood: ☺ ☺ ☹ Other

WEEK OF:
GOALS FOR WEEK:

WEEKLY TOTAL: _____

YEAR-TO-DATE TOTAL:

PENGUIN WORDS OF WISDOM

If the benefits of exercise could be put into a pill, it would be the most prescribed medication of all time.

MONDAY / Date: 8/7/06

Training notes: Ran 2 times around lake, hurting. Run after work @ 5:45. It was a good run except for my feet were

Today's goal: run 5 times around lake

Distance: 7.8
Time: 26.32
Heart Rate:
i-Rate (1-10):
X-Training:
Sleep Hours: 8
Weight: 128.2
Mood: ☺ (circled) ☺ ☹

WEATHER: SUN (circled) WIND RAIN CLOUDY SNOW TEMP: ___

FUEL LOG

WATER: 6-8 x 8 OZ.	FRUITS: 2-4	VEGGIES: 3-5	WHOLE GRAIN SERVINGS: 6-11	PROTEIN: 4-6 OZ.	LIMIT FAT?	ALCOHOLIC BEVERAGES?	LIMIT "EMPTY" CARBS?
☐☐☐☐	☐☐	☐☐	☐☐☐☐☐☐	☐☐☐	Y (N)	Y (N)	Y (N)

gallons 1½

TUESDAY / Date: 8/9/06

Training notes: Swimming for 3 hrs.

Today's goal: Run 3 times around lake

Distance:
Time:
Heart Rate:
i-Rate (1-10):
X-Training:
Sleep Hours:
Weight:
Mood: ☺ ☺ ☹

WEATHER: SUN WIND RAIN CLOUDY SNOW TEMP: ___

FUEL LOG

WATER: 6-8 x 8 OZ.	FRUITS: 2-4	VEGGIES: 3-5	WHOLE GRAIN SERVINGS: 6-11	PROTEIN: 4-6 OZ.	LIMIT FAT?	ALCOHOLIC BEVERAGES?	LIMIT "EMPTY" CARBS?
☐☐☐☐	☐☐	☐☐	☐☐☐☐☐☐	☐☐☐	Y N	Y N	Y N

WEDNESDAY / Date: 8/9/06

Training notes: Meeting got over too late rode bike for 40 min

Today's goal: Run 3 times around lake

Distance: 10 miles
Time: 40 min
Heart Rate:
i-Rate (1-10):
X-Training:
Sleep Hours:
Weight: 129.2
Mood: ☺ (circled) ☺ ☹

WEATHER: SUN (circled) WIND RAIN CLOUDY SNOW TEMP: ___

FUEL LOG

WATER: 6-8 x 8 OZ.	FRUITS: 2-4	VEGGIES: 3-5	WHOLE GRAIN SERVINGS: 6-11	PROTEIN: 4-6 OZ.	LIMIT FAT?	ALCOHOLIC BEVERAGES?	LIMIT "EMPTY" CARBS?
☐☐☐☐	☐☐	☐☐	☐☐☐☐☐☐	☐☐☐	Y N	Y (N)	Y (N)

THURSDAY / Date:

Training notes: Swimming for 3 hrs.

Today's goal:

Distance:
Time:
Heart Rate:
i-Rate (1-10):
X-Training:
Sleep Hours:
Weight:
Mood: ☺ ☺ ☹

WEATHER: SUN WIND RAIN CLOUDY SNOW TEMP: ___

FUEL LOG

WATER: 6-8 x 8 OZ.	FRUITS: 2-4	VEGGIES: 3-5	WHOLE GRAIN SERVINGS: 6-11	PROTEIN: 4-6 OZ.	LIMIT FAT?	ALCOHOLIC BEVERAGES?	LIMIT "EMPTY" CARBS?
☐☐☐☐	☐☐	☐☐	☐☐☐☐☐☐	☐☐☐	Y N	Y N	Y N

FRIDAY / Date:

Today's goal: _____

Training notes: _____

FUEL LOG

WATER: 6-8 x 8 OZ.	FRUITS: 2-4	VEGGIES: 3-5	WHOLE GRAIN SERVINGS: 6-11	PROTEIN: 4-6 OZ.	LIMIT FAT?	ALCOHOLIC BEVERAGES?	LIMIT "EMPTY" CARBS?
☐☐☐☐ ☐☐☐☐	☐☐ ☐☐	☐☐☐ ☐☐	☐☐☐☐☐ ☐☐☐☐☐	☐☐☐ ☐☐☐	Y N	Y N	Y N

WEATHER: SUN WIND RAIN CLOUDY SNOW TEMP:___

Distance: _____
Time: _____
Heart Rate: _____
i-Rate (1-10) _____
X-Training: _____
Sleep Hours: _____
Weight: _____
Mood: ☺ 😐 ☹ Other

SATURDAY / Date:

Today's goal: _____

Training notes: _____

FUEL LOG

WATER: 6-8 x 8 OZ.	FRUITS: 2-4	VEGGIES: 3-5	WHOLE GRAIN SERVINGS: 6-11	PROTEIN: 4-6 OZ.	LIMIT FAT?	ALCOHOLIC BEVERAGES?	LIMIT "EMPTY" CARBS?
☐☐☐☐ ☐☐☐☐	☐☐ ☐☐	☐☐☐ ☐☐	☐☐☐☐☐ ☐☐☐☐☐	☐☐☐ ☐☐☐	Y N	Y N	Y N

WEATHER: SUN WIND RAIN CLOUDY SNOW TEMP:___

Distance: _____
Time: _____
Heart Rate: _____
i-Rate (1-10) _____
X-Training: _____
Sleep Hours: _____
Weight: _____
Mood: ☺ 😐 ☹ Other

SUNDAY / Date:

Today's goal: _____

Training notes: _____

FUEL LOG

WATER: 6-8 x 8 OZ.	FRUITS: 2-4	VEGGIES: 3-5	WHOLE GRAIN SERVINGS: 6-11	PROTEIN: 4-6 OZ.	LIMIT FAT?	ALCOHOLIC BEVERAGES?	LIMIT "EMPTY" CARBS?
☐☐☐☐ ☐☐☐☐	☐☐ ☐☐	☐☐☐ ☐☐	☐☐☐☐☐ ☐☐☐☐☐	☐☐☐ ☐☐☐	Y N	Y N	Y N

WEATHER: SUN WIND RAIN CLOUDY SNOW TEMP:___

Distance: _____
Time: _____
Heart Rate: _____
i-Rate (1-10) _____
X-Training: _____
Sleep Hours: _____
Weight: _____
Mood: ☺ 😐 ☹ Other

WEEK OF: _____

GOALS FOR WEEK: _____

WEEKLY TOTAL: _____

YEAR-TO-DATE TOTAL: _____

PENGUIN WORDS OF WISDOM

Play is natural. The activity itself is not nearly as important as the fact that it is something that you enjoy doing, and that you can find time to do it for 20 minutes or so three to four times per week.

MONDAY / Date:

Today's goal:

Training notes:

FUEL LOG

WATER: 6-8 x 8 OZ.	FRUITS: 2-4	VEGGIES: 3-5	WHOLE GRAIN SERVINGS: 6-11	PROTEIN: 4-6 OZ.	LIMIT FAT?	ALCOHOLIC BEVERAGES?	LIMIT "EMPTY" CARBS?
☐☐☐☐ ☐☐☐☐	☐☐ ☐☐	☐☐ ☐☐	☐☐☐☐☐ ☐☐☐☐☐☐	☐☐☐ ☐☐	Y N	Y N	Y N

WEATHER: SUN WIND RAIN CLOUDY SNOW TEMP:____

Distance:
Time:
Heart Rate:
i-Rate (1-10)
X-Training:
Sleep Hours:
Weight:
Mood: ☺ ☺ ☹ Other

TUESDAY / Date:

Today's goal:

Training notes:

FUEL LOG

WATER: 6-8 x 8 OZ.	FRUITS: 2-4	VEGGIES: 3-5	WHOLE GRAIN SERVINGS: 6-11	PROTEIN: 4-6 OZ.	LIMIT FAT?	ALCOHOLIC BEVERAGES?	LIMIT "EMPTY" CARBS?
☐☐☐☐ ☐☐☐☐	☐☐ ☐☐	☐☐ ☐☐	☐☐☐☐☐ ☐☐☐☐☐☐	☐☐☐ ☐☐	Y N	Y N	Y N

WEATHER: SUN WIND RAIN CLOUDY SNOW TEMP:____

Distance:
Time:
Heart Rate:
i-Rate (1-10)
X-Training:
Sleep Hours:
Weight:
Mood: ☺ ☺ ☹ Other

WEDNESDAY / Date:

Today's goal:

Training notes:

FUEL LOG

WATER: 6-8 x 8 OZ.	FRUITS: 2-4	VEGGIES: 3-5	WHOLE GRAIN SERVINGS: 6-11	PROTEIN: 4-6 OZ.	LIMIT FAT?	ALCOHOLIC BEVERAGES?	LIMIT "EMPTY" CARBS?
☐☐☐☐ ☐☐☐☐	☐☐ ☐☐	☐☐ ☐☐	☐☐☐☐☐ ☐☐☐☐☐☐	☐☐☐ ☐☐	Y N	Y N	Y N

WEATHER: SUN WIND RAIN CLOUDY SNOW TEMP:____

Distance:
Time:
Heart Rate:
i-Rate (1-10)
X-Training:
Sleep Hours:
Weight:
Mood: ☺ ☺ ☹ Other

THURSDAY / Date:

Today's goal:

Training notes:

FUEL LOG

WATER: 6-8 x 8 OZ.	FRUITS: 2-4	VEGGIES: 3-5	WHOLE GRAIN SERVINGS: 6-11	PROTEIN: 4-6 OZ.	LIMIT FAT?	ALCOHOLIC BEVERAGES?	LIMIT "EMPTY" CARBS?
☐☐☐☐ ☐☐☐☐	☐☐ ☐☐	☐☐ ☐☐	☐☐☐☐☐ ☐☐☐☐☐☐	☐☐☐ ☐☐	Y N	Y N	Y N

WEATHER: SUN WIND RAIN CLOUDY SNOW TEMP:____

Distance:
Time:
Heart Rate:
i-Rate (1-10)
X-Training:
Sleep Hours:
Weight:
Mood: ☺ ☺ ☹ Other

FRIDAY / Date:

Today's goal: _____

Training notes: _____

FUEL LOG

WATER: 6-8 × 8 OZ.	FRUITS: 2-4	VEGGIES: 3-5	WHOLE GRAIN SERVINGS: 6-11	PROTEIN: 4-6 OZ.	LIMIT FAT?	ALCOHOLIC BEVERAGES?	LIMIT "EMPTY" CARBS?
☐☐☐☐ ☐☐☐☐	☐☐ ☐☐	☐☐ ☐☐	☐☐☐☐ ☐☐☐☐	☐☐☐ ☐☐☐	Y N	Y N	Y N

Distance:	
Time:	
Heart Rate:	
i-Rate (1-10)	
X-Training:	
Sleep Hours:	
Weight:	
Mood: ☺ ☺ ☹	

WEATHER: SUN WIND RAIN CLOUDY SNOW TEMP: _____
Mood: ☺ ☺ ☹ ☺ Other

SATURDAY / Date:

Today's goal: _____

Training notes: _____

FUEL LOG

WATER: 6-8 × 8 OZ.	FRUITS: 2-4	VEGGIES: 3-5	WHOLE GRAIN SERVINGS: 6-11	PROTEIN: 4-6 OZ.	LIMIT FAT?	ALCOHOLIC BEVERAGES?	LIMIT "EMPTY" CARBS?
☐☐☐☐ ☐☐☐☐	☐☐ ☐☐	☐☐ ☐☐	☐☐☐☐ ☐☐☐☐	☐☐☐ ☐☐☐	Y N	Y N	Y N

Distance:	
Time:	
Heart Rate:	
i-Rate (1-10)	
X-Training:	
Sleep Hours:	
Weight:	
Mood: ☺ ☺ ☹	

WEATHER: SUN WIND RAIN CLOUDY SNOW TEMP: _____
Mood: ☺ ☺ ☹ ☺ Other

SUNDAY / Date:

Today's goal: _____

Training notes: _____

FUEL LOG

WATER: 6-8 × 8 OZ.	FRUITS: 2-4	VEGGIES: 3-5	WHOLE GRAIN SERVINGS: 6-11	PROTEIN: 4-6 OZ.	LIMIT FAT?	ALCOHOLIC BEVERAGES?	LIMIT "EMPTY" CARBS?
☐☐☐☐ ☐☐☐☐	☐☐ ☐☐	☐☐ ☐☐	☐☐☐☐ ☐☐☐☐	☐☐☐ ☐☐☐	Y N	Y N	Y N

Distance:	
Time:	
Heart Rate:	
i-Rate (1-10)	
X-Training:	
Sleep Hours:	
Weight:	
Mood: ☺ ☺ ☹	

WEATHER: SUN WIND RAIN CLOUDY SNOW TEMP: _____
Mood: ☺ ☺ ☹ ☺ Other

WEEK OF:
GOALS FOR WEEK:

WEEKLY TOTAL: _____

YEAR-TO-DATE TOTAL:

PENGUIN WORDS OF WISDOM

It's never too late to gradually bring regular activity into your life. With a little common sense, nearly all of us can find something that helps more than it hurts.

MONDAY / Date:

Today's goal:

Training notes:

FUEL LOG

WATER: 6-8 x 8 OZ.	FRUITS: 2-4	VEGGIES: 3-5	WHOLE GRAIN SERVINGS: 6-11	PROTEIN: 4-6 OZ.	LIMIT FAT?	ALCOHOLIC BEVERAGES?	LIMIT "EMPTY" CARBS?
☐☐☐☐ ☐☐☐☐	☐☐ ☐☐	☐☐☐ ☐☐	☐☐☐☐ ☐☐☐ ☐	☐☐☐ ☐☐☐	Y N	Y N	Y N

WEATHER:
SUN WIND
RAIN CLOUDY
SNOW
TEMP: _____

Distance:
Time:
Heart Rate:
i-Rate (1-10)
X-Training:
Sleep Hours:
Weight:
Mood: ☺ ☺ ☹ Other

TUESDAY / Date:

Today's goal:

Training notes:

FUEL LOG

WATER: 6-8 x 8 OZ.	FRUITS: 2-4	VEGGIES: 3-5	WHOLE GRAIN SERVINGS: 6-11	PROTEIN: 4-6 OZ.	LIMIT FAT?	ALCOHOLIC BEVERAGES?	LIMIT "EMPTY" CARBS?
☐☐☐☐ ☐☐☐☐	☐☐ ☐☐	☐☐☐ ☐☐	☐☐☐☐ ☐☐☐ ☐	☐☐☐ ☐☐☐	Y N	Y N	Y N

WEATHER:
SUN WIND
RAIN CLOUDY
SNOW
TEMP: _____

Distance:
Time:
Heart Rate:
i-Rate (1-10)
X-Training:
Sleep Hours:
Weight:
Mood: ☺ ☺ ☹ Other

WEDNESDAY / Date:

Today's goal:

Training notes:

FUEL LOG

WATER: 6-8 x 8 OZ.	FRUITS: 2-4	VEGGIES: 3-5	WHOLE GRAIN SERVINGS: 6-11	PROTEIN: 4-6 OZ.	LIMIT FAT?	ALCOHOLIC BEVERAGES?	LIMIT "EMPTY" CARBS?
☐☐☐☐ ☐☐☐☐	☐☐ ☐☐	☐☐☐ ☐☐	☐☐☐☐ ☐☐☐ ☐	☐☐☐ ☐☐☐	Y N	Y N	Y N

WEATHER:
SUN WIND
RAIN CLOUDY
SNOW
TEMP: _____

Distance:
Time:
Heart Rate:
i-Rate (1-10)
X-Training:
Sleep Hours:
Weight:
Mood: ☺ ☺ ☹ Other

THURSDAY / Date:

Today's goal:

Training notes:

FUEL LOG

WATER: 6-8 x 8 OZ.	FRUITS: 2-4	VEGGIES: 3-5	WHOLE GRAIN SERVINGS: 6-11	PROTEIN: 4-6 OZ.	LIMIT FAT?	ALCOHOLIC BEVERAGES?	LIMIT "EMPTY" CARBS?
☐☐☐☐ ☐☐☐☐	☐☐ ☐☐	☐☐☐ ☐☐	☐☐☐☐ ☐☐☐ ☐	☐☐☐ ☐☐☐	Y N	Y N	Y N

WEATHER:
SUN WIND
RAIN CLOUDY
SNOW
TEMP: _____

Distance:
Time:
Heart Rate:
i-Rate (1-10)
X-Training:
Sleep Hours:
Weight:
Mood: ☺ ☺ ☹ Other

FRIDAY / Date:

Training notes:

Today's goal:

FUEL LOG

WATER: 6-8 × 8 OZ.	FRUITS: 2-4	VEGGIES: 3-5	WHOLE GRAIN SERVINGS: 6-11	PROTEIN: 2-4	LIMIT FAT?	ALCOHOLIC BEVERAGES?	LIMIT "EMPTY" CARBS?
☐☐☐☐ ☐☐☐☐	☐☐ ☐☐	☐☐☐ ☐☐	☐☐☐☐☐ ☐☐☐☐☐	☐☐☐ ☐☐	Y N	Y N	Y N

WEATHER:
SUN WIND
RAIN CLOUDY
SNOW
TEMP: _____

- Distance:
- Time:
- Heart Rate:
- i-Rate (1-10):
- X-Training:
- Sleep Hours:
- Weight:
- Mood: ☺ ☺ ☺ Other

SATURDAY / Date:

Training notes:

Today's goal:

FUEL LOG

WATER: 6-8 × 8 OZ.	FRUITS: 2-4	VEGGIES: 3-5	WHOLE GRAIN SERVINGS: 6-11	PROTEIN: 4-6 OZ.	LIMIT FAT?	ALCOHOLIC BEVERAGES?	LIMIT "EMPTY" CARBS?
☐☐☐☐ ☐☐☐☐	☐☐ ☐☐	☐☐☐ ☐☐	☐☐☐☐☐ ☐☐☐☐☐	☐☐☐ ☐☐	Y N	Y N	Y N

WEATHER:
SUN WIND
RAIN CLOUDY
SNOW
TEMP: _____

- Distance:
- Time:
- Heart Rate:
- i-Rate (1-10):
- X-Training:
- Sleep Hours:
- Weight:
- Mood: ☺ ☺ ☺ Other

SUNDAY / Date:

Training notes:

Today's goal:

FUEL LOG

WATER: 6-8 × 8 OZ.	FRUITS: 2-4	VEGGIES: 3-5	WHOLE GRAIN SERVINGS: 6-11	PROTEIN: 4-6 OZ.	LIMIT FAT?	ALCOHOLIC BEVERAGES?	LIMIT "EMPTY" CARBS?
☐☐☐☐ ☐☐☐☐	☐☐ ☐☐	☐☐☐ ☐☐	☐☐☐☐ ☐☐☐☐	☐☐☐ ☐☐	Y N	Y N	Y N

WEATHER:
SUN WIND
RAIN CLOUDY
SNOW
TEMP: _____

- Distance:
- Time:
- Heart Rate:
- i-Rate (1-10):
- X-Training:
- Sleep Hours:
- Weight:
- Mood: ☺ ☺ ☺ Other

WEEK OF:

GOALS FOR WEEK:

PENGUIN WORDS OF WISDOM

I believe the reason most folks give up running is because their expectations are completely out of line with reality.

WEEKLY TOTAL: _____

YEAR-TO-DATE TOTAL:

FEBRUARY

LABOR OF LOVE

There are hundreds of reasons to start an exercise program. You may have chosen to get more active because you want to lose weight, or lower your cholesterol, or lower your blood pressure. You may start walking or running because the forces of time and gravity have loaded up your body parts and moved them all South! You may start for those reasons, but you'll never stay with a program for those reasons.

Long term success in a program of activity comes down to one simple truth. You have to enjoy what you're doing.

You have to enjoy it. You can't just tolerate it. You can't just think it's something you should do . . . or worse . . . HAVE to do. You have to enjoy it. It has to be fun or you'll never stick with it.

The goal then, of every new athlete, has to be finding a way to make the activity fun. FUN. If going out three days a week and running so hard that your head hurts is fun for you, then by all means go to it. But if running so hard that you limp around for 24 hours doesn't sound like a good time, then don't.

There are no rules to becoming an active, healthy, adult-onset athlete. There are no standards that you have meet, no magic formula that you can apply that will tell you when you've moved from sedentary confinement to a life of activity. More importantly, no one else is ever going to know, for sure, when you get to call yourself an athlete.

The signs, though, that you are on the right track and heading in the right direction are straight forward. 1] Do you enjoy the activity for it's own sake, and 2] Can you imagine doing what you did this week for the rest of your life. If the answer to either of those questions is "no" then there may be trouble ahead.

To be successful, you have to allow yourself to enjoy the activity for it's own sake. Walking or running are, or can be, very pleasurable activities. Just look at any child on a playground. For them, running is one of life's greatest pleasures. Don't look beyond today's walk or run to see how it fits into some giant training plan. Just enjoy the moment.

And if you can't imagine still doing what you're doing a year from now . . . or 10 years from now . . . then change something. Go faster. Go slower. Go farther. Don't go so far. I don't know . . . but you do. If your workout isn't a labor of love, keep trying different things until it is.

MONDAY / Date:

Today's goal:

Training notes:

FUEL LOG

WATER: 6-8 x 8 OZ.	FRUITS: 2-4	VEGGIES: 3-5	WHOLE GRAIN SERVINGS: 6-11	PROTEIN: 4-6 OZ.	LIMIT FAT?	ALCOHOLIC BEVERAGES?	LIMIT "EMPTY" CARBS?
☐☐☐☐ ☐☐☐☐	☐☐ ☐☐	☐☐ ☐☐	☐☐☐☐☐ ☐	☐☐☐ ☐☐	Y N	Y N	Y N

WEATHER:
SUN   WIND
RAIN CLOUDY
SNOW
TEMP:_____

Distance:
Time:
Heart Rate:
i-Rate (1-10):
X-Training:
Sleep Hours:
Weight:
Mood: ☺ ☺ ☹ ☺ Other

TUESDAY / Date:

Today's goal:

Training notes:

FUEL LOG

WATER: 6-8 x 8 OZ.	FRUITS: 2-4	VEGGIES: 3-5	WHOLE GRAIN SERVINGS: 6-11	PROTEIN: 4-6 OZ.	LIMIT FAT?	ALCOHOLIC BEVERAGES?	LIMIT "EMPTY" CARBS?
☐☐☐☐ ☐☐☐☐	☐☐ ☐☐	☐☐ ☐☐	☐☐☐☐☐ ☐	☐☐☐ ☐☐	Y N	Y N	Y N

WEATHER:
SUN   WIND
RAIN CLOUDY
SNOW
TEMP:_____

Distance:
Time:
Heart Rate:
i-Rate (1-10):
X-Training:
Sleep Hours:
Weight:
Mood: ☺ ☺ ☹ ☺ Other

WEDNESDAY / Date:

Today's goal:

Training notes:

FUEL LOG

WATER: 6-8 x 8 OZ.	FRUITS: 2-4	VEGGIES: 3-5	WHOLE GRAIN SERVINGS: 6-11	PROTEIN: 4-6 OZ.	LIMIT FAT?	ALCOHOLIC BEVERAGES?	LIMIT "EMPTY" CARBS?
☐☐☐☐ ☐☐☐☐	☐☐ ☐☐	☐☐ ☐☐	☐☐☐☐☐ ☐	☐☐☐ ☐☐	Y N	Y N	Y N

WEATHER:
SUN   WIND
RAIN CLOUDY
SNOW
TEMP:_____

Distance:
Time:
Heart Rate:
i-Rate (1-10):
X-Training:
Sleep Hours:
Weight:
Mood: ☺ ☺ ☹ ☺ Other

THURSDAY / Date:

Today's goal:

Training notes:

FUEL LOG

WATER: 6-8 x 8 OZ.	FRUITS: 2-4	VEGGIES: 3-5	WHOLE GRAIN SERVINGS: 6-11	PROTEIN: 4-6 OZ.	LIMIT FAT?	ALCOHOLIC BEVERAGES?	LIMIT "EMPTY" CARBS?
☐☐☐☐ ☐☐☐☐	☐☐ ☐☐	☐☐ ☐☐	☐☐☐☐☐ ☐	☐☐☐ ☐☐	Y N	Y N	Y N

WEATHER:
SUN   WIND
RAIN CLOUDY
SNOW
TEMP:_____

Distance:
Time:
Heart Rate:
i-Rate (1-10):
X-Training:
Sleep Hours:
Weight:
Mood: ☺ ☺ ☹ ☺ Other

FRIDAY / Date:

Training notes: _____

Today's goal: _____

| Distance: |
| Time: |
| Heart Rate: |
| i-Rate (1-10): |
| X-Training: |
| Sleep Hours: |
| Weight: |
| Mood: ☺ ☺ ☹ ☹ Other |

FUEL LOG

WATER: 6-8 × 8 OZ.	FRUITS: 2-4	VEGGIES: 3-5	WHOLE GRAIN SERVINGS: 6-11	PROTEIN: 4-6 OZ.	LIMIT FAT?	ALCOHOLIC BEVERAGES?	LIMIT "EMPTY" CARBS?
☐☐☐☐ ☐☐☐☐	☐☐ ☐☐	☐☐ ☐	☐☐☐ ☐☐☐ ☐☐☐	☐☐☐ ☐☐☐	Y N	Y N	Y N

WEATHER:
SUN   WIND
RAIN CLOUDY
SNOW
TEMP: _____

SATURDAY / Date:

Training notes: _____

Today's goal: _____

| Distance: |
| Time: |
| Heart Rate: |
| i-Rate (1-10): |
| X-Training: |
| Sleep Hours: |
| Weight: |
| Mood: ☺ ☺ ☹ ☹ Other |

FUEL LOG

WATER: 6-8 × 8 OZ.	FRUITS: 2-4	VEGGIES: 3-5	WHOLE GRAIN SERVINGS: 6-11	PROTEIN: 4-6 OZ.	LIMIT FAT?	ALCOHOLIC BEVERAGES?	LIMIT "EMPTY" CARBS?
☐☐☐☐ ☐☐☐☐	☐☐ ☐☐	☐☐ ☐	☐☐☐ ☐☐☐ ☐☐☐	☐☐☐ ☐☐☐	Y N	Y N	Y N

WEATHER:
SUN   WIND
RAIN CLOUDY
SNOW
TEMP: _____

SUNDAY / Date:

Training notes: _____

Today's goal: _____

| Distance: |
| Time: |
| Heart Rate: |
| i-Rate (1-10): |
| X-Training: |
| Sleep Hours: |
| Weight: |
| Mood: ☺ ☺ ☹ ☹ Other |

FUEL LOG

WATER: 6-8 × 8 OZ.	FRUITS: 2-4	VEGGIES: 3-5	WHOLE GRAIN SERVINGS: 6-11	PROTEIN: 4-6 OZ.	LIMIT FAT?	ALCOHOLIC BEVERAGES?	LIMIT "EMPTY" CARBS?
☐☐☐☐ ☐☐☐☐	☐☐ ☐☐	☐☐ ☐	☐☐☐ ☐☐☐ ☐☐☐	☐☐☐ ☐☐☐	Y N	Y N	Y N

WEATHER:
SUN   WIND
RAIN CLOUDY
SNOW
TEMP: _____

WEEK OF: _____

GOALS FOR WEEK:

WEEKLY TOTAL: _____

YEAR-TO-DATE TOTAL: _____

PENGUIN WORDS OF WISDOM

For running to be a part of your life, it must become a part of who you are. For better or worse, being a runner is part of your definition of yourself.

MONDAY / Date:

Today's goal:

Training notes: ....

FUEL LOG

WATER: 6-8 × 8 OZ.	FRUITS: 2-4	VEGGIES: 3-5	WHOLE GRAIN SERVINGS: 6-11	PROTEIN: 4-6 OZ.	LIMIT FAT?	ALCOHOLIC BEVERAGES?	LIMIT "EMPTY" CARBS?
☐☐☐☐ ☐☐☐☐	☐☐ ☐☐	☐☐ ☐☐	☐☐☐☐ ☐☐☐☐	☐☐☐ ☐☐☐	Y N	Y N	Y N

Distance:
Time:
Heart Rate:
i-Rate (1-10):
X-Training:
Sleep Hours:
Weight:
Mood: ☺ ☺ ☹ ☹ Other

WEATHER:
SUN WIND
RAIN CLOUDY
SNOW
TEMP:_____

TUESDAY / Date:

Today's goal:

Training notes: ....

FUEL LOG

WATER: 6-8 × 8 OZ.	FRUITS: 2-4	VEGGIES: 3-5	WHOLE GRAIN SERVINGS: 6-11	PROTEIN: 4-6 OZ.	LIMIT FAT?	ALCOHOLIC BEVERAGES?	LIMIT "EMPTY" CARBS?
☐☐☐☐ ☐☐☐☐	☐☐ ☐☐	☐☐ ☐☐	☐☐☐☐ ☐☐☐☐	☐☐☐ ☐☐☐	Y N	Y N	Y N

Distance:
Time:
Heart Rate:
i-Rate (1-10):
X-Training:
Sleep Hours:
Weight:
Mood: ☺ ☺ ☹ ☹ Other

WEATHER:
SUN WIND
RAIN CLOUDY
SNOW
TEMP:_____

WEDNESDAY / Date:

Today's goal:

Training notes: ....

FUEL LOG

WATER: 6-8 × 8 OZ.	FRUITS: 2-4	VEGGIES: 3-5	WHOLE GRAIN SERVINGS: 6-11	PROTEIN: 4-6 OZ.	LIMIT FAT?	ALCOHOLIC BEVERAGES?	LIMIT "EMPTY" CARBS?
☐☐☐☐ ☐☐☐☐	☐☐ ☐☐	☐☐ ☐☐	☐☐☐☐ ☐☐☐☐	☐☐☐ ☐☐☐	Y N	Y N	Y N

Distance:
Time:
Heart Rate:
i-Rate (1-10):
X-Training:
Sleep Hours:
Weight:
Mood: ☺ ☺ ☹ ☹ Other

WEATHER:
SUN WIND
RAIN CLOUDY
SNOW
TEMP:_____

THURSDAY / Date:

Today's goal:

Training notes: ....

FUEL LOG

WATER: 6-8 × 8 OZ.	FRUITS: 2-4	VEGGIES: 3-5	WHOLE GRAIN SERVINGS: 6-11	PROTEIN: 4-6 OZ.	LIMIT FAT?	ALCOHOLIC BEVERAGES?	LIMIT "EMPTY" CARBS?
☐☐☐☐ ☐☐☐☐	☐☐ ☐☐	☐☐ ☐☐	☐☐☐☐ ☐☐☐☐	☐☐☐ ☐☐☐	Y N	Y N	Y N

Distance:
Time:
Heart Rate:
i-Rate (1-10):
X-Training:
Sleep Hours:
Weight:
Mood: ☺ ☺ ☹ ☹ Other

WEATHER:
SUN WIND
RAIN CLOUDY
SNOW
TEMP:_____

FRIDAY / Date:

Training notes:

Today's goal:

FUEL LOG

WATER: 6-8 × 8 OZ.	FRUITS: 2-4	VEGGIES: 3-5	WHOLE GRAIN SERVINGS: 6-11	PROTEIN: 4-6 OZ.	LIMIT FAT?	ALCOHOLIC BEVERAGES?	LIMIT "EMPTY" CARBS?
☐☐☐☐ ☐☐☐☐	☐☐ ☐☐	☐☐ ☐	☐☐☐ ☐☐☐	☐☐☐ ☐☐☐	Y N	Y N	Y N

WEATHER: SUN WIND RAIN CLOUDY SNOW TEMP:____

Distance:
Time:
Heart Rate:
i-Rate (1-10)
X-Training:
Sleep Hours:
Weight:
Mood: ☺ ☺ ☹ Other

SATURDAY / Date:

Training notes:

Today's goal:

FUEL LOG

WATER: 6-8 × 8 OZ.	FRUITS: 2-4	VEGGIES: 3-5	WHOLE GRAIN SERVINGS: 6-11	PROTEIN: 4-6 OZ.	LIMIT FAT?	ALCOHOLIC BEVERAGES?	LIMIT "EMPTY" CARBS?
☐☐☐☐ ☐☐☐☐	☐☐ ☐☐	☐☐ ☐	☐☐☐ ☐☐☐	☐☐☐ ☐☐☐	Y N	Y N	Y N

WEATHER: SUN WIND RAIN CLOUDY SNOW TEMP:____

Distance:
Time:
Heart Rate:
i-Rate (1-10)
X-Training:
Sleep Hours:
Weight:
Mood: ☺ ☺ ☹ Other

SUNDAY / Date:

Training notes:

Today's goal:

FUEL LOG

WATER: 6-8 × 8 OZ.	FRUITS: 2-4	VEGGIES: 3-5	WHOLE GRAIN SERVINGS: 6-11	PROTEIN: 4-6 OZ.	LIMIT FAT?	ALCOHOLIC BEVERAGES?	LIMIT "EMPTY" CARBS?
☐☐☐☐ ☐☐☐☐	☐☐ ☐☐	☐☐ ☐	☐☐☐ ☐☐☐	☐☐☐ ☐☐☐	Y N	Y N	Y N

WEATHER: SUN WIND RAIN CLOUDY SNOW TEMP:____

Distance:
Time:
Heart Rate:
i-Rate (1-10)
X-Training:
Sleep Hours:
Weight:
Mood: ☺ ☺ ☹ Other

WEEK OF:

GOALS FOR WEEK:

WEEKLY TOTAL: ____

YEAR-TO-DATE TOTAL: ____

PENGUIN WORDS OF WISDOM

For most of us our careers as runners are defined not by a singular moment or event, but rather by the accumulation of thousands of seemingly meaningless episodes.

MONDAY / Date:

Training notes: _____

Today's goal: _____

FUEL LOG

WATER: 6-8 × 8 OZ.	FRUITS: 2-4	VEGGIES: 3-5	WHOLE GRAIN SERVINGS: 6-11	PROTEIN: 4-6 OZ.	LIMIT FAT?	ALCOHOLIC BEVERAGES?	LIMIT "EMPTY" CARBS?
☐☐☐☐ ☐☐☐☐	☐☐ ☐☐	☐☐ ☐☐	☐☐☐☐☐ ☐☐☐☐☐☐	☐☐☐ ☐☐☐	Y N	Y N	Y N

WEATHER: SUN WIND RAIN CLOUDY SNOW TEMP: ____

Distance: _____
Time: _____
Heart Rate: _____
i-Rate (1-10): _____
X-Training: _____
Sleep Hours: _____
Weight: _____
Mood: ☺ ☺ ☹ Other

TUESDAY / Date:

Training notes: _____

Today's goal: _____

FUEL LOG

WATER: 6-8 × 8 OZ.	FRUITS: 2-4	VEGGIES: 3-5	WHOLE GRAIN SERVINGS: 6-11	PROTEIN: 4-6 OZ.	LIMIT FAT?	ALCOHOLIC BEVERAGES?	LIMIT "EMPTY" CARBS?
☐☐☐☐ ☐☐☐☐	☐☐ ☐☐	☐☐ ☐☐	☐☐☐☐☐ ☐☐☐☐☐☐	☐☐☐ ☐☐☐	Y N	Y N	Y N

WEATHER: SUN WIND RAIN CLOUDY SNOW TEMP: ____

Distance: _____
Time: _____
Heart Rate: _____
i-Rate (1-10): _____
X-Training: _____
Sleep Hours: _____
Weight: _____
Mood: ☺ ☺ ☹ Other

WEDNESDAY / Date:

Training notes: _____

Today's goal: _____

FUEL LOG

WATER: 6-8 × 8 OZ.	FRUITS: 2-4	VEGGIES: 3-5	WHOLE GRAIN SERVINGS: 6-11	PROTEIN: 4-6 OZ.	LIMIT FAT?	ALCOHOLIC BEVERAGES?	LIMIT "EMPTY" CARBS?
☐☐☐☐ ☐☐☐☐	☐☐ ☐☐	☐☐ ☐☐	☐☐☐☐☐ ☐☐☐☐☐☐	☐☐☐ ☐☐☐	Y N	Y N	Y N

WEATHER: SUN WIND RAIN CLOUDY SNOW TEMP: ____

Distance: _____
Time: _____
Heart Rate: _____
i-Rate (1-10): _____
X-Training: _____
Sleep Hours: _____
Weight: _____
Mood: ☺ ☺ ☹ Other

THURSDAY / Date:

Training notes: _____

Today's goal: _____

FUEL LOG

WATER: 6-8 × 8 OZ.	FRUITS: 2-4	VEGGIES: 3-5	WHOLE GRAIN SERVINGS: 6-11	PROTEIN: 4-6 OZ.	LIMIT FAT?	ALCOHOLIC BEVERAGES?	LIMIT "EMPTY" CARBS?
☐☐☐☐ ☐☐☐☐	☐☐ ☐☐	☐☐ ☐☐	☐☐☐☐☐ ☐☐☐☐☐☐	☐☐☐ ☐☐☐	Y N	Y N	Y N

WEATHER: SUN WIND RAIN CLOUDY SNOW TEMP: ____

Distance: _____
Time: _____
Heart Rate: _____
i-Rate (1-10): _____
X-Training: _____
Sleep Hours: _____
Weight: _____
Mood: ☺ ☺ ☹ Other

FRIDAY / Date:

Training notes:

Distance:
Time:
Heart Rate:
i-Rate (1-10)
X-Training:
Sleep Hours:
Weight:
Mood: ☺ ☺ ☹ Other

Today's goal:

WEATHER:
SUN WIND
RAIN CLOUDY
SNOW
TEMP: _____

FUEL LOG

WATER: 6-8 x 8 oz.	FRUITS: 2-4	VEGGIES: 3-5	WHOLE GRAIN SERVINGS: 6-11	PROTEIN: 4-6 oz.	LIMIT FAT?	ALCOHOLIC BEVERAGES?	LIMIT "EMPTY" CARBS?
☐☐☐☐ ☐☐☐☐	☐☐ ☐☐	☐☐ ☐☐	☐☐☐☐ ☐☐☐	☐☐☐ ☐☐☐	Y N	Y N	Y N

SATURDAY / Date:

Training notes:

Distance:
Time:
Heart Rate:
i-Rate (1-10)
X-Training:
Sleep Hours:
Weight:
Mood: ☺ ☺ ☹ Other

Today's goal:

WEATHER:
SUN WIND
RAIN CLOUDY
SNOW
TEMP: _____

FUEL LOG

WATER: 6-8 x 8 oz.	FRUITS: 2-4	VEGGIES: 3-5	WHOLE GRAIN SERVINGS: 6-11	PROTEIN: 4-6 oz.	LIMIT FAT?	ALCOHOLIC BEVERAGES?	LIMIT "EMPTY" CARBS?
☐☐☐☐ ☐☐☐☐	☐☐ ☐☐	☐☐ ☐☐	☐☐☐☐ ☐☐☐	☐☐☐ ☐☐☐	Y N	Y N	Y N

SUNDAY / Date:

Training notes:

Distance:
Time:
Heart Rate:
i-Rate (1-10)
X-Training:
Sleep Hours:
Weight:
Mood: ☺ ☺ ☹ Other

Today's goal:

WEATHER:
SUN WIND
RAIN CLOUDY
SNOW
TEMP: _____

FUEL LOG

WATER: 6-8 x 8 oz.	FRUITS: 2-4	VEGGIES: 3-5	WHOLE GRAIN SERVINGS: 6-11	PROTEIN: 4-6 oz.	LIMIT FAT?	ALCOHOLIC BEVERAGES?	LIMIT "EMPTY" CARBS?
☐☐☐☐ ☐☐☐☐	☐☐ ☐☐	☐☐ ☐☐	☐☐☐☐☐ ☐☐☐	☐☐☐ ☐☐☐	Y N	Y N	Y N

WEEK OF:

GOALS FOR WEEK:

WEEKLY TOTAL: _____

YEAR-TO-DATE TOTAL: _____

PENGUIN WORDS OF WISDOM

Every run, every decision to run, becomes a stone in our personal mosaic. Piece by piece we fashion a picture of ourselves that reflects not just who we are, but what we want to become.

MONDAY / Date:

Today's goal:

Training notes: _____

FUEL LOG

WATER: 6-8 x 8 OZ.	FRUITS: 2-4	VEGGIES: 3-5	WHOLE GRAIN SERVINGS: 6-11	PROTEIN: 4-6 OZ.	LIMIT FAT?	ALCOHOLIC BEVERAGES?	LIMIT "EMPTY" CARBS?
☐☐☐☐ ☐☐☐☐ ☐☐	☐☐ ☐☐	☐☐ ☐☐	☐☐☐☐☐ ☐☐	☐☐☐ ☐☐☐	Y N	Y N	Y N

Distance:
Time:
Heart Rate:
i-Rate (1-10)
X-Training:
Sleep Hours:
Weight:
Mood: ☺ ☺ ☹ ☹ Other

WEATHER:
SUN WIND
RAIN CLOUDY
SNOW
TEMP: _____

TUESDAY / Date:

Today's goal:

Training notes: _____

FUEL LOG

WATER: 6-8 x 8 OZ.	FRUITS: 2-4	VEGGIES: 3-5	WHOLE GRAIN SERVINGS: 6-11	PROTEIN: 4-6 OZ.	LIMIT FAT?	ALCOHOLIC BEVERAGES?	LIMIT "EMPTY" CARBS?
☐☐☐☐ ☐☐☐☐ ☐☐	☐☐ ☐☐	☐☐ ☐☐	☐☐☐ ☐☐☐	☐☐☐ ☐☐☐	Y N	Y N	Y N

Distance:
Time:
Heart Rate:
i-Rate (1-10)
X-Training:
Sleep Hours:
Weight:
Mood: ☺ ☺ ☹ ☹ Other

WEATHER:
SUN WIND
RAIN CLOUDY
SNOW
TEMP: _____

WEDNESDAY / Date:

Today's goal:

Training notes: _____

FUEL LOG

WATER: 6-8 x 8 OZ.	FRUITS: 2-4	VEGGIES: 3-5	WHOLE GRAIN SERVINGS: 6-11	PROTEIN: 4-6 OZ.	LIMIT FAT?	ALCOHOLIC BEVERAGES?	LIMIT "EMPTY" CARBS?
☐☐☐☐ ☐☐☐☐ ☐☐	☐☐ ☐☐	☐☐ ☐☐	☐☐☐ ☐☐☐	☐☐☐ ☐☐☐	Y N	Y N	Y N

Distance:
Time:
Heart Rate:
i-Rate (1-10)
X-Training:
Sleep Hours:
Weight:
Mood: ☺ ☺ ☹ ☹ Other

WEATHER:
SUN WIND
RAIN CLOUDY
SNOW
TEMP: _____

THURSDAY / Date:

Today's goal:

Training notes: _____

FUEL LOG

WATER: 6-8 x 8 OZ.	FRUITS: 2-4	VEGGIES: 3-5	WHOLE GRAIN SERVINGS: 6-11	PROTEIN: 4-6 OZ.	LIMIT FAT?	ALCOHOLIC BEVERAGES?	LIMIT "EMPTY" CARBS?
☐☐☐☐ ☐☐☐☐ ☐☐	☐☐ ☐☐	☐☐ ☐☐	☐☐☐ ☐☐☐	☐☐☐ ☐☐☐	Y N	Y N	Y N

Distance:
Time:
Heart Rate:
i-Rate (1-10)
X-Training:
Sleep Hours:
Weight:
Mood: ☺ ☺ ☹ ☹ Other

WEATHER:
SUN WIND
RAIN CLOUDY
SNOW
TEMP: _____

FRIDAY / Date:

Training notes: _____

Today's goal: _____

FUEL LOG

WATER: 6-8 x 8 OZ.	FRUITS: 2-4	VEGGIES: 3-5	WHOLE GRAIN SERVINGS: 6-11	PROTEIN: 4-6 OZ.	LIMIT FAT?	ALCOHOLIC BEVERAGES?	LIMIT "EMPTY" CARBS?
☐☐☐☐ ☐☐☐☐	☐☐ ☐☐	☐☐ ☐☐	☐☐☐☐☐ ☐☐☐☐☐☐	☐☐☐ ☐☐	Y N	Y N	Y N

Distance: _____
Time: _____
Heart Rate: _____
i-Rate (1-10) _____
X-Training: _____
Sleep Hours: _____
Weight: _____

WEATHER:
SUN WIND
RAIN CLOUDY
SNOW
TEMP: _____

Mood: ☺ ☺ ☺ Other

SATURDAY / Date:

Training notes: _____

Today's goal: _____

FUEL LOG

WATER: 6-8 x 8 OZ.	FRUITS: 2-4	VEGGIES: 3-5	WHOLE GRAIN SERVINGS: 6-11	PROTEIN: 4-6 OZ.	LIMIT FAT?	ALCOHOLIC BEVERAGES?	LIMIT "EMPTY" CARBS?
☐☐☐☐ ☐☐☐☐	☐☐ ☐☐	☐☐ ☐☐	☐☐☐☐☐ ☐☐☐☐☐☐	☐☐☐ ☐☐	Y N	Y N	Y N

Distance: _____
Time: _____
Heart Rate: _____
i-Rate (1-10) _____
X-Training: _____
Sleep Hours: _____
Weight: _____

WEATHER:
SUN WIND
RAIN CLOUDY
SNOW
TEMP: _____

Mood: ☺ ☺ ☺ Other

SUNDAY / Date:

Training notes: _____

Today's goal: _____

FUEL LOG

WATER: 6-8 x 8 OZ.	FRUITS: 2-4	VEGGIES: 3-5	WHOLE GRAIN SERVINGS: 6-11	PROTEIN: 4-6 OZ.	LIMIT FAT?	ALCOHOLIC BEVERAGES?	LIMIT "EMPTY" CARBS?
☐☐☐☐ ☐☐☐☐	☐☐ ☐☐	☐☐ ☐☐	☐☐☐☐☐ ☐☐☐☐☐☐	☐☐☐ ☐☐	Y N	Y N	Y N

Distance: _____
Time: _____
Heart Rate: _____
i-Rate (1-10) _____
X-Training: _____
Sleep Hours: _____
Weight: _____

WEATHER:
SUN WIND
RAIN CLOUDY
SNOW
TEMP: _____

Mood: ☺ ☺ ☺ Other

WEEK OF:

GOALS FOR WEEK:

WEEKLY TOTAL: _____

YEAR-TO-DATE TOTAL: _____

PENGUIN WORDS OF WISDOM

It may surprise some people that we, the penguins, are really doing the best that we can. One cannot undo the physical effects of 30 or 40 or more years of neglect and abuse in a matter of weeks or months.

MARCH

SPRING BREAK

After over twenty years as an academic, I know a thing of two about Spring Break. This long revered tradition in higher education ranks right up there with caps and gowns as an inescapable part of the college experience. Students were under the misguided notion that Spring Break was for them. They thought it was their time to let off steam, to party until they dropped. The students were wrong.

Spring Break was invented because by that time of year the faculty was just sick to death of the student body. We were tired of their youthful enthusiasm, challenged by their sophomoric intellect, and threatened by their dreams of a tomorrow in which we had no place.

Your walking and running program needs a Spring Break

just as surely as we did. Chances are that your body, like the faculty, is finding it more and more difficult to maintain the level of effort and frequency of the program you started with. Your may have over estimated your enthusiasm. You might have under estimated the time it was going to take to achieve your even your initial goals. You may have missed some important part of your life which is now beginning to intrude on your athletic life. You may have simply been wrong about what your were willing and capable of doing.

Now is NOT the time to quit. Now is the time to step back, take a break, and rethink your goals, your motives, your objectives, your discipline, and your ability. Maybe you will never have a bumper sticker on your car that says you are an outstanding athlete. Maybe you will have to accept that your progress will be slow and that your potential is much more modest that you thought.

We can all be athletes. We just can't all be really good athletes. The key to long term success is to discover what your athletic skills are and train in a way that you get the maximum from them. This is true whether you discover that at age fifty you can run a four-minute mile or whether you discover at age 30 that you'll never break six hours in a marathon. Neither is right. Neither is best. Both are just true.

Take a break in your training. Take a few days, or even a week, off. Take the time to rest, to recover, and to renew your enthusiasm. It worked for years as a student. It will work for you now.

MONDAY / Date:

Today's goal:

Training notes:

Distance:
Time:
Heart Rate:
i-Rate (1-10):
X-Training:
Sleep Hours:
Weight:
Mood: ☺ ☺ ☹ ☹ Other

FUEL LOG

WATER: 6-8 x 8 OZ.	FRUITS: 2-4	VEGGIES: 3-5	WHOLE GRAIN SERVINGS: 6-11	PROTEIN: 4-6 OZ.	LIMIT FAT?	ALCOHOLIC BEVERAGES?	LIMIT "EMPTY" CARBS?
☐☐☐☐ ☐☐☐☐	☐☐ ☐☐	☐☐ ☐☐	☐☐☐☐☐ ☐☐☐☐☐	☐☐☐ ☐☐☐	Y N	Y N	Y N

WEATHER: SUN WIND RAIN CLOUDY SNOW TEMP:_____

TUESDAY / Date:

Today's goal:

Training notes:

Distance:
Time:
Heart Rate:
i-Rate (1-10):
X-Training:
Sleep Hours:
Weight:
Mood: ☺ ☺ ☹ ☹ Other

FUEL LOG

WATER: 6-8 x 8 OZ.	FRUITS: 2-4	VEGGIES: 3-5	WHOLE GRAIN SERVINGS: 6-11	PROTEIN: 4-6 OZ.	LIMIT FAT?	ALCOHOLIC BEVERAGES?	LIMIT "EMPTY" CARBS?
☐☐☐☐ ☐☐☐☐	☐☐ ☐☐	☐☐ ☐☐	☐☐☐☐☐ ☐☐☐☐☐	☐☐☐ ☐☐☐	Y N	Y N	Y N

WEATHER: SUN WIND RAIN CLOUDY SNOW TEMP:_____

WEDNESDAY / Date:

Today's goal:

Training notes:

Distance:
Time:
Heart Rate:
i-Rate (1-10):
X-Training:
Sleep Hours:
Weight:
Mood: ☺ ☺ ☹ ☹ Other

FUEL LOG

WATER: 6-8 x 8 OZ.	FRUITS: 2-4	VEGGIES: 3-5	WHOLE GRAIN SERVINGS: 6-11	PROTEIN: 4-6 OZ.	LIMIT FAT?	ALCOHOLIC BEVERAGES?	LIMIT "EMPTY" CARBS?
☐☐☐☐ ☐☐☐☐	☐☐ ☐☐	☐☐ ☐☐	☐☐☐☐☐ ☐☐☐☐☐	☐☐☐ ☐☐☐	Y N	Y N	Y N

WEATHER: SUN WIND RAIN CLOUDY SNOW TEMP:_____

THURSDAY / Date:

Today's goal:

Training notes:

Distance:
Time:
Heart Rate:
i-Rate (1-10):
X-Training:
Sleep Hours:
Weight:
Mood: ☺ ☺ ☹ ☹ Other

FUEL LOG

WATER: 6-8 x 8 OZ.	FRUITS: 2-4	VEGGIES: 3-5	WHOLE GRAIN SERVINGS: 6-11	PROTEIN: 4-6 OZ.	LIMIT FAT?	ALCOHOLIC BEVERAGES?	LIMIT "EMPTY" CARBS?
☐☐☐☐ ☐☐☐☐	☐☐ ☐☐	☐☐ ☐☐	☐☐☐☐☐ ☐☐☐☐☐	☐☐☐ ☐☐☐	Y N	Y N	Y N

WEATHER: SUN WIND RAIN CLOUDY SNOW TEMP:_____

FRIDAY / Date:

Training notes:

Today's goal:

FUEL LOG

WATER: 6-8 x 8 OZ.	FRUITS: 2-4	VEGGIES: 3-5	WHOLE GRAIN SERVINGS: 6-11	PROTEIN: 4-6 OZ.	LIMIT FAT?	ALCOHOLIC BEVERAGES?	LIMIT "EMPTY" CARBS?
☐☐☐☐ ☐☐☐☐	☐☐ ☐☐	☐☐☐ ☐☐	☐☐☐☐☐ ☐☐☐☐☐	☐☐☐ ☐☐	Y N	Y N	Y N

Distance:
Time:
Heart Rate:
i-Rate (1-10)
X-Training:
Sleep Hours:
Weight:
Mood: ☺ ☺ ☹ Other

WEATHER:
SUN WIND
RAIN CLOUDY
SNOW
TEMP:___

SATURDAY / Date:

Training notes:

Today's goal:

FUEL LOG

WATER: 6-8 x 8 OZ.	FRUITS: 2-4	VEGGIES: 3-5	WHOLE GRAIN SERVINGS: 6-11	PROTEIN: 4-6 OZ.	LIMIT FAT?	ALCOHOLIC BEVERAGES?	LIMIT "EMPTY" CARBS?
☐☐☐☐ ☐☐☐☐	☐☐ ☐☐	☐☐☐ ☐☐	☐☐☐☐☐ ☐☐☐☐☐	☐☐☐ ☐☐	Y N	Y N	Y N

Distance:
Time:
Heart Rate:
i-Rate (1-10)
X-Training:
Sleep Hours:
Weight:
Mood: ☺ ☺ ☹ Other

WEATHER:
SUN WIND
RAIN CLOUDY
SNOW
TEMP:___

SUNDAY / Date:

Training notes:

Today's goal:

FUEL LOG

WATER: 6-8 x 8 OZ.	FRUITS: 2-4	VEGGIES: 3-5	WHOLE GRAIN SERVINGS: 6-11	PROTEIN: 4-6 OZ.	LIMIT FAT?	ALCOHOLIC BEVERAGES?	LIMIT "EMPTY" CARBS?
☐☐☐☐ ☐☐☐☐	☐☐ ☐☐	☐☐☐ ☐☐	☐☐☐☐☐ ☐☐☐☐☐	☐☐☐ ☐☐	Y N	Y N	Y N

Distance:
Time:
Heart Rate:
i-Rate (1-10)
X-Training:
Sleep Hours:
Weight:
Mood: ☺ ☺ ☹ Other

WEATHER:
SUN WIND
RAIN CLOUDY
SNOW
TEMP:___

WEEK OF:

GOALS FOR WEEK:

WEEKLY TOTAL: _____

YEAR-TO-DATE TOTAL:

PENGUIN WORDS OF WISDOM

We penguins run with more weight than the eagles and sparrows.
We run carrying the burden of failures past, present and future.

MONDAY / Date: ___

Today's goal: ___

Training notes: ___

FUEL LOG

WATER: 6-8 x 8 OZ.	FRUITS: 2-4	VEGGIES: 3-5	WHOLE GRAIN SERVINGS: 6-11	PROTEIN: 4-6 OZ.	LIMIT FAT?	ALCOHOLIC BEVERAGES?	LIMIT "EMPTY" CARBS?
☐☐☐☐ ☐☐☐☐	☐☐ ☐☐	☐☐ ☐☐	☐☐☐☐ ☐☐☐☐ ☐	☐☐☐ ☐☐☐	Y N	Y N	Y N

WEATHER: SUN WIND RAIN CLOUDY SNOW TEMP: ___

- Distance: ___
- Time: ___
- Heart Rate: ___
- i-Rate (1-10): ___
- X-Training: ___
- Sleep Hours: ___
- Weight: ___
- Mood: ☺ ☺ ☹ Other ___

TUESDAY / Date: ___

Today's goal: ___

Training notes: ___

FUEL LOG

WATER: 6-8 x 8 OZ.	FRUITS: 2-4	VEGGIES: 3-5	WHOLE GRAIN SERVINGS: 6-11	PROTEIN: 4-6 OZ.	LIMIT FAT?	ALCOHOLIC BEVERAGES?	LIMIT "EMPTY" CARBS?
☐☐☐☐ ☐☐☐☐	☐☐ ☐☐	☐☐ ☐☐	☐☐☐☐ ☐☐☐☐ ☐	☐☐☐ ☐☐☐	Y N	Y N	Y N

WEATHER: SUN WIND RAIN CLOUDY SNOW TEMP: ___

- Distance: ___
- Time: ___
- Heart Rate: ___
- i-Rate (1-10): ___
- X-Training: ___
- Sleep Hours: ___
- Weight: ___
- Mood: ☺ ☺ ☹ Other ___

WEDNESDAY / Date: ___

Today's goal: ___

Training notes: ___

FUEL LOG

WATER: 6-8 x 8 OZ.	FRUITS: 2-4	VEGGIES: 3-5	WHOLE GRAIN SERVINGS: 6-11	PROTEIN: 4-6 OZ.	LIMIT FAT?	ALCOHOLIC BEVERAGES?	LIMIT "EMPTY" CARBS?
☐☐☐☐ ☐☐☐☐	☐☐ ☐☐	☐☐ ☐☐	☐☐☐☐ ☐☐☐☐ ☐	☐☐☐ ☐☐☐	Y N	Y N	Y N

WEATHER: SUN WIND RAIN CLOUDY SNOW TEMP: ___

- Distance: ___
- Time: ___
- Heart Rate: ___
- i-Rate (1-10): ___
- X-Training: ___
- Sleep Hours: ___
- Weight: ___
- Mood: ☺ ☺ ☹ Other ___

THURSDAY / Date: ___

Today's goal: ___

Training notes: ___

FUEL LOG

WATER: 6-8 x 8 OZ.	FRUITS: 2-4	VEGGIES: 3-5	WHOLE GRAIN SERVINGS: 6-11	PROTEIN: 4-6 OZ.	LIMIT FAT?	ALCOHOLIC BEVERAGES?	LIMIT "EMPTY" CARBS?
☐☐☐☐ ☐☐☐☐	☐☐ ☐☐	☐☐ ☐☐	☐☐☐☐ ☐☐☐☐ ☐	☐☐☐ ☐☐☐	Y N	Y N	Y N

WEATHER: SUN WIND RAIN CLOUDY SNOW TEMP: ___

- Distance: ___
- Time: ___
- Heart Rate: ___
- i-Rate (1-10): ___
- X-Training: ___
- Sleep Hours: ___
- Weight: ___
- Mood: ☺ ☺ ☹ Other ___

FRIDAY / Date:

Today's goal:

Training notes:

Distance:
Time:
Heart Rate:
i-Rate (1-10):
X-Training:
Sleep Hours:
Weight:
Mood: ☺ ☺ ☹ Other

WEATHER:
SUN WIND
RAIN CLOUDY
SNOW
TEMP: _____

FUEL LOG

WATER: 6-8 x 8 OZ.	FRUITS: 2-4	VEGGIES: 3-5	WHOLE GRAIN SERVINGS: 6-11	PROTEIN: 4-6 OZ.	LIMIT FAT?	ALCOHOLIC BEVERAGES?	LIMIT "EMPTY" CARBS?
□□□□ □□□□	□□ □□	□□ □□	□□□□□ □□□□□ □	□□□ □□□	Y N	Y N	Y N

SATURDAY / Date:

Today's goal:

Training notes:

Distance:
Time:
Heart Rate:
i-Rate (1-10):
X-Training:
Sleep Hours:
Weight:
Mood: ☺ ☺ ☹ Other

WEATHER:
SUN WIND
RAIN CLOUDY
SNOW
TEMP: _____

FUEL LOG

WATER: 6-8 x 8 OZ.	FRUITS: 2-4	VEGGIES: 3-5	WHOLE GRAIN SERVINGS: 6-11	PROTEIN: 4-6 OZ.	LIMIT FAT?	ALCOHOLIC BEVERAGES?	LIMIT "EMPTY" CARBS?
□□□□ □□□□	□□ □□	□□ □□	□□□□□ □□□□□ □	□□□ □□□	Y N	Y N	Y N

SUNDAY / Date:

Today's goal:

Training notes:

Distance:
Time:
Heart Rate:
i-Rate (1-10):
X-Training:
Sleep Hours:
Weight:
Mood: ☺ ☺ ☹ Other

WEATHER:
SUN WIND
RAIN CLOUDY
SNOW
TEMP: _____

FUEL LOG

WATER: 6-8 x 8 OZ.	FRUITS: 2-4	VEGGIES: 3-5	WHOLE GRAIN SERVINGS: 6-11	PROTEIN: 4-6 OZ.	LIMIT FAT?	ALCOHOLIC BEVERAGES?	LIMIT "EMPTY" CARBS?
□□□□ □□□□	□□ □□	□□ □□	□□□□□ □□□□□ □	□□□ □□□	Y N	Y N	Y N

WEEK OF:

GOALS FOR WEEK:

WEEKLY TOTAL: _____

YEAR-TO-DATE TOTAL:

PENGUIN WORDS OF WISDOM

Our running shoes are really erasers. Every step erases some memory of a past failure. Every mile brings us closer to a clean slate. Each foot strike rubs away a word, a look, or an event which led us to believe that success was beyond our grasp.

MONDAY / Date: _____

Today's goal: _____

Training notes: _____

Distance: _____
Time: _____
Heart Rate: _____
i-Rate (1-10): _____
X-Training: _____
Sleep Hours: _____
Weight: _____
Mood: ☺ 😐 ☹ Other

FUEL LOG

WATER: 6-8 x 8 OZ.	FRUITS: 2-4	VEGGIES: 3-5	WHOLE GRAIN SERVINGS: 6-11	PROTEIN: 4-6 OZ.	LIMIT FAT?	ALCOHOLIC BEVERAGES?	LIMIT "EMPTY" CARBS?
☐☐☐☐ ☐☐☐☐	☐☐ ☐☐	☐☐ ☐	☐☐☐☐☐ ☐	☐☐ ☐☐	Y N	Y N	Y N

WEATHER: SUN WIND RAIN CLOUDY SNOW TEMP: _____

TUESDAY / Date: _____

Today's goal: _____

Training notes: _____

Distance: _____
Time: _____
Heart Rate: _____
i-Rate (1-10): _____
X-Training: _____
Sleep Hours: _____
Weight: _____
Mood: ☺ 😐 ☹ Other

FUEL LOG

WATER: 6-8 x 8 OZ.	FRUITS: 2-4	VEGGIES: 3-5	WHOLE GRAIN SERVINGS: 6-11	PROTEIN: 4-6 OZ.	LIMIT FAT?	ALCOHOLIC BEVERAGES?	LIMIT "EMPTY" CARBS?
☐☐☐☐ ☐☐☐☐	☐☐ ☐☐	☐☐ ☐	☐☐☐☐☐ ☐	☐☐ ☐☐	Y N	Y N	Y N

WEATHER: SUN WIND RAIN CLOUDY SNOW TEMP: _____

WEDNESDAY / Date: _____

Today's goal: _____

Training notes: _____

Distance: _____
Time: _____
Heart Rate: _____
i-Rate (1-10): _____
X-Training: _____
Sleep Hours: _____
Weight: _____
Mood: ☺ 😐 ☹ Other

FUEL LOG

WATER: 6-8 x 8 OZ.	FRUITS: 2-4	VEGGIES: 3-5	WHOLE GRAIN SERVINGS: 6-11	PROTEIN: 4-6 OZ.	LIMIT FAT?	ALCOHOLIC BEVERAGES?	LIMIT "EMPTY" CARBS?
☐☐☐☐ ☐☐☐☐	☐☐ ☐☐	☐☐ ☐	☐☐☐☐☐ ☐	☐☐ ☐☐	Y N	Y N	Y N

WEATHER: SUN WIND RAIN CLOUDY SNOW TEMP: _____

THURSDAY / Date: _____

Today's goal: _____

Training notes: _____

Distance: _____
Time: _____
Heart Rate: _____
i-Rate (1-10): _____
X-Training: _____
Sleep Hours: _____
Weight: _____
Mood: ☺ 😐 ☹ Other

FUEL LOG

WATER: 6-8 x 8 OZ.	FRUITS: 2-4	VEGGIES: 3-5	WHOLE GRAIN SERVINGS: 6-11	PROTEIN: 4-6 OZ.	LIMIT FAT?	ALCOHOLIC BEVERAGES?	LIMIT "EMPTY" CARBS?
☐☐☐☐ ☐☐☐☐	☐☐ ☐☐	☐☐ ☐	☐☐☐☐☐ ☐	☐☐ ☐☐	Y N	Y N	Y N

WEATHER: SUN WIND RAIN CLOUDY SNOW TEMP: _____

FRIDAY / Date: _____

Today's goal: _____

Training notes: _____

FUEL LOG

WATER: 6-8 x 8 OZ.	FRUITS: 2-4	VEGGIES: 3-5	WHOLE GRAIN SERVINGS: 6-11	PROTEIN: 4-6 OZ.	LIMIT FAT?	ALCOHOLIC BEVERAGES?	LIMIT "EMPTY" CARBS?
☐☐☐☐ ☐☐☐☐	☐☐ ☐☐	☐☐ ☐	☐☐☐☐ ☐☐☐☐ ☐☐☐	☐☐☐ ☐☐☐	Y N	Y N	Y N

WEATHER:
SUN WIND
RAIN CLOUDY
SNOW
TEMP:_____

Distance: _____
Time: _____
Heart Rate: _____
i-Rate (1-10) _____
X-Training: _____
Sleep Hours: _____
Weight: _____
Mood: ☺ ☺ ☹ Other

SATURDAY / Date: _____

Today's goal: _____

Training notes: _____

FUEL LOG

WATER: 6-8 x 8 OZ.	FRUITS: 2-4	VEGGIES: 3-5	WHOLE GRAIN SERVINGS: 6-11	PROTEIN: 4-6 OZ.	LIMIT FAT?	ALCOHOLIC BEVERAGES?	LIMIT "EMPTY" CARBS?
☐☐☐☐ ☐☐☐☐	☐☐ ☐☐	☐☐ ☐	☐☐☐☐ ☐☐☐☐ ☐☐☐	☐☐☐ ☐☐☐	Y N	Y N	Y N

WEATHER:
SUN WIND
RAIN CLOUDY
SNOW
TEMP:_____

Distance: _____
Time: _____
Heart Rate: _____
i-Rate (1-10) _____
X-Training: _____
Sleep Hours: _____
Weight: _____
Mood: ☺ ☺ ☹ Other

SUNDAY / Date: _____

Today's goal: _____

Training notes: _____

FUEL LOG

WATER: 6-8 x 8 OZ.	FRUITS: 2-4	VEGGIES: 3-5	WHOLE GRAIN SERVINGS: 6-11	PROTEIN: 4-6 OZ.	LIMIT FAT?	ALCOHOLIC BEVERAGES?	LIMIT "EMPTY" CARBS?
☐☐☐☐ ☐☐☐☐	☐☐ ☐☐	☐☐ ☐	☐☐☐☐ ☐☐☐☐ ☐☐☐	☐☐☐ ☐☐☐	Y N	Y N	Y N

WEATHER:
SUN WIND
RAIN CLOUDY
SNOW
TEMP:_____

Distance: _____
Time: _____
Heart Rate: _____
i-Rate (1-10) _____
X-Training: _____
Sleep Hours: _____
Weight: _____
Mood: ☺ ☺ ☹ Other

WEEK OF: _____

GOALS FOR WEEK: _____

WEEKLY TOTAL: _____

YEAR-TO-DATE TOTAL: _____

PENGUIN WORDS OF WISDOM

We do not march to the beat of a different drummer. We ramble to the syncopation of our own existence.

MONDAY / Date:

Training notes:

Today's goal:

FUEL LOG

WATER: 6-8 × 8 OZ.	FRUITS: 2-4	VEGGIES: 3-5	WHOLE GRAIN SERVINGS: 6-11	PROTEIN: 4-6 OZ.	LIMIT FAT?	ALCOHOLIC BEVERAGES?	LIMIT "EMPTY" CARBS?
☐☐☐☐ ☐☐☐☐	☐☐ ☐☐	☐☐ ☐	☐☐☐☐ ☐☐☐☐	☐☐ ☐☐ ☐☐	Y N	Y N	Y N

WEATHER:
SUN WIND
RAIN CLOUDY
SNOW
TEMP: _____

Distance:
Time:
Heart Rate:
i-Rate (1-10)
X-Training:
Sleep Hours:
Weight:
Mood: ☺ ☺ ☹ ☹ Other

TUESDAY / Date:

Training notes:

Today's goal:

FUEL LOG

WATER: 6-8 × 8 OZ.	FRUITS: 2-4	VEGGIES: 3-5	WHOLE GRAIN SERVINGS: 6-11	PROTEIN: 4-6 OZ.	LIMIT FAT?	ALCOHOLIC BEVERAGES?	LIMIT "EMPTY" CARBS?
☐☐☐☐ ☐☐☐☐	☐☐ ☐☐	☐☐ ☐	☐☐☐☐ ☐☐☐☐	☐☐ ☐☐ ☐☐	Y N	Y N	Y N

WEATHER:
SUN WIND
RAIN CLOUDY
SNOW
TEMP: _____

Distance:
Time:
Heart Rate:
i-Rate (1-10)
X-Training:
Sleep Hours:
Weight:
Mood: ☺ ☺ ☹ ☹ Other

WEDNESDAY / Date:

Training notes:

Today's goal:

FUEL LOG

WATER: 6-8 × 8 OZ.	FRUITS: 2-4	VEGGIES: 3-5	WHOLE GRAIN SERVINGS: 6-11	PROTEIN: 4-6 OZ.	LIMIT FAT?	ALCOHOLIC BEVERAGES?	LIMIT "EMPTY" CARBS?
☐☐☐☐ ☐☐☐☐	☐☐ ☐☐	☐☐ ☐	☐☐☐☐ ☐☐☐☐	☐☐ ☐☐ ☐☐	Y N	Y N	Y N

WEATHER:
SUN WIND
RAIN CLOUDY
SNOW
TEMP: _____

Distance:
Time:
Heart Rate:
i-Rate (1-10)
X-Training:
Sleep Hours:
Weight:
Mood: ☺ ☺ ☹ ☹ Other

THURSDAY / Date:

Training notes:

Today's goal:

FUEL LOG

WATER: 6-8 × 8 OZ.	FRUITS: 2-4	VEGGIES: 3-5	WHOLE GRAIN SERVINGS: 6-11	PROTEIN: 4-6 OZ.	LIMIT FAT?	ALCOHOLIC BEVERAGES?	LIMIT "EMPTY" CARBS?
☐☐☐☐ ☐☐☐☐	☐☐ ☐☐	☐☐ ☐	☐☐☐☐ ☐☐☐☐	☐☐ ☐☐ ☐☐	Y N	Y N	Y N

WEATHER:
SUN WIND
RAIN CLOUDY
SNOW
TEMP: _____

Distance:
Time:
Heart Rate:
i-Rate (1-10)
X-Training:
Sleep Hours:
Weight:
Mood: ☺ ☺ ☹ ☹ Other

FRIDAY / Date:

Training notes:

Today's goal:

FUEL LOG

WATER: 6-8 × 8 OZ.	FRUITS: 2-4	VEGGIES: 3-5	WHOLE GRAIN SERVINGS: 6-11	PROTEIN: 4-6 OZ.	LIMIT FAT?	ALCOHOLIC BEVERAGES?	LIMIT "EMPTY" CARBS?
☐☐☐☐ ☐☐☐☐	☐☐ ☐☐	☐☐ ☐	☐☐☐☐ ☐☐☐☐ ☐☐☐	☐☐☐ ☐☐	Y N	Y N	Y N

WEATHER:
SUN WIND
RAIN CLOUDY
SNOW
TEMP: _____

Distance:
Time:
Heart Rate:
i-Rate (1-10)
X-Training:
Sleep Hours:
Weight:
Mood: ☺ ☺ ☹ ☹ Other

SATURDAY / Date:

Training notes:

Today's goal:

FUEL LOG

WATER: 6-8 × 8 OZ.	FRUITS: 2-4	VEGGIES: 3-5	WHOLE GRAIN SERVINGS: 6-11	PROTEIN: 4-6 OZ.	LIMIT FAT?	ALCOHOLIC BEVERAGES?	LIMIT "EMPTY" CARBS?
☐☐☐☐ ☐☐☐☐	☐☐ ☐☐	☐☐ ☐	☐☐☐☐ ☐☐☐☐ ☐☐☐	☐☐☐ ☐☐	Y N	Y N	Y N

WEATHER:
SUN WIND
RAIN CLOUDY
SNOW
TEMP: _____

Distance:
Time:
Heart Rate:
i-Rate (1-10)
X-Training:
Sleep Hours:
Weight:
Mood: ☺ ☺ ☹ ☹ Other

SUNDAY / Date:

Training notes:

Today's goal:

FUEL LOG

WATER: 6-8 × 8 OZ.	FRUITS: 2-4	VEGGIES: 3-5	WHOLE GRAIN SERVINGS: 6-11	PROTEIN: 4-6 OZ.	LIMIT FAT?	ALCOHOLIC BEVERAGES?	LIMIT "EMPTY" CARBS?
☐☐☐☐ ☐☐☐☐	☐☐ ☐☐	☐☐ ☐	☐☐☐☐ ☐☐☐☐ ☐☐☐	☐☐☐ ☐☐	Y N	Y N	Y N

WEATHER:
SUN WIND
RAIN CLOUDY
SNOW
TEMP: _____

Distance:
Time:
Heart Rate:
i-Rate (1-10)
X-Training:
Sleep Hours:
Weight:
Mood: ☺ ☺ ☹ ☹ Other

WEEK OF:

GOALS FOR WEEK:

WEEKLY TOTAL: _____

YEAR-TO-DATE TOTAL:

PENGUIN WORDS OF WISDOM

There are many advantages to starting to run later in life. Among them is the ability to use running as a means to rediscover memories long forgotten.

MONDAY / Date:

Today's goal:

Training notes:

FUEL LOG

WATER: 6-8 × 8 OZ.	FRUITS: 2-4	VEGGIES: 3-5	WHOLE GRAIN SERVINGS: 6-11	PROTEIN: 4-6 OZ.	LIMIT FAT?	ALCOHOLIC BEVERAGES?	LIMIT "EMPTY" CARBS?
☐☐☐☐ ☐☐☐☐	☐☐ ☐☐	☐☐ ☐	☐☐☐☐ ☐☐☐☐ ☐☐☐	☐☐☐ ☐☐☐	Y N	Y N	Y N

WEATHER: SUN WIND RAIN CLOUDY SNOW TEMP:_____

Distance:
Time:
Heart Rate:
i-Rate (1-10)
X-Training:
Sleep Hours:
Weight:
Mood: ☺ ☺ ☹ Other

TUESDAY / Date:

Today's goal:

Training notes:

FUEL LOG

WATER: 6-8 × 8 OZ.	FRUITS: 2-4	VEGGIES: 3-5	WHOLE GRAIN SERVINGS: 6-11	PROTEIN: 4-6 OZ.	LIMIT FAT?	ALCOHOLIC BEVERAGES?	LIMIT "EMPTY" CARBS?
☐☐☐☐ ☐☐☐☐	☐☐ ☐☐	☐☐ ☐	☐☐☐☐ ☐☐☐☐ ☐☐☐	☐☐☐ ☐☐☐	Y N	Y N	Y N

WEATHER: SUN WIND RAIN CLOUDY SNOW TEMP:_____

Distance:
Time:
Heart Rate:
i-Rate (1-10)
X-Training:
Sleep Hours:
Weight:
Mood: ☺ ☺ ☹ Other

WEDNESDAY / Date:

Today's goal:

Training notes:

FUEL LOG

WATER: 6-8 × 8 OZ.	FRUITS: 2-4	VEGGIES: 3-5	WHOLE GRAIN SERVINGS: 6-11	PROTEIN: 4-6 OZ.	LIMIT FAT?	ALCOHOLIC BEVERAGES?	LIMIT "EMPTY" CARBS?
☐☐☐☐ ☐☐☐☐	☐☐ ☐☐	☐☐ ☐	☐☐☐☐ ☐☐☐☐ ☐☐☐	☐☐☐ ☐☐☐	Y N	Y N	Y N

WEATHER: SUN WIND RAIN CLOUDY SNOW TEMP:_____

Distance:
Time:
Heart Rate:
i-Rate (1-10)
X-Training:
Sleep Hours:
Weight:
Mood: ☺ ☺ ☹ Other

THURSDAY / Date:

Today's goal:

Training notes:

FUEL LOG

WATER: 6-8 × 8 OZ.	FRUITS: 2-4	VEGGIES: 3-5	WHOLE GRAIN SERVINGS: 6-11	PROTEIN: 4-6 OZ.	LIMIT FAT?	ALCOHOLIC BEVERAGES?	LIMIT "EMPTY" CARBS?
☐☐☐☐ ☐☐☐☐	☐☐ ☐☐	☐☐ ☐	☐☐☐☐ ☐☐☐☐ ☐☐☐	☐☐☐ ☐☐☐	Y N	Y N	Y N

WEATHER: SUN WIND RAIN CLOUDY SNOW TEMP:_____

Distance:
Time:
Heart Rate:
i-Rate (1-10)
X-Training:
Sleep Hours:
Weight:
Mood: ☺ ☺ ☹ Other

FRIDAY / Date:

Training notes: _____

Today's goal: _____

FUEL LOG

WATER: 6-8 × 8 OZ.	FRUITS: 2-4	VEGGIES: 3-5	WHOLE GRAIN SERVINGS: 6-11	PROTEIN: 4-6 OZ.	LIMIT FAT?	ALCOHOLIC BEVERAGES?	LIMIT "EMPTY" CARBS?
☐☐☐☐ ☐☐☐☐	☐☐ ☐☐	☐☐☐ ☐☐	☐☐☐☐☐☐ ☐☐☐☐☐	☐☐☐ ☐☐	Y N	Y N	Y N

WEATHER: SUN WIND RAIN CLOUDY SNOW TEMP: ____

Distance: ____
Time: ____
Heart Rate: ____
i-Rate (1-10): ____
X-Training: ____
Sleep Hours: ____
Weight: ____
Mood: ☺ ☺ ☹ ☹ Other

SATURDAY / Date:

Training notes: _____

Today's goal: _____

FUEL LOG

WATER: 6-8 × 8 OZ.	FRUITS: 2-4	VEGGIES: 3-5	WHOLE GRAIN SERVINGS: 6-11	PROTEIN: 4-6 OZ.	LIMIT FAT?	ALCOHOLIC BEVERAGES?	LIMIT "EMPTY" CARBS?
☐☐☐☐ ☐☐☐☐	☐☐ ☐☐	☐☐☐ ☐☐	☐☐☐☐☐☐ ☐☐☐☐☐	☐☐☐ ☐☐	Y N	Y N	Y N

WEATHER: SUN WIND RAIN CLOUDY SNOW TEMP: ____

Distance: ____
Time: ____
Heart Rate: ____
i-Rate (1-10): ____
X-Training: ____
Sleep Hours: ____
Weight: ____
Mood: ☺ ☺ ☹ ☹ Other

SUNDAY / Date:

Training notes: _____

Today's goal: _____

FUEL LOG

WATER: 6-8 × 8 OZ.	FRUITS: 2-4	VEGGIES: 3-5	WHOLE GRAIN SERVINGS: 6-11	PROTEIN: 4-6 OZ.	LIMIT FAT?	ALCOHOLIC BEVERAGES?	LIMIT "EMPTY" CARBS?
☐☐☐☐ ☐☐☐☐	☐☐ ☐☐	☐☐☐ ☐☐	☐☐☐☐☐☐ ☐☐☐☐☐	☐☐☐ ☐☐	Y N	Y N	Y N

WEATHER: SUN WIND RAIN CLOUDY SNOW TEMP: ____

Distance: ____
Time: ____
Heart Rate: ____
i-Rate (1-10): ____
X-Training: ____
Sleep Hours: ____
Weight: ____
Mood: ☺ ☺ ☹ ☹ Other

WEEK OF:

GOALS FOR WEEK:

WEEKLY TOTAL: _____

YEAR-TO-DATE TOTAL: _____

PENGUIN WORDS OF WISDOM

The battles I fought as a child are being refought every day in my adult world. I am still seeking to prove to myself and others that I can play their game, that I should be on their team, and that I shouldn't be picked last.

APRIL

SINGING IN THE RAIN

Ah, Springtime, when flowers bloom, birds sing, allergies flare, and rain pours. Ah, Springtime, when you never know from day to day what the temperature will be. Ah, Springtime, when [if you live in a part of the country with seasons] you get to run in everything from freezing temperatures to blistering heat. Sometimes on the same run.

April is a great month for excuses. I think it's easier to not run at this time of year than almost any other. If the weather's nice, there's all those springtime things to do from planting flowers to seeding the lawn to washing the windows and cleaning the gutters. If the weather is lousy, it's just too easy to convince yourself that tomorrow will be better so you'll just wait.

As months go, April requires discipline. It requires planning with the ability to adjust, scheduling with the ability to change, and forethought with the understanding that all the planning, scheduling and forethought might have to be disregarded. April is a difficult month. April will challenge every part of you and it will frustrate you if you let it.

Checking off the days in April when I can stay true to my schedule, though, is one of life's great satisfactions. I know that the excuses are there if I look for them. I know that the sun and moon and stars and planets are all conspiring against me. I know that a cold front will come through and the temperature will drop 20 degrees in the middle of a 10 mile run that I started wearing shorts and a t-shirt. I know that it will get to 90 degrees on the day that the only clothes I have to run in are a pair of tights and a fleece top.

That's why I accept the challenge of April with so much determination. I am a warrior in the battle against the ravages and vagaries of the weather. I am a soldier in a war against complacency. I will not give in to the temptations of April. I will accept April as it is, and conquer it.

Every day in April, then, becomes an opportunity for growth and achievement. Every day is a chance to redefine the experience into terms of victory rather than defeat. And a well fought April is the best foundation for a year of success.

MONDAY / Date:

Today's goal:

Training notes:

FUEL LOG

WATER: 6-8 × 8 OZ.	FRUITS: 2-4	VEGGIES: 3-5	WHOLE GRAIN SERVINGS: 6-11	PROTEIN: 4-6 OZ.	LIMIT FAT?	ALCOHOLIC BEVERAGES?	LIMIT "EMPTY" CARBS?
☐☐☐☐ ☐☐☐☐	☐☐ ☐☐	☐☐ ☐☐	☐☐☐☐ ☐☐☐☐ ☐☐☐	☐☐☐ ☐☐☐	Y N	Y N	Y N

WEATHER: SUN WIND RAIN CLOUDY SNOW TEMP:_____

Distance:
Time:
Heart Rate:
i-Rate (1-10)
X-Training:
Sleep Hours:
Weight:
Mood: ☺ ☺ ☹ Other

TUESDAY / Date:

Today's goal:

Training notes:

FUEL LOG

WATER: 6-8 × 8 OZ.	FRUITS: 2-4	VEGGIES: 3-5	WHOLE GRAIN SERVINGS: 6-11	PROTEIN: 4-6 OZ.	LIMIT FAT?	ALCOHOLIC BEVERAGES?	LIMIT "EMPTY" CARBS?
☐☐☐☐ ☐☐☐☐	☐☐ ☐☐	☐☐ ☐☐	☐☐☐☐ ☐☐☐☐ ☐☐☐	☐☐☐ ☐☐☐	Y N	Y N	Y N

WEATHER: SUN WIND RAIN CLOUDY SNOW TEMP:_____

Distance:
Time:
Heart Rate:
i-Rate (1-10)
X-Training:
Sleep Hours:
Weight:
Mood: ☺ ☺ ☹ Other

WEDNESDAY / Date:

Today's goal:

Training notes:

FUEL LOG

WATER: 6-8 × 8 OZ.	FRUITS: 2-4	VEGGIES: 3-5	WHOLE GRAIN SERVINGS: 6-11	PROTEIN: 4-6 OZ.	LIMIT FAT?	ALCOHOLIC BEVERAGES?	LIMIT "EMPTY" CARBS?
☐☐☐☐ ☐☐☐☐	☐☐ ☐☐	☐☐ ☐☐	☐☐☐☐ ☐☐☐☐ ☐☐☐	☐☐☐ ☐☐☐	Y N	Y N	Y N

WEATHER: SUN WIND RAIN CLOUDY SNOW TEMP:_____

Distance:
Time:
Heart Rate:
i-Rate (1-10)
X-Training:
Sleep Hours:
Weight:
Mood: ☺ ☺ ☹ Other

THURSDAY / Date:

Today's goal:

Training notes:

FUEL LOG

WATER: 6-8 × 8 OZ.	FRUITS: 2-4	VEGGIES: 3-5	WHOLE GRAIN SERVINGS: 6-11	PROTEIN: 4-6 OZ.	LIMIT FAT?	ALCOHOLIC BEVERAGES?	LIMIT "EMPTY" CARBS?
☐☐☐☐ ☐☐☐☐	☐☐ ☐☐	☐☐ ☐☐	☐☐☐☐ ☐☐☐☐ ☐☐☐	☐☐☐ ☐☐☐	Y N	Y N	Y N

WEATHER: SUN WIND RAIN CLOUDY SNOW TEMP:_____

Distance:
Time:
Heart Rate:
i-Rate (1-10)
X-Training:
Sleep Hours:
Weight:
Mood: ☺ ☺ ☹ Other

FRIDAY / Date:

Today's goal: _____

Training notes: _____

	Distance:
	Time:
	Heart Rate:
	i-Rate (1-10)
	X-Training:
	Sleep Hours:
	Weight:
	Mood: ☺ 😐 ☹ Other

FUEL LOG

WATER: 6-8 x 8 OZ.	FRUITS: 2-4	VEGGIES: 3-5	WHOLE GRAIN SERVINGS: 6-11	PROTEIN: 4-6 OZ.	LIMIT FAT?	ALCOHOLIC BEVERAGES?	LIMIT "EMPTY" CARBS?
☐☐☐☐ ☐☐☐☐	☐☐ ☐☐	☐☐ ☐☐	☐☐☐☐☐ ☐☐☐☐☐☐	☐☐☐ ☐☐☐	Y N	Y N	Y N

WEATHER: SUN WIND RAIN CLOUDY SNOW TEMP: _____

SATURDAY / Date:

Today's goal: _____

Training notes: _____

	Distance:
	Time:
	Heart Rate:
	i-Rate (1-10)
	X-Training:
	Sleep Hours:
	Weight:
	Mood: ☺ 😐 ☹ Other

FUEL LOG

WATER: 6-8 x 8 OZ.	FRUITS: 2-4	VEGGIES: 3-5	WHOLE GRAIN SERVINGS: 6-11	PROTEIN: 4-6 OZ.	LIMIT FAT?	ALCOHOLIC BEVERAGES?	LIMIT "EMPTY" CARBS?
☐☐☐☐ ☐☐☐☐	☐☐ ☐☐	☐☐ ☐☐	☐☐☐☐☐ ☐☐☐☐☐☐	☐☐☐ ☐☐☐	Y N	Y N	Y N

WEATHER: SUN WIND RAIN CLOUDY SNOW TEMP: _____

SUNDAY / Date:

Today's goal: _____

Training notes: _____

	Distance:
	Time:
	Heart Rate:
	i-Rate (1-10)
	X-Training:
	Sleep Hours:
	Weight:
	Mood: ☺ 😐 ☹ Other

FUEL LOG

WATER: 6-8 x 8 OZ.	FRUITS: 2-4	VEGGIES: 3-5	WHOLE GRAIN SERVINGS: 6-11	PROTEIN: 4-6 OZ.	LIMIT FAT?	ALCOHOLIC BEVERAGES?	LIMIT "EMPTY" CARBS?
☐☐☐☐ ☐☐☐☐	☐☐ ☐☐	☐☐ ☐☐	☐☐☐☐☐ ☐☐☐☐☐☐	☐☐☐ ☐☐☐	Y N	Y N	Y N

WEATHER: SUN WIND RAIN CLOUDY SNOW TEMP: _____

WEEK OF: _____

GOALS FOR WEEK:

WEEKLY TOTAL: _____

YEAR-TO-DATE TOTAL: _____

PENGUIN WORDS OF WISDOM

It happens to all of us I think. The moment comes when what was impossible is possible, the unthinkable thinkable, the undoable done.

MONDAY / Date:

Today's goal: _____

Training notes: _____

Distance: _____
Time: _____
Heart Rate: _____
i-Rate (1-10): _____
X-Training: _____
Sleep Hours: _____
Weight: _____
Mood: ☺ ☺ ☹ Other _____

WEATHER:
SUN   WIND
RAIN CLOUDY
SNOW
TEMP: _____

FUEL LOG

WATER: 6-8 × 8 OZ.	FRUITS: 2-4	VEGGIES: 3-5	WHOLE GRAIN SERVINGS: 6-11	PROTEIN: 4-6 OZ.	LIMIT FAT?	ALCOHOLIC BEVERAGES?	LIMIT "EMPTY" CARBS?
☐☐☐☐ ☐☐☐☐	☐☐ ☐☐	☐☐☐ ☐☐	☐☐☐☐☐ ☐☐☐☐☐ ☐	☐☐☐ ☐☐☐	Y N	Y N	Y N

TUESDAY / Date:

Today's goal: _____

Training notes: _____

Distance: _____
Time: _____
Heart Rate: _____
i-Rate (1-10): _____
X-Training: _____
Sleep Hours: _____
Weight: _____
Mood: ☺ ☺ ☹ Other _____

WEATHER:
SUN   WIND
RAIN CLOUDY
SNOW
TEMP: _____

FUEL LOG

WATER: 6-8 × 8 OZ.	FRUITS: 2-4	VEGGIES: 3-5	WHOLE GRAIN SERVINGS: 6-11	PROTEIN: 4-6 OZ.	LIMIT FAT?	ALCOHOLIC BEVERAGES?	LIMIT "EMPTY" CARBS?
☐☐☐☐ ☐☐☐☐	☐☐ ☐☐	☐☐☐ ☐☐	☐☐☐☐☐ ☐☐☐☐☐ ☐	☐☐☐ ☐☐☐	Y N	Y N	Y N

WEDNESDAY / Date:

Today's goal: _____

Training notes: _____

Distance: _____
Time: _____
Heart Rate: _____
i-Rate (1-10): _____
X-Training: _____
Sleep Hours: _____
Weight: _____
Mood: ☺ ☺ ☹ Other _____

WEATHER:
SUN   WIND
RAIN CLOUDY
SNOW
TEMP: _____

FUEL LOG

WATER: 6-8 × 8 OZ.	FRUITS: 2-4	VEGGIES: 3-5	WHOLE GRAIN SERVINGS: 6-11	PROTEIN: 4-6 OZ.	LIMIT FAT?	ALCOHOLIC BEVERAGES?	LIMIT "EMPTY" CARBS?
☐☐☐☐ ☐☐☐☐	☐☐ ☐☐	☐☐☐ ☐☐	☐☐☐☐☐ ☐☐☐☐☐ ☐	☐☐☐ ☐☐☐	Y N	Y N	Y N

THURSDAY / Date:

Today's goal: _____

Training notes: _____

Distance: _____
Time: _____
Heart Rate: _____
i-Rate (1-10): _____
X-Training: _____
Sleep Hours: _____
Weight: _____
Mood: ☺ ☺ ☹ Other _____

WEATHER:
SUN   WIND
RAIN CLOUDY
SNOW
TEMP: _____

FUEL LOG

WATER: 6-8 × 8 OZ.	FRUITS: 2-4	VEGGIES: 3-5	WHOLE GRAIN SERVINGS: 6-11	PROTEIN: 4-6 OZ.	LIMIT FAT?	ALCOHOLIC BEVERAGES?	LIMIT "EMPTY" CARBS?
☐☐☐☐ ☐☐☐☐	☐☐ ☐☐	☐☐☐ ☐☐	☐☐☐☐☐ ☐☐☐☐☐ ☐	☐☐☐ ☐☐☐	Y N	Y N	Y N

FRIDAY / Date: _____

Training notes: _____

Today's goal: _____

Distance: _____
Time: _____
Heart Rate: _____
i-Rate (1-10): _____
X-Training: _____
Sleep Hours: _____
Weight: _____
Mood: ☺ ☺ ☹ Other

FUEL LOG

WATER: 6-8 x 8 OZ.	FRUITS: 2-4	VEGGIES: 3-5	WHOLE GRAIN SERVINGS: 6-11	PROTEIN: 4-6 OZ.	LIMIT FAT?	ALCOHOLIC BEVERAGES?	LIMIT "EMPTY" CARBS?
☐☐☐☐ ☐☐☐☐	☐☐ ☐☐	☐☐☐ ☐☐	☐☐☐☐☐ ☐☐☐☐☐	☐☐☐ ☐☐☐	Y N	Y N	Y N

WEATHER: SUN WIND RAIN CLOUDY SNOW TEMP: _____

SATURDAY / Date: _____

Training notes: _____

Today's goal: _____

Distance: _____
Time: _____
Heart Rate: _____
i-Rate (1-10): _____
X-Training: _____
Sleep Hours: _____
Weight: _____
Mood: ☺ ☺ ☹ Other

FUEL LOG

WATER: 6-8 x 8 OZ.	FRUITS: 2-4	VEGGIES: 3-5	WHOLE GRAIN SERVINGS: 6-11	PROTEIN: 4-6 OZ.	LIMIT FAT?	ALCOHOLIC BEVERAGES?	LIMIT "EMPTY" CARBS?
☐☐☐☐ ☐☐☐☐	☐☐ ☐☐	☐☐☐ ☐☐	☐☐☐☐☐ ☐☐☐☐☐	☐☐☐ ☐☐☐	Y N	Y N	Y N

WEATHER: SUN WIND RAIN CLOUDY SNOW TEMP: _____

SUNDAY / Date: _____

Training notes: _____

Today's goal: _____

Distance: _____
Time: _____
Heart Rate: _____
i-Rate (1-10): _____
X-Training: _____
Sleep Hours: _____
Weight: _____
Mood: ☺ ☺ ☹ Other

FUEL LOG

WATER: 6-8 x 8 OZ.	FRUITS: 2-4	VEGGIES: 3-5	WHOLE GRAIN SERVINGS: 6-11	PROTEIN: 4-6 OZ.	LIMIT FAT?	ALCOHOLIC BEVERAGES?	LIMIT "EMPTY" CARBS?
☐☐☐☐ ☐☐☐☐	☐☐ ☐☐	☐☐☐ ☐☐	☐☐☐☐☐ ☐☐☐☐☐	☐☐☐ ☐☐☐	Y N	Y N	Y N

WEATHER: SUN WIND RAIN CLOUDY SNOW TEMP: _____

WEEK OF: _____

GOALS FOR WEEK: _____

PENGUIN WORDS OF WISDOM

As runners, we have only a few choices when we're ready to take the next step. We can run farther, run faster, or learn to be happy with what we have.

WEEKLY TOTAL: _____

YEAR-TO-DATE TOTAL: _____

MONDAY / Date:

Training notes: _____

Today's goal: _____

FUEL LOG

WATER: 6-8 × 8 OZ.	FRUITS: 2-4	VEGGIES: 3-5	WHOLE GRAIN SERVINGS: 6-11	PROTEIN: 4-6 OZ.	LIMIT FAT?	ALCOHOLIC BEVERAGES?	LIMIT "EMPTY" CARBS?
☐☐☐☐ ☐☐☐☐	☐☐ ☐☐	☐☐ ☐☐	☐☐☐☐ ☐☐☐☐ ☐☐☐	☐☐☐ ☐☐☐ ☐☐☐	Y N	Y N	Y N

WEATHER: SUN WIND RAIN CLOUDY SNOW
TEMP: _____

Distance: _____
Time: _____
Heart Rate: _____
i-Rate (1-10): _____
X-Training: _____
Sleep Hours: _____
Weight: _____
Mood: ☺ ☺ ☹   Other

TUESDAY / Date:

Training notes: _____

Today's goal: _____

FUEL LOG

WATER: 6-8 × 8 OZ.	FRUITS: 2-4	VEGGIES: 3-5	WHOLE GRAIN SERVINGS: 6-11	PROTEIN: 4-6 OZ.	LIMIT FAT?	ALCOHOLIC BEVERAGES?	LIMIT "EMPTY" CARBS?
☐☐☐☐ ☐☐☐☐	☐☐ ☐☐	☐☐ ☐☐	☐☐☐☐ ☐☐☐☐ ☐☐☐	☐☐☐ ☐☐☐ ☐☐☐	Y N	Y N	Y N

WEATHER: SUN WIND RAIN CLOUDY SNOW
TEMP: _____

Distance: _____
Time: _____
Heart Rate: _____
i-Rate (1-10): _____
X-Training: _____
Sleep Hours: _____
Weight: _____
Mood: ☺ ☺ ☹   Other

WEDNESDAY / Date:

Training notes: _____

Today's goal: _____

FUEL LOG

WATER: 6-8 × 8 OZ.	FRUITS: 2-4	VEGGIES: 3-5	WHOLE GRAIN SERVINGS: 6-11	PROTEIN: 4-6 OZ.	LIMIT FAT?	ALCOHOLIC BEVERAGES?	LIMIT "EMPTY" CARBS?
☐☐☐☐ ☐☐☐☐	☐☐ ☐☐	☐☐ ☐☐	☐☐☐☐ ☐☐☐☐ ☐☐☐	☐☐☐ ☐☐☐ ☐☐☐	Y N	Y N	Y N

WEATHER: SUN WIND RAIN CLOUDY SNOW
TEMP: _____

Distance: _____
Time: _____
Heart Rate: _____
i-Rate (1-10): _____
X-Training: _____
Sleep Hours: _____
Weight: _____
Mood: ☺ ☺ ☹   Other

THURSDAY / Date:

Training notes: _____

Today's goal: _____

FUEL LOG

WATER: 6-8 × 8 OZ.	FRUITS: 2-4	VEGGIES: 3-5	WHOLE GRAIN SERVINGS: 6-11	PROTEIN: 4-6 OZ.	LIMIT FAT?	ALCOHOLIC BEVERAGES?	LIMIT "EMPTY" CARBS?
☐☐☐☐ ☐☐☐☐	☐☐ ☐☐	☐☐ ☐☐	☐☐☐☐ ☐☐☐☐ ☐☐☐	☐☐☐ ☐☐☐ ☐☐☐	Y N	Y N	Y N

WEATHER: SUN WIND RAIN CLOUDY SNOW
TEMP: _____

Distance: _____
Time: _____
Heart Rate: _____
i-Rate (1-10): _____
X-Training: _____
Sleep Hours: _____
Weight: _____
Mood: ☺ ☺ ☹   Other

FRIDAY / Date:

Today's goal: _____

Training notes: _____

Distance: _____
Time: _____
Heart Rate: _____
i-Rate (1-10): _____
X-Training: _____
Sleep Hours: _____
Weight: _____
Mood: ☺ ☺ ☹ ☹ Other

FUEL LOG

WATER: 6-8 × 8 OZ.	FRUITS: 2-4	VEGGIES: 3-5	WHOLE GRAIN SERVINGS: 6-11	PROTEIN: 4-6 OZ.	LIMIT FAT?	ALCOHOLIC BEVERAGES?	LIMIT "EMPTY" CARBS?
☐☐☐☐ ☐☐☐☐	☐☐ ☐☐	☐☐ ☐☐☐	☐☐☐☐ ☐☐☐	☐☐☐ ☐☐☐	Y N	Y N	Y N

WEATHER: SUN WIND RAIN CLOUDY SNOW TEMP: _____

SATURDAY / Date:

Today's goal: _____

Training notes: _____

Distance: _____
Time: _____
Heart Rate: _____
i-Rate (1-10): _____
X-Training: _____
Sleep Hours: _____
Weight: _____
Mood: ☺ ☺ ☹ ☹ Other

FUEL LOG

WATER: 6-8 × 8 OZ.	FRUITS: 2-4	VEGGIES: 3-5	WHOLE GRAIN SERVINGS: 6-11	PROTEIN: 4-6 OZ.	LIMIT FAT?	ALCOHOLIC BEVERAGES?	LIMIT "EMPTY" CARBS?
☐☐☐☐ ☐☐☐☐	☐☐ ☐☐	☐☐ ☐☐☐	☐☐☐☐ ☐☐☐	☐☐☐ ☐☐☐	Y N	Y N	Y N

WEATHER: SUN WIND RAIN CLOUDY SNOW TEMP: _____

SUNDAY / Date:

Today's goal: _____

Training notes: _____

Distance: _____
Time: _____
Heart Rate: _____
i-Rate (1-10): _____
X-Training: _____
Sleep Hours: _____
Weight: _____
Mood: ☺ ☺ ☹ ☹ Other

FUEL LOG

WATER: 6-8 × 8 OZ.	FRUITS: 2-4	VEGGIES: 3-5	WHOLE GRAIN SERVINGS: 6-11	PROTEIN: 4-6 OZ.	LIMIT FAT?	ALCOHOLIC BEVERAGES?	LIMIT "EMPTY" CARBS?
☐☐☐☐ ☐☐☐☐	☐☐ ☐☐	☐☐ ☐☐☐	☐☐☐☐ ☐☐☐	☐☐☐ ☐☐☐	Y N	Y N	Y N

WEATHER: SUN WIND RAIN CLOUDY SNOW TEMP: _____

WEEK OF:

GOALS FOR WEEK:

WEEKLY TOTAL: _____

YEAR-TO-DATE TOTAL: _____

PENGUIN WORDS OF WISDOM

If I'm content too long I get stale. If I push my limits too often I get frustrated. So, as best I can, I give in to the moods.

MONDAY / Date:

Today's goal:

Training notes:
....

FUEL LOG

WATER: 6-8 x 8 oz.	FRUITS: 2-4	VEGGIES: 3-5	WHOLE GRAIN SERVINGS: 6-11	PROTEIN: 4-6 oz.	LIMIT FAT?	ALCOHOLIC BEVERAGES?	LIMIT "EMPTY" CARBS?
☐☐☐☐	☐☐	☐☐	☐☐☐☐	☐☐	Y N	Y N	Y N
☐☐☐☐	☐☐	☐☐	☐☐☐☐	☐☐			
			☐	☐☐			

WEATHER:
SUN WIND
RAIN CLOUDY
SNOW
TEMP:_____

Distance:
Time:
Heart Rate:
i-Rate (1-10)
X-Training:
Sleep Hours:
Weight:
Mood: ☺ ☺ ☹ ☹ Other

TUESDAY / Date:

Today's goal:

Training notes:
....

FUEL LOG

WATER: 6-8 x 8 oz.	FRUITS: 2-4	VEGGIES: 3-5	WHOLE GRAIN SERVINGS: 6-11	PROTEIN: 4-6 oz.	LIMIT FAT?	ALCOHOLIC BEVERAGES?	LIMIT "EMPTY" CARBS?
☐☐☐☐	☐☐	☐☐	☐☐☐☐	☐☐	Y N	Y N	Y N
☐☐☐☐	☐☐	☐☐	☐☐☐☐	☐☐			
			☐	☐☐			

WEATHER:
SUN WIND
RAIN CLOUDY
SNOW
TEMP:_____

Distance:
Time:
Heart Rate:
i-Rate (1-10)
X-Training:
Sleep Hours:
Weight:
Mood: ☺ ☺ ☹ ☹ Other

WEDNESDAY / Date:

Today's goal:

Training notes:
....

FUEL LOG

WATER: 6-8 x 8 oz.	FRUITS: 2-4	VEGGIES: 3-5	WHOLE GRAIN SERVINGS: 6-11	PROTEIN: 4-6 oz.	LIMIT FAT?	ALCOHOLIC BEVERAGES?	LIMIT "EMPTY" CARBS?
☐☐☐☐	☐☐	☐☐	☐☐☐☐	☐☐	Y N	Y N	Y N
☐☐☐☐	☐☐	☐☐	☐☐☐☐	☐☐			
			☐	☐☐			

WEATHER:
SUN WIND
RAIN CLOUDY
SNOW
TEMP:_____

Distance:
Time:
Heart Rate:
i-Rate (1-10)
X-Training:
Sleep Hours:
Weight:
Mood: ☺ ☺ ☹ ☹ Other

THURSDAY / Date:

Today's goal:

Training notes:
....

FUEL LOG

WATER: 6-8 x 8 oz.	FRUITS: 2-4	VEGGIES: 3-5	WHOLE GRAIN SERVINGS: 6-11	PROTEIN: 4-6 oz.	LIMIT FAT?	ALCOHOLIC BEVERAGES?	LIMIT "EMPTY" CARBS?
☐☐☐☐	☐☐	☐☐	☐☐☐☐	☐☐	Y N	Y N	Y N
☐☐☐☐	☐☐	☐☐	☐☐☐☐	☐☐			
			☐	☐☐			

WEATHER:
SUN WIND
RAIN CLOUDY
SNOW
TEMP:_____

Distance:
Time:
Heart Rate:
i-Rate (1-10)
X-Training:
Sleep Hours:
Weight:
Mood: ☺ ☺ ☹ ☹ Other

FRIDAY / Date: _____

Training notes: _____

Distance: _____
Time: _____
Heart Rate: _____
i-Rate (1-10): _____
X-Training: _____
Sleep Hours: _____
Weight: _____
Mood: ☺ ☺ ☹ ☹ Other

Today's goal: _____

FUEL LOG

WATER: 6-8 × 8 OZ.	FRUITS: 2-4	VEGGIES: 3-5	WHOLE GRAIN SERVINGS: 6-11	PROTEIN: 4-6 OZ.	LIMIT FAT?	ALCOHOLIC BEVERAGES?	LIMIT "EMPTY" CARBS?	WEATHER:
☐☐☐☐ ☐☐☐☐	☐☐ ☐☐	☐☐☐ ☐☐☐	☐☐☐☐☐ ☐☐☐☐☐ ☐	☐☐☐ ☐☐☐ ☐	Y N	Y N	Y N	SUN WIND RAIN CLOUDY SNOW TEMP: ____

SATURDAY / Date: _____

Training notes: _____

Distance: _____
Time: _____
Heart Rate: _____
i-Rate (1-10): _____
X-Training: _____
Sleep Hours: _____
Weight: _____
Mood: ☺ ☺ ☹ ☹ Other

Today's goal: _____

FUEL LOG

WATER: 6-8 × 8 OZ.	FRUITS: 2-4	VEGGIES: 3-5	WHOLE GRAIN SERVINGS: 6-11	PROTEIN: 4-6 OZ.	LIMIT FAT?	ALCOHOLIC BEVERAGES?	LIMIT "EMPTY" CARBS?	WEATHER:
☐☐☐☐ ☐☐☐☐	☐☐ ☐☐	☐☐☐ ☐☐☐	☐☐☐☐☐ ☐☐☐☐☐ ☐	☐☐☐ ☐☐☐ ☐	Y N	Y N	Y N	SUN WIND RAIN CLOUDY SNOW TEMP: ____

SUNDAY / Date: _____

Training notes: _____

Distance: _____
Time: _____
Heart Rate: _____
i-Rate (1-10): _____
X-Training: _____
Sleep Hours: _____
Weight: _____
Mood: ☺ ☺ ☹ ☹ Other

Today's goal: _____

FUEL LOG

WATER: 6-8 × 8 OZ.	FRUITS: 2-4	VEGGIES: 3-5	WHOLE GRAIN SERVINGS: 6-11	PROTEIN: 4-6 OZ.	LIMIT FAT?	ALCOHOLIC BEVERAGES?	LIMIT "EMPTY" CARBS?	WEATHER:
☐☐☐☐ ☐☐☐☐	☐☐ ☐☐	☐☐☐ ☐☐☐	☐☐☐☐☐ ☐☐☐☐☐ ☐	☐☐☐ ☐☐☐ ☐	Y N	Y N	Y N	SUN WIND RAIN CLOUDY SNOW TEMP: ____

WEEK OF: _____

GOALS FOR WEEK: _____

WEEKLY TOTAL: _____

YEAR-TO-DATE TOTAL: _____

PENGUIN WORDS OF WISDOM

In the back, we are worried about the really big issues: Will I be able to go the distance? Will there be any food left by the time I finish? And most importantly: Where can I go to the bathroom on the course?

MAY

SMELLING THE FLOWERS

A woman asked me recently how long it takes to feel the runner's high. I told her that I didn't know for sure. If by runner's high she meant the sort of all encompassing euphoria that some people describe, then the answer might be never. I've known people who have been runners for years and never felt anything close to euphoria.

If, on the other hand, she meant the kind of quiet satisfaction that comes from running or walking on the perfect morning, with wonderful friends, on a beautiful path, then that kind of "high" can happen at almost anytime. It can happen when you notice something new on your regular run, when you go a little farther, or a little faster than you expected, or when you are simply happy that you were able to be active on that day. The high is elusive. The joy is right there in front of you.

How often you experience the joy comes down to how often you are available to it. So often we strap on our shoes and try to sneak in a workout in the middle of an already hectic life. We get up early, we skip lunch, or get home late all in the desperate attempt to find the time to do the one thing we enjoy most. The time we spend running or walking is viewed as the least valuable minutes of our day, and the ones that we are most likely to give up.

I would argue that the time we spend being active, whether that means a solo run before work, or track workout with our club in the evening, or a social long run on the weekends, is the most important time of our life. It is the time that not only strengthens our bodies, but refreshes our minds and renews our spirits.

For one month, try making your workouts your number one priority. Schedule you training with the same precision and dedication that you would use to plan and complete an important project. Make the time for your training FIRST, and then go back and fill in your calendar with things like work and other responsibilities. Try it. Just for a month.

My guess is that at the end of May you will realize a calmness and energy that you never dreamed possible. You'll realize, as many have before you, that being active allows you to be a better employee, or employer, or parent, or friend. Running and walking on a regular basis is the quickest path to becoming yourself.

MONDAY / Date: _____

Today's goal: _____

Training notes: _____

FUEL LOG

WATER: 6-8 x 8 OZ.	FRUITS: 2-4	VEGGIES: 3-5	WHOLE GRAIN SERVINGS: 6-11	PROTEIN: 4-6 OZ.	LIMIT FAT?	ALCOHOLIC BEVERAGES?	LIMIT "EMPTY" CARBS?
☐☐☐☐ ☐☐☐☐	☐☐ ☐☐	☐☐☐ ☐☐	☐☐☐☐ ☐	☐☐☐ ☐☐	Y N	Y N	Y N

WEATHER: SUN WIND RAIN CLOUDY SNOW   TEMP: _____

Distance: _____
Time: _____
Heart Rate: _____
i-Rate (1-10): _____
X-Training: _____
Sleep Hours: _____
Weight: _____
Mood: ☺ ☺ ☹ Other

TUESDAY / Date: _____

Today's goal: _____

Training notes: _____

FUEL LOG

WATER: 6-8 x 8 OZ.	FRUITS: 2-4	VEGGIES: 3-5	WHOLE GRAIN SERVINGS: 6-11	PROTEIN: 4-6 OZ.	LIMIT FAT?	ALCOHOLIC BEVERAGES?	LIMIT "EMPTY" CARBS?
☐☐☐☐ ☐☐☐☐	☐☐ ☐☐	☐☐☐ ☐☐	☐☐☐☐ ☐	☐☐☐ ☐☐	Y N	Y N	Y N

WEATHER: SUN WIND RAIN CLOUDY SNOW   TEMP: _____

Distance: _____
Time: _____
Heart Rate: _____
i-Rate (1-10): _____
X-Training: _____
Sleep Hours: _____
Weight: _____
Mood: ☺ ☺ ☹ Other

WEDNESDAY / Date: _____

Today's goal: _____

Training notes: _____

FUEL LOG

WATER: 6-8 x 8 OZ.	FRUITS: 2-4	VEGGIES: 3-5	WHOLE GRAIN SERVINGS: 6-11	PROTEIN: 4-6 OZ.	LIMIT FAT?	ALCOHOLIC BEVERAGES?	LIMIT "EMPTY" CARBS?
☐☐☐☐ ☐☐☐☐	☐☐ ☐☐	☐☐☐ ☐☐	☐☐☐☐ ☐	☐☐☐ ☐☐	Y N	Y N	Y N

WEATHER: SUN WIND RAIN CLOUDY SNOW   TEMP: _____

Distance: _____
Time: _____
Heart Rate: _____
i-Rate (1-10): _____
X-Training: _____
Sleep Hours: _____
Weight: _____
Mood: ☺ ☺ ☹ Other

THURSDAY / Date: _____

Today's goal: _____

Training notes: _____

FUEL LOG

WATER: 6-8 x 8 OZ.	FRUITS: 2-4	VEGGIES: 3-5	WHOLE GRAIN SERVINGS: 6-11	PROTEIN: 4-6 OZ.	LIMIT FAT?	ALCOHOLIC BEVERAGES?	LIMIT "EMPTY" CARBS?
☐☐☐☐ ☐☐☐☐	☐☐ ☐☐	☐☐☐ ☐☐	☐☐☐☐ ☐	☐☐☐ ☐☐	Y N	Y N	Y N

WEATHER: SUN WIND RAIN CLOUDY SNOW   TEMP: _____

Distance: _____
Time: _____
Heart Rate: _____
i-Rate (1-10): _____
X-Training: _____
Sleep Hours: _____
Weight: _____
Mood: ☺ ☺ ☹ Other

FRIDAY / Date:

Today's goal:

Training notes:

Distance:
Time:
Heart Rate:
i-Rate (1-10):
X-Training:
Sleep Hours:
Weight:
Mood: ☺ 😐 ☹ Other

FUEL LOG

WATER: 6-8 x 8 OZ.	FRUITS: 2-4	VEGGIES: 3-5	WHOLE GRAIN SERVINGS: 6-11	PROTEIN: 4-6 OZ.	LIMIT FAT?	ALCOHOLIC BEVERAGES?	LIMIT "EMPTY" CARBS?
☐☐☐☐ ☐☐☐☐	☐☐ ☐☐	☐☐ ☐	☐☐☐ ☐☐☐	☐☐☐ ☐	Y N	Y N	Y N

WEATHER: SUN WIND RAIN CLOUDY SNOW TEMP: ___

SATURDAY / Date:

Today's goal:

Training notes:

Distance:
Time:
Heart Rate:
i-Rate (1-10):
X-Training:
Sleep Hours:
Weight:
Mood: ☺ 😐 ☹ Other

FUEL LOG

WATER: 6-8 x 8 OZ.	FRUITS: 2-4	VEGGIES: 3-5	WHOLE GRAIN SERVINGS: 6-11	PROTEIN: 4-6 OZ.	LIMIT FAT?	ALCOHOLIC BEVERAGES?	LIMIT "EMPTY" CARBS?
☐☐☐☐ ☐☐☐☐	☐☐ ☐☐	☐☐ ☐	☐☐☐ ☐☐☐	☐☐☐ ☐	Y N	Y N	Y N

WEATHER: SUN WIND RAIN CLOUDY SNOW TEMP: ___

SUNDAY / Date:

Today's goal:

Training notes:

Distance:
Time:
Heart Rate:
i-Rate (1-10):
X-Training:
Sleep Hours:
Weight:
Mood: ☺ 😐 ☹ Other

FUEL LOG

WATER: 6-8 x 8 OZ.	FRUITS: 2-4	VEGGIES: 3-5	WHOLE GRAIN SERVINGS: 6-11	PROTEIN: 4-6 OZ.	LIMIT FAT?	ALCOHOLIC BEVERAGES?	LIMIT "EMPTY" CARBS?
☐☐☐☐ ☐☐☐☐	☐☐ ☐☐	☐☐ ☐	☐☐☐ ☐☐☐	☐☐☐ ☐	Y N	Y N	Y N

WEATHER: SUN WIND RAIN CLOUDY SNOW TEMP: ___

WEEK OF:

GOALS FOR WEEK:

WEEKLY TOTAL: ___

YEAR-TO-DATE TOTAL:

PENGUIN WORDS OF WISDOM

As tempting as it may be to view one's life as a single season, our experience tells us that it is not. Life is a succession of seasons.

MONDAY / Date:

Today's goal:

Training notes: _____

FUEL LOG

WATER: 6-8 × 8 OZ.	FRUITS: 2-4	VEGGIES: 3-5	WHOLE GRAIN SERVINGS: 6-11	PROTEIN: 4-6 OZ.	LIMIT FAT?	ALCOHOLIC BEVERAGES?	LIMIT "EMPTY" CARBS?
☐☐☐☐ ☐☐☐☐	☐☐ ☐☐	☐☐☐ ☐☐	☐☐☐☐☐ ☐☐☐☐☐ ☐	☐☐☐ ☐☐☐	Y N	Y N	Y N

WEATHER: SUN WIND RAIN CLOUDY SNOW TEMP:_____

Distance:
Time:
Heart Rate:
i-Rate (1-10)
X-Training:
Sleep Hours:
Weight:
Mood: ☺ ☺ ☺ Other

TUESDAY / Date:

Today's goal:

Training notes: _____

FUEL LOG

WATER: 6-8 × 8 OZ.	FRUITS: 2-4	VEGGIES: 3-5	WHOLE GRAIN SERVINGS: 6-11	PROTEIN: 4-6 OZ.	LIMIT FAT?	ALCOHOLIC BEVERAGES?	LIMIT "EMPTY" CARBS?
☐☐☐☐ ☐☐☐☐	☐☐ ☐☐	☐☐☐ ☐☐	☐☐☐☐☐ ☐☐☐☐☐ ☐	☐☐☐ ☐☐☐	Y N	Y N	Y N

WEATHER: SUN WIND RAIN CLOUDY SNOW TEMP:_____

Distance:
Time:
Heart Rate:
i-Rate (1-10)
X-Training:
Sleep Hours:
Weight:
Mood: ☺ ☺ ☺ Other

WEDNESDAY / Date:

Today's goal:

Training notes: _____

FUEL LOG

WATER: 6-8 × 8 OZ.	FRUITS: 2-4	VEGGIES: 3-5	WHOLE GRAIN SERVINGS: 6-11	PROTEIN: 4-6 OZ.	LIMIT FAT?	ALCOHOLIC BEVERAGES?	LIMIT "EMPTY" CARBS?
☐☐☐☐ ☐☐☐☐	☐☐ ☐☐	☐☐☐ ☐☐	☐☐☐☐☐ ☐☐☐☐☐ ☐	☐☐☐ ☐☐☐	Y N	Y N	Y N

WEATHER: SUN WIND RAIN CLOUDY SNOW TEMP:_____

Distance:
Time:
Heart Rate:
i-Rate (1-10)
X-Training:
Sleep Hours:
Weight:
Mood: ☺ ☺ ☺ Other

THURSDAY / Date:

Today's goal:

Training notes: _____

FUEL LOG

WATER: 6-8 × 8 OZ.	FRUITS: 2-4	VEGGIES: 3-5	WHOLE GRAIN SERVINGS: 6-11	PROTEIN: 4-6 OZ.	LIMIT FAT?	ALCOHOLIC BEVERAGES?	LIMIT "EMPTY" CARBS?
☐☐☐☐ ☐☐☐☐	☐☐ ☐☐	☐☐☐ ☐☐	☐☐☐☐☐ ☐☐☐☐☐ ☐	☐☐☐ ☐☐☐	Y N	Y N	Y N

WEATHER: SUN WIND RAIN CLOUDY SNOW TEMP:_____

Distance:
Time:
Heart Rate:
i-Rate (1-10)
X-Training:
Sleep Hours:
Weight:
Mood: ☺ ☺ ☺ Other

FRIDAY / Date: _____

Today's goal: _____

Training notes: _____

FUEL LOG

WATER: 6-8 x 8 oz.	FRUITS: 2-4	VEGGIES: 3-5	WHOLE GRAIN SERVINGS: 6-11	PROTEIN: 4-6 oz.	LIMIT FAT?	ALCOHOLIC BEVERAGES?	LIMIT "EMPTY" CARBS?
☐☐☐☐ ☐☐☐☐	☐☐ ☐☐	☐☐ ☐☐	☐☐☐☐ ☐☐☐☐ ☐☐☐	☐☐☐ ☐☐☐	Y N	Y N	Y N

Distance: _____
Time: _____
Heart Rate: _____
i-Rate (1-10): _____
X-Training: _____
Sleep Hours: _____
Weight: _____
Mood: ☺ ☺ ☹ ☹ Other

WEATHER: SUN WIND RAIN CLOUDY SNOW TEMP:_____

SATURDAY / Date: _____

Today's goal: _____

Training notes: _____

FUEL LOG

WATER: 6-8 x 8 oz.	FRUITS: 2-4	VEGGIES: 3-5	WHOLE GRAIN SERVINGS: 6-11	PROTEIN: 4-6 oz.	LIMIT FAT?	ALCOHOLIC BEVERAGES?	LIMIT "EMPTY" CARBS?
☐☐☐☐ ☐☐☐☐	☐☐ ☐☐	☐☐ ☐☐	☐☐☐☐ ☐☐☐☐ ☐☐☐	☐☐☐ ☐☐☐	Y N	Y N	Y N

Distance: _____
Time: _____
Heart Rate: _____
i-Rate (1-10): _____
X-Training: _____
Sleep Hours: _____
Weight: _____
Mood: ☺ ☺ ☹ ☹ Other

WEATHER: SUN WIND RAIN CLOUDY SNOW TEMP:_____

SUNDAY / Date: _____

Today's goal: _____

Training notes: _____

FUEL LOG

WATER: 6-8 x 8 oz.	FRUITS: 2-4	VEGGIES: 3-5	WHOLE GRAIN SERVINGS: 6-11	PROTEIN: 4-6 oz.	LIMIT FAT?	ALCOHOLIC BEVERAGES?	LIMIT "EMPTY" CARBS?
☐☐☐☐ ☐☐☐☐	☐☐ ☐☐	☐☐ ☐☐	☐☐☐☐ ☐☐☐☐ ☐☐☐	☐☐☐ ☐☐☐	Y N	Y N	Y N

Distance: _____
Time: _____
Heart Rate: _____
i-Rate (1-10): _____
X-Training: _____
Sleep Hours: _____
Weight: _____
Mood: ☺ ☺ ☹ ☹ Other

WEATHER: SUN WIND RAIN CLOUDY SNOW TEMP:_____

WEEK OF: _____

GOALS FOR WEEK: _____

WEEKLY TOTAL: _____

YEAR-TO-DATE TOTAL: _____

PENGUIN WORDS OF WISDOM

At times I find myself sitting and staring at my shoes, waiting for them to somehow find the energy to begin running by themselves. It is almost as if, like a squirrel, I have been hiding good feelings inside my shoes for the days when I need them.

MONDAY / Date:

Today's goal:

Training notes:
_____
_____

FUEL LOG

WATER: 6-8 × 8 OZ.	FRUITS: 2-4	VEGGIES: 3-5	WHOLE GRAIN SERVINGS: 6-11	PROTEIN: 4-6 OZ.	LIMIT FAT?	ALCOHOLIC BEVERAGES?	LIMIT "EMPTY" CARBS?
☐☐☐☐ ☐☐☐☐	☐☐ ☐☐	☐☐ ☐☐	☐☐☐☐☐ ☐☐☐☐☐☐	☐☐☐ ☐☐☐	Y N	Y N	Y N

WEATHER:
SUN WIND
RAIN CLOUDY
SNOW
TEMP:_____

Distance:
Time:
Heart Rate:
i-Rate (1-10)
X-Training:
Sleep Hours:
Weight:
Mood: ☺ ☺ ☹ Other

TUESDAY / Date:

Today's goal:

Training notes:
_____
_____

FUEL LOG

WATER: 6-8 × 8 OZ.	FRUITS: 2-4	VEGGIES: 3-5	WHOLE GRAIN SERVINGS: 6-11	PROTEIN: 4-6 OZ.	LIMIT FAT?	ALCOHOLIC BEVERAGES?	LIMIT "EMPTY" CARBS?
☐☐☐☐ ☐☐☐☐	☐☐ ☐☐	☐☐ ☐☐	☐☐☐☐☐ ☐☐☐☐☐☐	☐☐☐ ☐☐☐	Y N	Y N	Y N

WEATHER:
SUN WIND
RAIN CLOUDY
SNOW
TEMP:_____

Distance:
Time:
Heart Rate:
i-Rate (1-10)
X-Training:
Sleep Hours:
Weight:
Mood: ☺ ☺ ☹ Other

WEDNESDAY / Date:

Today's goal:

Training notes:
_____
_____

FUEL LOG

WATER: 6-8 × 8 OZ.	FRUITS: 2-4	VEGGIES: 3-5	WHOLE GRAIN SERVINGS: 6-11	PROTEIN: 4-6 OZ.	LIMIT FAT?	ALCOHOLIC BEVERAGES?	LIMIT "EMPTY" CARBS?
☐☐☐☐ ☐☐☐☐	☐☐ ☐☐	☐☐ ☐☐	☐☐☐☐☐ ☐☐☐☐☐☐	☐☐☐ ☐☐☐	Y N	Y N	Y N

WEATHER:
SUN WIND
RAIN CLOUDY
SNOW
TEMP:_____

Distance:
Time:
Heart Rate:
i-Rate (1-10)
X-Training:
Sleep Hours:
Weight:
Mood: ☺ ☺ ☹ Other

THURSDAY / Date:

Today's goal:

Training notes:
_____
_____

FUEL LOG

WATER: 6-8 × 8 OZ.	FRUITS: 2-4	VEGGIES: 3-5	WHOLE GRAIN SERVINGS: 6-11	PROTEIN: 4-6 OZ.	LIMIT FAT?	ALCOHOLIC BEVERAGES?	LIMIT "EMPTY" CARBS?
☐☐☐☐ ☐☐☐☐	☐☐ ☐☐	☐☐ ☐☐	☐☐☐☐☐ ☐☐☐☐☐☐	☐☐☐ ☐☐☐	Y N	Y N	Y N

WEATHER:
SUN WIND
RAIN CLOUDY
SNOW
TEMP:_____

Distance:
Time:
Heart Rate:
i-Rate (1-10)
X-Training:
Sleep Hours:
Weight:
Mood: ☺ ☺ ☹ Other

FRIDAY / Date:

Training notes:

Today's goal:

- Distance:
- Time:
- Heart Rate:
- i-Rate (1-10)
- X-Training:
- Sleep Hours:
- Weight:
- Mood: ☺ 😐 ☹ Other

FUEL LOG

WATER: 6-8 × 8 OZ.	FRUITS: 2-4	VEGGIES: 3-5	WHOLE GRAIN SERVINGS: 6-11	PROTEIN: 4-6 OZ.	LIMIT FAT?	ALCOHOLIC BEVERAGES?	LIMIT "EMPTY" CARBS?
☐☐☐☐	☐☐	☐☐	☐☐☐☐☐	☐☐☐	Y N	Y N	Y N
☐☐☐☐	☐☐	☐	☐☐☐☐☐	☐☐☐			

WEATHER:
SUN WIND
RAIN CLOUDY
SNOW
TEMP:___

SATURDAY / Date:

Training notes:

Today's goal:

- Distance:
- Time:
- Heart Rate:
- i-Rate (1-10)
- X-Training:
- Sleep Hours:
- Weight:
- Mood: ☺ 😐 ☹ Other

FUEL LOG

WATER: 6-8 × 8 OZ.	FRUITS: 2-4	VEGGIES: 3-5	WHOLE GRAIN SERVINGS: 6-11	PROTEIN: 4-6 OZ.	LIMIT FAT?	ALCOHOLIC BEVERAGES?	LIMIT "EMPTY" CARBS?
☐☐☐☐	☐☐	☐☐	☐☐☐☐☐	☐☐☐	Y N	Y N	Y N
☐☐☐☐	☐☐	☐	☐☐☐☐☐	☐☐☐			

WEATHER:
SUN WIND
RAIN CLOUDY
SNOW
TEMP:___

SUNDAY / Date:

Training notes:

Today's goal:

- Distance:
- Time:
- Heart Rate:
- i-Rate (1-10)
- X-Training:
- Sleep Hours:
- Weight:
- Mood: ☺ 😐 ☹ Other

FUEL LOG

WATER: 6-8 × 8 OZ.	FRUITS: 2-4	VEGGIES: 3-5	WHOLE GRAIN SERVINGS: 6-11	PROTEIN: 4-6 OZ.	LIMIT FAT?	ALCOHOLIC BEVERAGES?	LIMIT "EMPTY" CARBS?
☐☐☐☐	☐☐	☐☐	☐☐☐☐☐	☐☐☐	Y N	Y N	Y N
☐☐☐☐	☐☐	☐	☐☐☐☐☐	☐☐☐			

WEATHER:
SUN WIND
RAIN CLOUDY
SNOW
TEMP:___

WEEK OF:

GOALS FOR WEEK:

WEEKLY TOTAL: _____

YEAR-TO-DATE TOTAL:

PENGUIN WORDS OF WISDOM

Even when I am running alone, I know that somewhere, at the same time, hundreds of other people are doing the same thing. Some, perhaps, for the same reasons.

MONDAY / Date:

Today's goal:

Training notes: _____

FUEL LOG

WATER: 6-8 × 8 OZ.	FRUITS: 2-4	VEGGIES: 3-5	WHOLE GRAIN SERVINGS: 6-11	PROTEIN: 4-6 OZ.	LIMIT FAT?	ALCOHOLIC BEVERAGES?	LIMIT "EMPTY" CARBS?
☐☐☐☐ ☐☐☐☐	☐☐ ☐☐	☐☐ ☐	☐☐☐☐☐ ☐☐☐☐☐ ☐	☐☐☐ ☐☐☐	Y N	Y N	Y N

WEATHER:
SUN WIND
RAIN CLOUDY
SNOW
TEMP:_____

Distance:
Time:
Heart Rate:
i-Rate (1-10)
X-Training:
Sleep Hours:
Weight:
Mood: ☺ ☺ ☹ Other

TUESDAY / Date:

Today's goal:

Training notes: _____

FUEL LOG

WATER: 6-8 × 8 OZ.	FRUITS: 2-4	VEGGIES: 3-5	WHOLE GRAIN SERVINGS: 6-11	PROTEIN: 4-6 OZ.	LIMIT FAT?	ALCOHOLIC BEVERAGES?	LIMIT "EMPTY" CARBS?
☐☐☐☐ ☐☐☐☐	☐☐ ☐☐	☐☐ ☐	☐☐☐☐☐ ☐☐☐☐☐ ☐	☐☐☐ ☐☐☐	Y N	Y N	Y N

WEATHER:
SUN WIND
RAIN CLOUDY
SNOW
TEMP:_____

Distance:
Time:
Heart Rate:
i-Rate (1-10)
X-Training:
Sleep Hours:
Weight:
Mood: ☺ ☺ ☹ Other

WEDNESDAY / Date:

Today's goal:

Training notes: _____

FUEL LOG

WATER: 6-8 × 8 OZ.	FRUITS: 2-4	VEGGIES: 3-5	WHOLE GRAIN SERVINGS: 6-11	PROTEIN: 4-6 OZ.	LIMIT FAT?	ALCOHOLIC BEVERAGES?	LIMIT "EMPTY" CARBS?
☐☐☐☐ ☐☐☐☐	☐☐ ☐☐	☐☐ ☐	☐☐☐☐☐ ☐☐☐☐☐ ☐	☐☐☐ ☐☐☐	Y N	Y N	Y N

WEATHER:
SUN WIND
RAIN CLOUDY
SNOW
TEMP:_____

Distance:
Time:
Heart Rate:
i-Rate (1-10)
X-Training:
Sleep Hours:
Weight:
Mood: ☺ ☺ ☹ Other

THURSDAY / Date:

Today's goal:

Training notes: _____

FUEL LOG

WATER: 6-8 × 8 OZ.	FRUITS: 2-4	VEGGIES: 3-5	WHOLE GRAIN SERVINGS: 6-11	PROTEIN: 4-6 OZ.	LIMIT FAT?	ALCOHOLIC BEVERAGES?	LIMIT "EMPTY" CARBS?
☐☐☐☐ ☐☐☐☐	☐☐ ☐☐	☐☐ ☐	☐☐☐☐☐ ☐☐☐☐☐ ☐	☐☐☐ ☐☐☐	Y N	Y N	Y N

WEATHER:
SUN WIND
RAIN CLOUDY
SNOW
TEMP:_____

Distance:
Time:
Heart Rate:
i-Rate (1-10)
X-Training:
Sleep Hours:
Weight:
Mood: ☺ ☺ ☹ Other

FRIDAY / Date: _____   Training notes: _____

Today's goal: _____

Distance: _____
Time: _____
Heart Rate: _____
i-Rate (1-10) _____
X-Training: _____
Sleep Hours: _____
Weight: _____
Mood: ☺ ☺ ☹ ☹ Other _____

WEATHER:
SUN   WIND
RAIN CLOUDY
SNOW
TEMP: _____

FUEL LOG

WATER: 6-8 x 8 OZ.	FRUITS: 2-4	VEGGIES: 3-5	WHOLE GRAIN SERVINGS: 6-11	PROTEIN: 4-6 OZ.	LIMIT FAT?	ALCOHOLIC BEVERAGES?	LIMIT "EMPTY" CARBS?
☐☐☐☐ ☐☐☐☐	☐☐ ☐☐	☐☐ ☐☐	☐☐☐☐ ☐☐☐☐ ☐☐☐	☐☐☐ ☐☐☐	Y N	Y N	Y N

SATURDAY / Date: _____   Training notes: _____

Today's goal: _____

Distance: _____
Time: _____
Heart Rate: _____
i-Rate (1-10) _____
X-Training: _____
Sleep Hours: _____
Weight: _____
Mood: ☺ ☺ ☹ ☹ Other _____

WEATHER:
SUN   WIND
RAIN CLOUDY
SNOW
TEMP: _____

FUEL LOG

WATER: 6-8 x 8 OZ.	FRUITS: 2-4	VEGGIES: 3-5	WHOLE GRAIN SERVINGS: 6-11	PROTEIN: 4-6 OZ.	LIMIT FAT?	ALCOHOLIC BEVERAGES?	LIMIT "EMPTY" CARBS?
☐☐☐☐ ☐☐☐☐	☐☐ ☐☐	☐☐ ☐☐	☐☐☐☐ ☐☐☐☐ ☐☐☐	☐☐☐ ☐☐☐	Y N	Y N	Y N

SUNDAY / Date: _____   Training notes: _____

Today's goal: _____

Distance: _____
Time: _____
Heart Rate: _____
i-Rate (1-10) _____
X-Training: _____
Sleep Hours: _____
Weight: _____
Mood: ☺ ☺ ☹ ☹ Other _____

WEATHER:
SUN   WIND
RAIN CLOUDY
SNOW
TEMP: _____

FUEL LOG

WATER: 6-8 x 8 OZ.	FRUITS: 2-4	VEGGIES: 3-5	WHOLE GRAIN SERVINGS: 6-11	PROTEIN: 4-6 OZ.	LIMIT FAT?	ALCOHOLIC BEVERAGES?	LIMIT "EMPTY" CARBS?
☐☐☐☐ ☐☐☐☐	☐☐ ☐☐	☐☐ ☐☐	☐☐☐☐ ☐☐☐☐ ☐☐☐	☐☐☐ ☐☐☐	Y N	Y N	Y N

WEEK OF: _____

GOALS FOR WEEK: _____

WEEKLY TOTAL: _____

YEAR-TO-DATE TOTAL: _____

PENGUIN WORDS OF WISDOM

As runners, we face our moment of truth every time we put on our running shoes. In fact, it may be that the more important moment of truth comes just before we decide to put on our running shoes. In that powder flash of decision, we affirm our identity as runners.

JUNE

JUNE GLOOM

I'm going to let you in on a little secret about running and walking. This is the best kept secret in the running community and one that everyone is afraid will get out. This is the secret that brings fear into the hearts of the giant shoe companies and running magazine editors. This is what they are afraid that you are going to discover.

Some runs just aren't any fun at all.

There, now you know. You know that it's true for me, that it's true for world class athletes, that it's true for those that have been running for a lifetime, that it's true for those that have been running for less than a year, and it's going to be true for you. It is. Some runs start badly, get worse, and end horribly. You never know when it will happen, you rarely know why, but you can count on it happening to you.

When it does (and it will) the real question is what are you going to do about it. How are your going to react when the one activity in your life that you count on to relieve your stress, to bring some fun into your life, suddenly turns ugly on you. How are you going to react when even your feet have deserted you? What will you do when there's nothing that you can do?

The answer is simple, if you're willing to hear it. When there's nothing you can do, do nothing. Nothing. If you haven't started on your run yet and you sense the gloom coming over you . . . don't run. If you're headed out the door when it hits you, don't go out. And if it hits you in the middle of a run just stop, turn around, and go home. Immediately. Nothing good ever comes from making a bad run worse by banging your head against it.

Accept the fact that you, like all of us, are human and that your running is an extension of every part of you. The parts that you like, the parts that you don't, the parts that you want to keep, and the parts that you'd like to change. You are, like all of us, a complicated blend of discipline and irresponsibility, ambition and complacency, and courage and fear. Your running life will not be composed of only the best of you. It will also have a full measure of the rest of you.

So when that grumpy part of you steals the joy from your run, don't resist. Tomorrow is another day.

MONDAY / Date:

Today's goal:

Training notes:
_____
_____
_____

FUEL LOG

WATER: 6-8 × 8 OZ.	FRUITS: 2-4	VEGGIES: 3-5	WHOLE GRAIN SERVINGS: 6-11	PROTEIN: 4-6 OZ.	LIMIT FAT?	ALCOHOLIC BEVERAGES?	LIMIT "EMPTY" CARBS?
☐☐☐☐ ☐☐☐☐	☐☐ ☐☐	☐☐ ☐☐	☐☐☐☐☐ ☐☐☐☐☐ ☐	☐☐☐ ☐☐☐	Y N	Y N	Y N

WEATHER:
SUN WIND
RAIN CLOUDY
SNOW
TEMP:_____

Distance:
Time:
Heart Rate:
i-Rate (1-10)
X-Training:
Sleep Hours:
Weight:
Mood: ☺ ☺ ☹ ☹ Other

TUESDAY / Date:

Today's goal:

Training notes:
_____
_____
_____

FUEL LOG

WATER: 6-8 × 8 OZ.	FRUITS: 2-4	VEGGIES: 3-5	WHOLE GRAIN SERVINGS: 6-11	PROTEIN: 4-6 OZ.	LIMIT FAT?	ALCOHOLIC BEVERAGES?	LIMIT "EMPTY" CARBS?
☐☐☐☐ ☐☐☐☐	☐☐ ☐☐	☐☐ ☐☐	☐☐☐☐☐ ☐☐☐☐☐ ☐	☐☐☐ ☐☐☐	Y N	Y N	Y N

WEATHER:
SUN WIND
RAIN CLOUDY
SNOW
TEMP:_____

Distance:
Time:
Heart Rate:
i-Rate (1-10)
X-Training:
Sleep Hours:
Weight:
Mood: ☺ ☺ ☹ ☹ Other

WEDNESDAY / Date:

Today's goal:

Training notes:
_____
_____
_____

FUEL LOG

WATER: 6-8 × 8 OZ.	FRUITS: 2-4	VEGGIES: 3-5	WHOLE GRAIN SERVINGS: 6-11	PROTEIN: 4-6 OZ.	LIMIT FAT?	ALCOHOLIC BEVERAGES?	LIMIT "EMPTY" CARBS?
☐☐☐☐ ☐☐☐☐	☐☐ ☐☐	☐☐ ☐☐	☐☐☐☐☐ ☐☐☐☐☐ ☐	☐☐☐ ☐☐☐	Y N	Y N	Y N

WEATHER:
SUN WIND
RAIN CLOUDY
SNOW
TEMP:_____

Distance:
Time:
Heart Rate:
i-Rate (1-10)
X-Training:
Sleep Hours:
Weight:
Mood: ☺ ☺ ☹ ☹ Other

THURSDAY / Date:

Today's goal:

Training notes:
_____
_____
_____

FUEL LOG

WATER: 6-8 × 8 OZ.	FRUITS: 2-4	VEGGIES: 3-5	WHOLE GRAIN SERVINGS: 6-11	PROTEIN: 4-6 OZ.	LIMIT FAT?	ALCOHOLIC BEVERAGES?	LIMIT "EMPTY" CARBS?
☐☐☐☐ ☐☐☐☐	☐☐ ☐☐	☐☐ ☐☐	☐☐☐☐☐ ☐☐☐☐☐ ☐	☐☐☐ ☐☐☐	Y N	Y N	Y N

WEATHER:
SUN WIND
RAIN CLOUDY
SNOW
TEMP:_____

Distance:
Time:
Heart Rate:
i-Rate (1-10)
X-Training:
Sleep Hours:
Weight:
Mood: ☺ ☺ ☹ ☹ Other

FRIDAY / Date: _____   Training notes: _____

Today's goal: _____

Distance: _____
Time: _____
Heart Rate: _____
i-Rate (1-10): _____
X-Training: _____
Sleep Hours: _____
Weight: _____
Mood: ☺ 😐 ☹ Other

WEATHER:
SUN WIND
RAIN CLOUDY
SNOW
TEMP: _____

FUEL LOG

WATER: 6-8 × 8 OZ.	FRUITS: 2-4	VEGGIES: 3-5	WHOLE GRAIN SERVINGS: 6-11	PROTEIN: 4-6 OZ.	LIMIT FAT?	ALCOHOLIC BEVERAGES?	LIMIT "EMPTY" CARBS?
☐☐☐☐ ☐☐☐☐	☐☐ ☐☐	☐☐☐ ☐☐	☐☐☐☐☐☐ ☐☐☐☐☐	☐☐☐ ☐☐	Y N	Y N	Y N

SATURDAY / Date: _____   Training notes: _____

Today's goal: _____

Distance: _____
Time: _____
Heart Rate: _____
i-Rate (1-10): _____
X-Training: _____
Sleep Hours: _____
Weight: _____
Mood: ☺ 😐 ☹ Other

WEATHER:
SUN WIND
RAIN CLOUDY
SNOW
TEMP: _____

FUEL LOG

WATER: 6-8 × 8 OZ.	FRUITS: 2-4	VEGGIES: 3-5	WHOLE GRAIN SERVINGS: 6-11	PROTEIN: 4-6 OZ.	LIMIT FAT?	ALCOHOLIC BEVERAGES?	LIMIT "EMPTY" CARBS?
☐☐☐☐ ☐☐☐☐	☐☐ ☐☐	☐☐☐ ☐☐	☐☐☐☐☐☐ ☐☐☐☐☐	☐☐☐ ☐☐	Y N	Y N	Y N

SUNDAY / Date: _____   Training notes: _____

Today's goal: _____

Distance: _____
Time: _____
Heart Rate: _____
i-Rate (1-10): _____
X-Training: _____
Sleep Hours: _____
Weight: _____
Mood: ☺ 😐 ☹ Other

WEATHER:
SUN WIND
RAIN CLOUDY
SNOW
TEMP: _____

FUEL LOG

WATER: 6-8 × 8 OZ.	FRUITS: 2-4	VEGGIES: 3-5	WHOLE GRAIN SERVINGS: 6-11	PROTEIN: 4-6 OZ.	LIMIT FAT?	ALCOHOLIC BEVERAGES?	LIMIT "EMPTY" CARBS?
☐☐☐☐ ☐☐☐☐	☐☐ ☐☐	☐☐☐ ☐☐	☐☐☐☐☐☐ ☐☐☐☐☐	☐☐☐ ☐☐	Y N	Y N	Y N

WEEK OF: _____

GOALS FOR WEEK: _____

WEEKLY TOTAL: _____

YEAR-TO-DATE TOTAL: _____

PENGUIN WORDS OF WISDOM

It never bothered me to finish last, or nearly last. No matter how silly I might have looked running, it was nothing compared to how stupid I looked drunk.

MONDAY / Date: _____ Training notes: _____

Today's goal: _____

Distance: _____
Time: _____
Heart Rate: _____
i-Rate (1-10): _____
X-Training: _____
Sleep Hours: _____
Weight: _____
Mood: ☺ ☺ ☹ Other

FUEL LOG

WEATHER: SUN WIND RAIN CLOUDY SNOW   TEMP: _____

WATER: 6-8 x 8 OZ.	FRUITS: 2-4	VEGGIES: 3-5	WHOLE GRAIN SERVINGS: 6-11	PROTEIN: 4-6 OZ.	LIMIT FAT?	ALCOHOLIC BEVERAGES?	LIMIT "EMPTY" CARBS?
☐☐☐☐☐ ☐☐☐☐	☐☐ ☐☐	☐☐ ☐☐	☐☐☐☐☐ ☐	☐☐ ☐☐ ☐☐	Y N	Y N	Y N

TUESDAY / Date: _____ Training notes: _____

Today's goal: _____

Distance: _____
Time: _____
Heart Rate: _____
i-Rate (1-10): _____
X-Training: _____
Sleep Hours: _____
Weight: _____
Mood: ☺ ☺ ☹ Other

FUEL LOG

WEATHER: SUN WIND RAIN CLOUDY SNOW   TEMP: _____

WATER: 6-8 x 8 OZ.	FRUITS: 2-4	VEGGIES: 3-5	WHOLE GRAIN SERVINGS: 6-11	PROTEIN: 4-6 OZ.	LIMIT FAT?	ALCOHOLIC BEVERAGES?	LIMIT "EMPTY" CARBS?
☐☐☐☐☐ ☐☐☐☐	☐☐ ☐☐	☐☐ ☐☐	☐☐☐☐☐ ☐	☐☐ ☐☐ ☐☐	Y N	Y N	Y N

WEDNESDAY / Date: _____ Training notes: _____

Today's goal: _____

Distance: _____
Time: _____
Heart Rate: _____
i-Rate (1-10): _____
X-Training: _____
Sleep Hours: _____
Weight: _____
Mood: ☺ ☺ ☹ Other

FUEL LOG

WEATHER: SUN WIND RAIN CLOUDY SNOW   TEMP: _____

WATER: 6-8 x 8 OZ.	FRUITS: 2-4	VEGGIES: 3-5	WHOLE GRAIN SERVINGS: 6-11	PROTEIN: 4-6 OZ.	LIMIT FAT?	ALCOHOLIC BEVERAGES?	LIMIT "EMPTY" CARBS?
☐☐☐☐☐ ☐☐☐☐	☐☐ ☐☐	☐☐ ☐☐	☐☐☐☐☐ ☐	☐☐ ☐☐ ☐☐	Y N	Y N	Y N

THURSDAY / Date: _____ Training notes: _____

Today's goal: _____

Distance: _____
Time: _____
Heart Rate: _____
i-Rate (1-10): _____
X-Training: _____
Sleep Hours: _____
Weight: _____
Mood: ☺ ☺ ☹ Other

FUEL LOG

WEATHER: SUN WIND RAIN CLOUDY SNOW   TEMP: _____

WATER: 6-8 x 8 OZ.	FRUITS: 2-4	VEGGIES: 3-5	WHOLE GRAIN SERVINGS: 6-11	PROTEIN: 4-6 OZ.	LIMIT FAT?	ALCOHOLIC BEVERAGES?	LIMIT "EMPTY" CARBS?
☐☐☐☐☐ ☐☐☐☐	☐☐ ☐☐	☐☐ ☐☐	☐☐☐☐☐ ☐	☐☐ ☐☐ ☐☐	Y N	Y N	Y N

FRIDAY / Date:

Today's goal: _____

Training notes: _____

Distance: _____
Time: _____
Heart Rate: _____
i-Rate (1-10): _____
X-Training: _____
Sleep Hours: _____
Weight: _____
Mood: ☺ 😐 ☹ Other _____

WEATHER:
SUN WIND
RAIN CLOUDY
SNOW
TEMP: _____

FUEL LOG

WATER: 6-8 x 8 OZ.	FRUITS: 2-4	VEGGIES: 3-5	WHOLE GRAIN SERVINGS: 6-11	PROTEIN: 4-6 OZ.	LIMIT FAT?	ALCOHOLIC BEVERAGES?	LIMIT "EMPTY" CARBS?
☐☐☐☐ ☐☐☐☐	☐☐ ☐☐	☐☐☐ ☐☐	☐☐☐☐☐ ☐☐☐☐☐ ☐	☐☐☐ ☐☐☐	Y N	Y N	Y N

SATURDAY / Date:

Today's goal: _____

Training notes: _____

Distance: _____
Time: _____
Heart Rate: _____
i-Rate (1-10): _____
X-Training: _____
Sleep Hours: _____
Weight: _____
Mood: ☺ 😐 ☹ Other _____

WEATHER:
SUN WIND
RAIN CLOUDY
SNOW
TEMP: _____

FUEL LOG

WATER: 6-8 x 8 OZ.	FRUITS: 2-4	VEGGIES: 3-5	WHOLE GRAIN SERVINGS: 6-11	PROTEIN: 4-6 OZ.	LIMIT FAT?	ALCOHOLIC BEVERAGES?	LIMIT "EMPTY" CARBS?
☐☐☐☐ ☐☐☐☐	☐☐ ☐☐	☐☐☐ ☐☐	☐☐☐☐☐ ☐☐☐☐☐ ☐	☐☐☐ ☐☐☐	Y N	Y N	Y N

SUNDAY / Date:

Today's goal: _____

Training notes: _____

Distance: _____
Time: _____
Heart Rate: _____
i-Rate (1-10): _____
X-Training: _____
Sleep Hours: _____
Weight: _____
Mood: ☺ 😐 ☹ Other _____

WEATHER:
SUN WIND
RAIN CLOUDY
SNOW
TEMP: _____

FUEL LOG

WATER: 6-8 x 8 OZ.	FRUITS: 2-4	VEGGIES: 3-5	WHOLE GRAIN SERVINGS: 6-11	PROTEIN: 4-6 OZ.	LIMIT FAT?	ALCOHOLIC BEVERAGES?	LIMIT "EMPTY" CARBS?
☐☐☐☐ ☐☐☐☐	☐☐ ☐☐	☐☐☐ ☐☐	☐☐☐☐☐ ☐☐☐☐☐ ☐	☐☐☐ ☐☐☐	Y N	Y N	Y N

WEEK OF: _____

GOALS FOR WEEK: _____

WEEKLY TOTAL: _____

YEAR-TO-DATE TOTAL: _____

PENGUIN WORDS OF WISDOM

I didn't start running with a goal in mind. I didn't get fired up about running a 5K or marathon. I didn't have a grand plan, or even a not-so-grand plan. I started running so that I could quit running.

MONDAY / Date:

Today's goal:

Training notes:

Distance:
Time:
Heart Rate:
i-Rate (1-10)
X-Training:
Sleep Hours:
Weight:
Mood: ☺ ☺ ☹ ⊗ Other

FUEL LOG

WATER: 6-8 x 8 OZ.	FRUITS: 2-4	VEGGIES: 3-5	WHOLE GRAIN SERVINGS: 6-11	PROTEIN: 4-6 OZ.	LIMIT FAT?	ALCOHOLIC BEVERAGES?	LIMIT "EMPTY" CARBS?
☐☐☐☐ ☐☐☐☐	☐☐ ☐☐	☐☐ ☐☐	☐☐☐☐☐ ☐☐☐☐☐ ☐	☐☐ ☐☐ ☐☐	Y N	Y N	Y N

WEATHER: SUN WIND RAIN CLOUDY SNOW TEMP:_____

TUESDAY / Date:

Today's goal:

Training notes:

Distance:
Time:
Heart Rate:
i-Rate (1-10)
X-Training:
Sleep Hours:
Weight:
Mood: ☺ ☺ ☹ ⊗ Other

FUEL LOG

WATER: 6-8 x 8 OZ.	FRUITS: 2-4	VEGGIES: 3-5	WHOLE GRAIN SERVINGS: 6-11	PROTEIN: 4-6 OZ.	LIMIT FAT?	ALCOHOLIC BEVERAGES?	LIMIT "EMPTY" CARBS?
☐☐☐☐ ☐☐☐☐	☐☐ ☐☐	☐☐ ☐☐	☐☐☐☐☐ ☐☐☐☐☐ ☐	☐☐ ☐☐ ☐☐	Y N	Y N	Y N

WEATHER: SUN WIND RAIN CLOUDY SNOW TEMP:_____

WEDNESDAY / Date:

Today's goal:

Training notes:

Distance:
Time:
Heart Rate:
i-Rate (1-10)
X-Training:
Sleep Hours:
Weight:
Mood: ☺ ☺ ☹ ⊗ Other

FUEL LOG

WATER: 6-8 x 8 OZ.	FRUITS: 2-4	VEGGIES: 3-5	WHOLE GRAIN SERVINGS: 6-11	PROTEIN: 4-6 OZ.	LIMIT FAT?	ALCOHOLIC BEVERAGES?	LIMIT "EMPTY" CARBS?
☐☐☐☐ ☐☐☐☐	☐☐ ☐☐	☐☐ ☐☐	☐☐☐☐☐ ☐☐☐☐☐ ☐	☐☐ ☐☐ ☐☐	Y N	Y N	Y N

WEATHER: SUN WIND RAIN CLOUDY SNOW TEMP:_____

THURSDAY / Date:

Today's goal:

Training notes:

Distance:
Time:
Heart Rate:
i-Rate (1-10)
X-Training:
Sleep Hours:
Weight:
Mood: ☺ ☺ ☹ ⊗ Other

FUEL LOG

WATER: 6-8 x 8 OZ.	FRUITS: 2-4	VEGGIES: 3-5	WHOLE GRAIN SERVINGS: 6-11	PROTEIN: 4-6 OZ.	LIMIT FAT?	ALCOHOLIC BEVERAGES?	LIMIT "EMPTY" CARBS?
☐☐☐☐ ☐☐☐☐	☐☐ ☐☐	☐☐ ☐☐	☐☐☐☐☐ ☐☐☐☐☐ ☐	☐☐ ☐☐ ☐☐	Y N	Y N	Y N

WEATHER: SUN WIND RAIN CLOUDY SNOW TEMP:_____

FRIDAY / Date:

Training notes: _____

Today's goal: _____

FUEL LOG

WATER: 6-8 x 8 OZ.	FRUITS: 2-4	VEGGIES: 3-5	PROTEIN: 4-6 OZ.	WHOLE GRAIN SERVINGS: 6-11	LIMIT FAT?	ALCOHOLIC BEVERAGES?	LIMIT "EMPTY" CARBS?
☐☐☐☐ ☐☐☐☐	☐☐ ☐☐	☐☐☐ ☐☐	☐☐☐ ☐☐	☐☐☐☐☐☐ ☐☐☐☐☐	Y N	Y N	Y N

WEATHER: SUN WIND RAIN CLOUDY SNOW TEMP: _____

Distance: _____
Time: _____
Heart Rate: _____
i-Rate (1-10): _____
X-Training: _____
Sleep Hours: _____
Weight: _____
Mood: ☺ ☺ ☹ ☹ Other

SATURDAY / Date:

Training notes: _____

Today's goal: _____

FUEL LOG

WATER: 6-8 x 8 OZ.	FRUITS: 2-4	VEGGIES: 3-5	PROTEIN: 4-6 OZ.	WHOLE GRAIN SERVINGS: 6-11	LIMIT FAT?	ALCOHOLIC BEVERAGES?	LIMIT "EMPTY" CARBS?
☐☐☐☐ ☐☐☐☐	☐☐ ☐☐	☐☐☐ ☐☐	☐☐☐ ☐☐	☐☐☐☐☐☐ ☐☐☐☐☐	Y N	Y N	Y N

WEATHER: SUN WIND RAIN CLOUDY SNOW TEMP: _____

Distance: _____
Time: _____
Heart Rate: _____
i-Rate (1-10): _____
X-Training: _____
Sleep Hours: _____
Weight: _____
Mood: ☺ ☺ ☹ ☹ Other

SUNDAY / Date:

Training notes: _____

Today's goal: _____

FUEL LOG

WATER: 6-8 x 8 OZ.	FRUITS: 2-4	VEGGIES: 3-5	PROTEIN: 4-6 OZ.	WHOLE GRAIN SERVINGS: 6-11	LIMIT FAT?	ALCOHOLIC BEVERAGES?	LIMIT "EMPTY" CARBS?
☐☐☐☐ ☐☐☐☐	☐☐ ☐☐	☐☐☐ ☐☐	☐☐☐ ☐☐	☐☐☐☐☐☐ ☐☐☐☐☐	Y N	Y N	Y N

WEATHER: SUN WIND RAIN CLOUDY SNOW TEMP: _____

Distance: _____
Time: _____
Heart Rate: _____
i-Rate (1-10): _____
X-Training: _____
Sleep Hours: _____
Weight: _____
Mood: ☺ ☺ ☹ ☹ Other

WEEK OF:

GOALS FOR WEEK: _____

WEEKLY TOTAL: _____

YEAR-TO-DATE TOTAL: _____

PENGUIN WORDS OF WISDOM

My early training was equally divided between sheer lunacy and pure stupidity. I foolishly believed that tearing my body down was the way to build my body up.

MONDAY / Date:

Today's goal:

Training notes:
_____
_____

FUEL LOG

WATER: 6-8 x 8 OZ.	FRUITS: 2-4	VEGGIES: 3-5	WHOLE GRAIN SERVINGS: 6-11	PROTEIN: 4-6 OZ.	LIMIT FAT?	ALCOHOLIC BEVERAGES?	LIMIT "EMPTY" CARBS?
☐☐☐☐ ☐☐☐☐	☐☐ ☐☐	☐☐☐☐ ☐☐	☐☐☐☐☐☐ ☐☐☐☐☐	☐☐☐ ☐☐☐	Y N	Y N	Y N

WEATHER: SUN WIND RAIN CLOUDY SNOW TEMP: ____

Distance:
Time:
Heart Rate:
i-Rate (1-10)
X-Training:
Sleep Hours:
Weight:
Mood: ☺ ☹ ☻ Other

TUESDAY / Date:

Today's goal:

Training notes:
_____
_____

FUEL LOG

WATER: 6-8 x 8 OZ.	FRUITS: 2-4	VEGGIES: 3-5	WHOLE GRAIN SERVINGS: 6-11	PROTEIN: 4-6 OZ.	LIMIT FAT?	ALCOHOLIC BEVERAGES?	LIMIT "EMPTY" CARBS?
☐☐☐☐ ☐☐☐☐	☐☐ ☐☐	☐☐☐☐ ☐☐	☐☐☐☐☐☐ ☐☐☐☐☐	☐☐☐ ☐☐☐	Y N	Y N	Y N

WEATHER: SUN WIND RAIN CLOUDY SNOW TEMP: ____

Distance:
Time:
Heart Rate:
i-Rate (1-10)
X-Training:
Sleep Hours:
Weight:
Mood: ☺ ☹ ☻ Other

WEDNESDAY / Date:

Today's goal:

Training notes:
_____
_____

FUEL LOG

WATER: 6-8 x 8 OZ.	FRUITS: 2-4	VEGGIES: 3-5	WHOLE GRAIN SERVINGS: 6-11	PROTEIN: 4-6 OZ.	LIMIT FAT?	ALCOHOLIC BEVERAGES?	LIMIT "EMPTY" CARBS?
☐☐☐☐ ☐☐☐☐	☐☐ ☐☐	☐☐☐☐ ☐☐	☐☐☐☐☐☐ ☐☐☐☐☐	☐☐☐ ☐☐☐	Y N	Y N	Y N

WEATHER: SUN WIND RAIN CLOUDY SNOW TEMP: ____

Distance:
Time:
Heart Rate:
i-Rate (1-10)
X-Training:
Sleep Hours:
Weight:
Mood: ☺ ☹ ☻ Other

THURSDAY / Date:

Today's goal:

Training notes:
_____
_____

FUEL LOG

WATER: 6-8 x 8 OZ.	FRUITS: 2-4	VEGGIES: 3-5	WHOLE GRAIN SERVINGS: 6-11	PROTEIN: 4-6 OZ.	LIMIT FAT?	ALCOHOLIC BEVERAGES?	LIMIT "EMPTY" CARBS?
☐☐☐☐ ☐☐☐☐	☐☐ ☐☐	☐☐☐☐ ☐☐	☐☐☐☐☐☐ ☐☐☐☐☐	☐☐☐ ☐☐☐	Y N	Y N	Y N

WEATHER: SUN WIND RAIN CLOUDY SNOW TEMP: ____

Distance:
Time:
Heart Rate:
i-Rate (1-10)
X-Training:
Sleep Hours:
Weight:
Mood: ☺ ☹ ☻ Other

FRIDAY / Date:

Today's goal:

Training notes:

Distance:
Time:
Heart Rate:
i-Rate (1-10)
X-Training:
Sleep Hours:
Weight:
Mood: ☺ ☺ ☹ Other

FUEL LOG

WATER: 6-8 × 8 OZ.	FRUITS: 2-4	VEGGIES: 3-5	WHOLE GRAIN SERVINGS: 6-11	PROTEIN: 4-6 OZ.	LIMIT FAT?	ALCOHOLIC BEVERAGES?	LIMIT "EMPTY" CARBS?
☐☐☐☐ ☐☐☐☐	☐☐ ☐☐	☐☐ ☐☐	☐☐☐☐☐ ☐☐☐☐☐	☐☐☐ ☐☐	Y N	Y N	Y N

WEATHER:
SUN WIND
RAIN CLOUDY
SNOW
TEMP:_____

SATURDAY / Date:

Today's goal:

Training notes:

Distance:
Time:
Heart Rate:
i-Rate (1-10)
X-Training:
Sleep Hours:
Weight:
Mood: ☺ ☺ ☹ Other

FUEL LOG

WATER: 6-8 × 8 OZ.	FRUITS: 2-4	VEGGIES: 3-5	WHOLE GRAIN SERVINGS: 6-11	PROTEIN: 4-6 OZ.	LIMIT FAT?	ALCOHOLIC BEVERAGES?	LIMIT "EMPTY" CARBS?
☐☐☐☐ ☐☐☐☐	☐☐ ☐☐	☐☐ ☐☐	☐☐☐☐☐ ☐☐☐☐☐	☐☐☐ ☐☐	Y N	Y N	Y N

WEATHER:
SUN WIND
RAIN CLOUDY
SNOW
TEMP:_____

SUNDAY / Date:

Today's goal:

Training notes:

Distance:
Time:
Heart Rate:
i-Rate (1-10)
X-Training:
Sleep Hours:
Weight:
Mood: ☺ ☺ ☹ Other

FUEL LOG

WATER: 6-8 × 8 OZ.	FRUITS: 2-4	VEGGIES: 3-5	WHOLE GRAIN SERVINGS: 6-11	PROTEIN: 4-6 OZ.	LIMIT FAT?	ALCOHOLIC BEVERAGES?	LIMIT "EMPTY" CARBS?
☐☐☐☐ ☐☐☐☐	☐☐ ☐☐	☐☐ ☐☐	☐☐☐☐☐ ☐☐☐☐☐	☐☐☐ ☐☐	Y N	Y N	Y N

WEATHER:
SUN WIND
RAIN CLOUDY
SNOW
TEMP:_____

WEEK OF:

GOALS FOR WEEK:

WEEKLY TOTAL: _____

YEAR-TO-DATE TOTAL:

PENGUIN WORDS OF WISDOM

The struggle to find one's potential as a runner is the most frustrat-
ingly satisfying pursuit that many of us ever embrace. Running is both
the cause and effect of our desire to find that element of heroism in
ourselves.

MONDAY / Date:

Training notes:

Today's goal:

FUEL LOG

WATER: 6-8 x 8 OZ.	FRUITS: 2-4	VEGGIES: 3-5	WHOLE GRAIN SERVINGS: 6-11	PROTEIN: 4-6 OZ.	LIMIT FAT?	ALCOHOLIC BEVERAGES?	LIMIT "EMPTY" CARBS?
☐☐☐☐ ☐☐☐☐	☐☐ ☐☐	☐☐☐ ☐☐	☐☐☐☐ ☐☐☐☐ ☐	☐☐☐ ☐☐	Y N	Y N	Y N

WEATHER: SUN WIND RAIN CLOUDY SNOW TEMP:____

Distance:
Time:
Heart Rate:
i-Rate (1-10):
X-Training:
Sleep Hours:
Weight:
Mood: ☺ ☺ ☹ Other

TUESDAY / Date:

Training notes:

Today's goal:

FUEL LOG

WATER: 6-8 x 8 OZ.	FRUITS: 2-4	VEGGIES: 3-5	WHOLE GRAIN SERVINGS: 6-11	PROTEIN: 4-6 OZ.	LIMIT FAT?	ALCOHOLIC BEVERAGES?	LIMIT "EMPTY" CARBS?
☐☐☐☐ ☐☐☐☐	☐☐ ☐☐	☐☐☐ ☐☐	☐☐☐☐ ☐☐☐☐ ☐	☐☐☐ ☐☐	Y N	Y N	Y N

WEATHER: SUN WIND RAIN CLOUDY SNOW TEMP:____

Distance:
Time:
Heart Rate:
i-Rate (1-10):
X-Training:
Sleep Hours:
Weight:
Mood: ☺ ☺ ☹ Other

WEDNESDAY / Date:

Training notes:

Today's goal:

FUEL LOG

WATER: 6-8 x 8 OZ.	FRUITS: 2-4	VEGGIES: 3-5	WHOLE GRAIN SERVINGS: 6-11	PROTEIN: 4-6 OZ.	LIMIT FAT?	ALCOHOLIC BEVERAGES?	LIMIT "EMPTY" CARBS?
☐☐☐☐ ☐☐☐☐	☐☐ ☐☐	☐☐☐ ☐☐	☐☐☐☐ ☐☐☐☐ ☐	☐☐☐ ☐☐	Y N	Y N	Y N

WEATHER: SUN WIND RAIN CLOUDY SNOW TEMP:____

Distance:
Time:
Heart Rate:
i-Rate (1-10):
X-Training:
Sleep Hours:
Weight:
Mood: ☺ ☺ ☹ Other

THURSDAY / Date:

Training notes:

Today's goal:

FUEL LOG

WATER: 6-8 x 8 OZ.	FRUITS: 2-4	VEGGIES: 3-5	WHOLE GRAIN SERVINGS: 6-11	PROTEIN: 4-6 OZ.	LIMIT FAT?	ALCOHOLIC BEVERAGES?	LIMIT "EMPTY" CARBS?
☐☐☐☐ ☐☐☐☐	☐☐ ☐☐	☐☐☐ ☐☐	☐☐☐☐ ☐☐☐☐ ☐	☐☐☐ ☐☐	Y N	Y N	Y N

WEATHER: SUN WIND RAIN CLOUDY SNOW TEMP:____

Distance:
Time:
Heart Rate:
i-Rate (1-10):
X-Training:
Sleep Hours:
Weight:
Mood: ☺ ☺ ☹ Other

FRIDAY / Date: _____

Training notes: _____

Today's goal: _____

FUEL LOG

WATER: 6-8 × 8 OZ.	FRUITS: 2-4	VEGGIES: 3-5	WHOLE GRAIN SERVINGS: 6-11	PROTEIN: 4-6 OZ.	LIMIT FAT?	ALCOHOLIC BEVERAGES?	LIMIT "EMPTY" CARBS?
☐☐☐☐ ☐☐☐☐	☐☐ ☐☐	☐☐☐ ☐☐	☐☐☐☐☐☐ ☐☐☐☐☐	☐☐☐ ☐☐☐	Y N	Y N	Y N

WEATHER: SUN WIND RAIN CLOUDY SNOW TEMP:____

Distance: _____
Time: _____
Heart Rate: _____
i-Rate (1-10) _____
X-Training: _____
Sleep Hours: _____
Weight: _____
Mood: ☺ ☺ ☹ Other

SATURDAY / Date: _____

Training notes: _____

Today's goal: _____

FUEL LOG

WATER: 6-8 × 8 OZ.	FRUITS: 2-4	VEGGIES: 3-5	WHOLE GRAIN SERVINGS: 6-11	PROTEIN: 4-6 OZ.	LIMIT FAT?	ALCOHOLIC BEVERAGES?	LIMIT "EMPTY" CARBS?
☐☐☐☐ ☐☐☐☐	☐☐ ☐☐	☐☐☐ ☐☐	☐☐☐☐☐☐ ☐☐☐☐☐	☐☐☐ ☐☐☐	Y N	Y N	Y N

WEATHER: SUN WIND RAIN CLOUDY SNOW TEMP:____

Distance: _____
Time: _____
Heart Rate: _____
i-Rate (1-10) _____
X-Training: _____
Sleep Hours: _____
Weight: _____
Mood: ☺ ☺ ☹ Other

SUNDAY / Date: _____

Training notes: _____

Today's goal: _____

FUEL LOG

WATER: 6-8 × 8 OZ.	FRUITS: 2-4	VEGGIES: 3-5	WHOLE GRAIN SERVINGS: 6-11	PROTEIN: 4-6 OZ.	LIMIT FAT?	ALCOHOLIC BEVERAGES?	LIMIT "EMPTY" CARBS?
☐☐☐☐ ☐☐☐☐	☐☐ ☐☐	☐☐☐ ☐☐	☐☐☐☐☐☐ ☐☐☐☐☐	☐☐☐ ☐☐☐	Y N	Y N	Y N

WEATHER: SUN WIND RAIN CLOUDY SNOW TEMP:____

Distance: _____
Time: _____
Heart Rate: _____
i-Rate (1-10) _____
X-Training: _____
Sleep Hours: _____
Weight: _____
Mood: ☺ ☺ ☹ Other

WEEK OF: _____

PENGUIN WORDS OF WISDOM

Some of the best parts of being a runner have nothing to do with run-ning. Knowing how difficult it was to overcome the bad habits of my early life, and knowing that I have, has given me the courage to try almost anything.

GOALS FOR WEEK: _____

WEEKLY TOTAL: _____

YEAR-TO-DATE TOTAL: _____

JULY

FIREWORKS

For me, the greatest moments in my running career have happened out on a race course. It's not that there haven't been some times of serene pleasure when I haven't been on a race course, but the times when I have felt most closely aligned with all the hopes and dreams that running has released in me have been when there were mile markers and timing clocks to record my progress.

Racing is the act of letting go. It is the ultimate leap of faith. Racing is the only time when we can risk abject failure in the hope of unrestrained success. Racing is when we can be most fully unfettered, when we can hoist our sails and let the wind of competition carry us along. Racing is when we measure the quality of our effort against the quality of those around us.

There are "Firecracker 5K's" in nearly every city on the 4th of July. It doesn't matter if you are in the heart of the big city or miles from the next town, everybody can find a 5K to on or around July 4th. And for most of us, a full on, take-no-prisoners, let it all hang out, "damn the torpedoes-full speed ahead" 5K is one of life's and running's most enduring pleasures.

You know it's going to hurt. You know because you know that you are going to find your comfort zone early in the first mile and then you are going to immediately exceed it. You are going to get locked into your regular pace and then immediately start going faster. You are going to find people ahead of you that your are going to chase and overcome. You are gong to race every person out there, whether they are in your age group or not. You are going to wage a battle to the death with every one who comes near you.

Your heart is going to pound, your lungs are going to be sucking air, and your legs are going to feel like they are going to quit at any moment. But you are not going to quit. You are going to see the 2 mile marker and pick up the pace. You'll find more people to run down, more people to hold off, and more courage to not give in.

And when you see the finish line you are going to let out a primal scream and run like your shorts are on fire. You will cross the finish line in a daze . . . you mind clouded by the blood rushing through your head. The volunteers will hold you up and walk you through the chutes. You will have run the race of your life.

Nothing can replace the feeling of an all out effort. It may not be your cup of tea every week, or even every month. But once a year you owe it to yourself to go just a little bit crazy. And a 5K on the 4th of July seems like the perfect time to do it.

MONDAY / Date: _____   Training notes: _____

Today's goal: _____

FUEL LOG

WATER: 6-8 × 8 OZ.	FRUITS: 2-4	VEGGIES: 3-5	WHOLE GRAIN SERVINGS: 6-11	PROTEIN: 4-6 OZ.	LIMIT FAT?	ALCOHOLIC BEVERAGES?	LIMIT "EMPTY" CARBS?
☐☐☐☐ ☐☐☐☐	☐☐ ☐☐	☐☐☐ ☐☐	☐☐☐☐ ☐☐☐☐	☐☐☐ ☐☐☐	Y N	Y N	Y N

Distance: _____
Time: _____
Heart Rate: _____
i-Rate (1-10): _____
X-Training: _____
Sleep Hours: _____
Weight: _____
Mood: ☺ ☺ ☹ ☹

WEATHER: SUN WIND RAIN CLOUDY SNOW TEMP: ____

TUESDAY / Date: _____   Training notes: _____

Today's goal: _____

FUEL LOG

WATER: 6-8 × 8 OZ.	FRUITS: 2-4	VEGGIES: 3-5	WHOLE GRAIN SERVINGS: 6-11	PROTEIN: 4-6 OZ.	LIMIT FAT?	ALCOHOLIC BEVERAGES?	LIMIT "EMPTY" CARBS?
☐☐☐☐ ☐☐☐☐	☐☐ ☐☐	☐☐☐ ☐☐	☐☐☐☐ ☐☐☐☐	☐☐☐ ☐☐☐	Y N	Y N	Y N

Distance: _____
Time: _____
Heart Rate: _____
i-Rate (1-10): _____
X-Training: _____
Sleep Hours: _____
Weight: _____
Mood: ☺ ☺ ☹ ☹

WEATHER: SUN WIND RAIN CLOUDY SNOW TEMP: ____

WEDNESDAY / Date: _____   Training notes: _____

Today's goal: _____

FUEL LOG

WATER: 6-8 × 8 OZ.	FRUITS: 2-4	VEGGIES: 3-5	WHOLE GRAIN SERVINGS: 6-11	PROTEIN: 4-6 OZ.	LIMIT FAT?	ALCOHOLIC BEVERAGES?	LIMIT "EMPTY" CARBS?
☐☐☐☐ ☐☐☐☐	☐☐ ☐☐	☐☐☐ ☐☐	☐☐☐☐ ☐☐☐☐	☐☐☐ ☐☐☐	Y N	Y N	Y N

Distance: _____
Time: _____
Heart Rate: _____
i-Rate (1-10): _____
X-Training: _____
Sleep Hours: _____
Weight: _____
Mood: ☺ ☺ ☹ ☹

WEATHER: SUN WIND RAIN CLOUDY SNOW TEMP: ____

THURSDAY / Date: _____   Training notes: _____

Today's goal: _____

FUEL LOG

WATER: 6-8 × 8 OZ.	FRUITS: 2-4	VEGGIES: 3-5	WHOLE GRAIN SERVINGS: 6-11	PROTEIN: 4-6 OZ.	LIMIT FAT?	ALCOHOLIC BEVERAGES?	LIMIT "EMPTY" CARBS?
☐☐☐☐ ☐☐☐☐	☐☐ ☐☐	☐☐☐ ☐☐	☐☐☐☐ ☐☐☐☐	☐☐☐ ☐☐☐	Y N	Y N	Y N

Distance: _____
Time: _____
Heart Rate: _____
i-Rate (1-10): _____
X-Training: _____
Sleep Hours: _____
Weight: _____
Mood: ☺ ☺ ☹ ☹ Other

WEATHER: SUN WIND RAIN CLOUDY SNOW TEMP: ____

FRIDAY / Date:

Today's goal:

Training notes:

FUEL LOG

WATER: 6-8 x 8 OZ.	FRUITS: 2-4	VEGGIES: 3-5	WHOLE GRAIN SERVINGS: 6-11	PROTEIN: 4-6 OZ.	LIMIT FAT?	ALCOHOLIC BEVERAGES?	LIMIT "EMPTY" CARBS?
☐☐☐☐ ☐☐☐☐	☐☐ ☐☐	☐☐☐ ☐☐	☐☐☐☐☐☐ ☐☐☐☐☐	☐☐☐ ☐☐☐	Y N	Y N	Y N

WEATHER: SUN WIND RAIN CLOUDY SNOW TEMP: _____

- Distance:
- Time:
- Heart Rate:
- i-Rate (1-10):
- X-Training:
- Sleep Hours:
- Weight:
- Mood: ☺ ☺ ☹ ☹ Other

SATURDAY / Date:

Today's goal:

Training notes:

FUEL LOG

WATER: 6-8 x 8 OZ.	FRUITS: 2-4	VEGGIES: 3-5	WHOLE GRAIN SERVINGS: 6-11	PROTEIN: 4-6 OZ.	LIMIT FAT?	ALCOHOLIC BEVERAGES?	LIMIT "EMPTY" CARBS?
☐☐☐☐ ☐☐☐☐	☐☐ ☐☐	☐☐☐ ☐☐	☐☐☐☐☐☐ ☐☐☐☐☐	☐☐☐ ☐☐☐	Y N	Y N	Y N

WEATHER: SUN WIND RAIN CLOUDY SNOW TEMP: _____

- Distance:
- Time:
- Heart Rate:
- i-Rate (1-10):
- X-Training:
- Sleep Hours:
- Weight:
- Mood: ☺ ☺ ☹ ☹ Other

SUNDAY / Date:

Today's goal:

Training notes:

FUEL LOG

WATER: 6-8 x 8 OZ.	FRUITS: 2-4	VEGGIES: 3-5	WHOLE GRAIN SERVINGS: 6-11	PROTEIN: 4-6 OZ.	LIMIT FAT?	ALCOHOLIC BEVERAGES?	LIMIT "EMPTY" CARBS?
☐☐☐☐ ☐☐☐☐	☐☐ ☐☐	☐☐☐ ☐☐	☐☐☐☐☐☐ ☐☐☐☐☐	☐☐☐ ☐☐☐	Y N	Y N	Y N

WEATHER: SUN WIND RAIN CLOUDY SNOW TEMP: _____

- Distance:
- Time:
- Heart Rate:
- i-Rate (1-10):
- X-Training:
- Sleep Hours:
- Weight:
- Mood: ☺ ☺ ☹ ☹ Other

WEEK OF:

GOALS FOR WEEK:

PENGUIN WORDS OF WISDOM

Finishing last in your first race is a sure-fire way to have lots to look forward to in your running career. I know. In my first race I finished just ahead of the ambulance.

WEEKLY TOTAL: _____

YEAR-TO-DATE TOTAL:

MONDAY / Date:

Today's goal:

Training notes:

FUEL LOG

WATER: 6-8 × 8 OZ.	FRUITS: 2-4	VEGGIES: 3-5	WHOLE GRAIN SERVINGS: 6-11	PROTEIN: 4-6 OZ.	LIMIT FAT?	ALCOHOLIC BEVERAGES?	LIMIT "EMPTY" CARBS?
☐☐☐☐ ☐☐☐☐	☐☐ ☐☐	☐☐☐ ☐☐	☐☐☐☐☐ ☐☐☐☐☐ ☐	☐☐☐ ☐☐☐	Y N	Y N	Y N

Distance:
Time:
Heart Rate:
i-Rate (1-10):
X-Training:
Sleep Hours:
Weight:
Mood: ☺ ☺ ☹ Other

WEATHER:
SUN WIND
RAIN CLOUDY
SNOW
TEMP:

TUESDAY / Date:

Today's goal:

Training notes:

FUEL LOG

WATER: 6-8 × 8 OZ.	FRUITS: 2-4	VEGGIES: 3-5	WHOLE GRAIN SERVINGS: 6-11	PROTEIN: 4-6 OZ.	LIMIT FAT?	ALCOHOLIC BEVERAGES?	LIMIT "EMPTY" CARBS?
☐☐☐☐ ☐☐☐☐	☐☐ ☐☐	☐☐☐ ☐☐	☐☐☐☐☐ ☐☐☐☐☐ ☐	☐☐☐ ☐☐☐	Y N	Y N	Y N

Distance:
Time:
Heart Rate:
i-Rate (1-10):
X-Training:
Sleep Hours:
Weight:
Mood: ☺ ☺ ☹ Other

WEATHER:
SUN WIND
RAIN CLOUDY
SNOW
TEMP:

WEDNESDAY / Date:

Today's goal:

Training notes:

FUEL LOG

WATER: 6-8 × 8 OZ.	FRUITS: 2-4	VEGGIES: 3-5	WHOLE GRAIN SERVINGS: 6-11	PROTEIN: 4-6 OZ.	LIMIT FAT?	ALCOHOLIC BEVERAGES?	LIMIT "EMPTY" CARBS?
☐☐☐☐ ☐☐☐☐	☐☐ ☐☐	☐☐☐ ☐☐	☐☐☐☐☐ ☐☐☐☐☐ ☐	☐☐☐ ☐☐☐	Y N	Y N	Y N

Distance:
Time:
Heart Rate:
i-Rate (1-10):
X-Training:
Sleep Hours:
Weight:
Mood: ☺ ☺ ☹ Other

WEATHER:
SUN WIND
RAIN CLOUDY
SNOW
TEMP:

THURSDAY / Date:

Today's goal:

Training notes:

FUEL LOG

WATER: 6-8 × 8 OZ.	FRUITS: 2-4	VEGGIES: 3-5	WHOLE GRAIN SERVINGS: 6-11	PROTEIN: 4-6 OZ.	LIMIT FAT?	ALCOHOLIC BEVERAGES?	LIMIT "EMPTY" CARBS?
☐☐☐☐ ☐☐☐☐	☐☐ ☐☐	☐☐☐ ☐☐	☐☐☐☐☐ ☐☐☐☐☐ ☐	☐☐☐ ☐☐☐	Y N	Y N	Y N

Distance:
Time:
Heart Rate:
i-Rate (1-10):
X-Training:
Sleep Hours:
Weight:
Mood: ☺ ☺ ☹ Other

WEATHER:
SUN WIND
RAIN CLOUDY
SNOW
TEMP:

FRIDAY / Date:

Today's goal:

Training notes:

FUEL LOG

WATER: 6-8 x 8 OZ.	FRUITS: 2-4	VEGGIES: 3-5	WHOLE GRAIN SERVINGS: 6-11	PROTEIN: 4-6 OZ.	LIMIT FAT?	ALCOHOLIC BEVERAGES?	LIMIT "EMPTY" CARBS?
☐☐☐☐ ☐☐☐☐	☐☐ ☐☐	☐☐☐ ☐☐	☐☐☐☐☐ ☐☐☐☐☐☐	☐☐☐ ☐☐☐	Y N	Y N	Y N

WEATHER: SUN WIND RAIN CLOUDY SNOW TEMP:____

Distance:
Time:
Heart Rate:
i-Rate (1-10):
X-Training:
Sleep Hours:
Weight:
Mood: ☺ ☺ ☹ Other

SATURDAY / Date:

Today's goal:

Training notes:

FUEL LOG

WATER: 6-8 x 8 OZ.	FRUITS: 2-4	VEGGIES: 3-5	WHOLE GRAIN SERVINGS: 6-11	PROTEIN: 4-6 OZ.	LIMIT FAT?	ALCOHOLIC BEVERAGES?	LIMIT "EMPTY" CARBS?
☐☐☐☐ ☐☐☐☐	☐☐ ☐☐	☐☐☐ ☐☐	☐☐☐☐☐ ☐☐☐☐☐☐	☐☐☐ ☐☐☐	Y N	Y N	Y N

WEATHER: SUN WIND RAIN CLOUDY SNOW TEMP:____

Distance:
Time:
Heart Rate:
i-Rate (1-10):
X-Training:
Sleep Hours:
Weight:
Mood: ☺ ☺ ☹ Other

SUNDAY / Date:

Today's goal:

Training notes:

FUEL LOG

WATER: 6-8 x 8 OZ.	FRUITS: 2-4	VEGGIES: 3-5	WHOLE GRAIN SERVINGS: 6-11	PROTEIN: 4-6 OZ.	LIMIT FAT?	ALCOHOLIC BEVERAGES?	LIMIT "EMPTY" CARBS?
☐☐☐☐ ☐☐☐☐	☐☐ ☐☐	☐☐☐ ☐☐	☐☐☐☐☐ ☐☐☐☐☐☐	☐☐☐ ☐☐☐	Y N	Y N	Y N

WEATHER: SUN WIND RAIN CLOUDY SNOW TEMP:____

Distance:
Time:
Heart Rate:
i-Rate (1-10):
X-Training:
Sleep Hours:
Weight:
Mood: ☺ ☺ ☹ Other

WEEK OF:

GOALS FOR WEEK:

WEEKLY TOTAL: _____

YEAR-TO-DATE TOTAL:

PENGUIN WORDS OF WISDOM

Somewhere between those runs that tax our reserves and those that are simply too easy are the countless runs that are just right.

MONDAY / Date:

Today's goal:

Training notes:

FUEL LOG

WATER: 6-8 x 8 OZ.	FRUITS: 2-4	VEGGIES: 3-5	WHOLE GRAIN SERVINGS: 6-11	PROTEIN: 4-6 OZ.	LIMIT FAT?	ALCOHOLIC BEVERAGES?	LIMIT "EMPTY" CARBS?
☐☐☐☐ ☐☐☐☐	☐☐ ☐☐	☐☐☐ ☐☐	☐☐☐☐ ☐☐☐☐ ☐	☐☐☐ ☐☐☐	Y N	Y N	Y N

WEATHER: SUN WIND RAIN CLOUDY SNOW TEMP:____

Distance:
Time:
Heart Rate:
i-Rate (1-10)
X-Training:
Sleep Hours:
Weight:
Mood: ☺ ☺ ☹ Other

TUESDAY / Date:

Today's goal:

Training notes:

FUEL LOG

WATER: 6-8 x 8 OZ.	FRUITS: 2-4	VEGGIES: 3-5	WHOLE GRAIN SERVINGS: 6-11	PROTEIN: 4-6 OZ.	LIMIT FAT?	ALCOHOLIC BEVERAGES?	LIMIT "EMPTY" CARBS?
☐☐☐☐ ☐☐☐☐	☐☐ ☐☐	☐☐☐ ☐☐	☐☐☐☐ ☐☐☐☐ ☐	☐☐☐ ☐☐☐	Y N	Y N	Y N

WEATHER: SUN WIND RAIN CLOUDY SNOW TEMP:____

Distance:
Time:
Heart Rate:
i-Rate (1-10)
X-Training:
Sleep Hours:
Weight:
Mood: ☺ ☺ ☹ Other

WEDNESDAY / Date:

Today's goal:

Training notes:

FUEL LOG

WATER: 6-8 x 8 OZ.	FRUITS: 2-4	VEGGIES: 3-5	WHOLE GRAIN SERVINGS: 6-11	PROTEIN: 4-6 OZ.	LIMIT FAT?	ALCOHOLIC BEVERAGES?	LIMIT "EMPTY" CARBS?
☐☐☐☐ ☐☐☐☐	☐☐ ☐☐	☐☐☐ ☐☐	☐☐☐☐ ☐☐☐☐ ☐	☐☐☐ ☐☐☐	Y N	Y N	Y N

WEATHER: SUN WIND RAIN CLOUDY SNOW TEMP:____

Distance:
Time:
Heart Rate:
i-Rate (1-10)
X-Training:
Sleep Hours:
Weight:
Mood: ☺ ☺ ☹ Other

THURSDAY / Date:

Today's goal:

Training notes:

FUEL LOG

WATER: 6-8 x 8 OZ.	FRUITS: 2-4	VEGGIES: 3-5	WHOLE GRAIN SERVINGS: 6-11	PROTEIN: 4-6 OZ.	LIMIT FAT?	ALCOHOLIC BEVERAGES?	LIMIT "EMPTY" CARBS?
☐☐☐☐ ☐☐☐☐	☐☐ ☐☐	☐☐☐ ☐☐	☐☐☐☐ ☐☐☐☐ ☐	☐☐☐ ☐☐☐	Y N	Y N	Y N

WEATHER: SUN WIND RAIN CLOUDY SNOW TEMP:____

Distance:
Time:
Heart Rate:
i-Rate (1-10)
X-Training:
Sleep Hours:
Weight:
Mood: ☺ ☺ ☹ Other

FRIDAY / Date:

Today's goal:

Training notes: _____

Distance: _____
Time: _____
Heart Rate: _____
i-Rate (1-10): _____
X-Training: _____
Sleep Hours: _____
Weight: _____
Mood: ☺ ☺ ☹ Other

WEATHER:
SUN WIND
RAIN CLOUDY
SNOW
TEMP: _____

FUEL LOG

WATER: 6-8 x 8 OZ.	FRUITS: 2-4	VEGGIES: 3-5	WHOLE GRAIN SERVINGS: 6-11	PROTEIN: 4-6 OZ.	LIMIT FAT?	ALCOHOLIC BEVERAGES?	LIMIT "EMPTY" CARBS?
☐☐☐☐ ☐☐☐☐	☐☐ ☐☐	☐☐☐ ☐☐	☐☐☐☐☐☐ ☐☐☐☐☐	☐☐☐ ☐☐☐	Y N	Y N	Y N

SATURDAY / Date:

Today's goal:

Training notes: _____

Distance: _____
Time: _____
Heart Rate: _____
i-Rate (1-10): _____
X-Training: _____
Sleep Hours: _____
Weight: _____
Mood: ☺ ☺ ☹ Other

WEATHER:
SUN WIND
RAIN CLOUDY
SNOW
TEMP: _____

FUEL LOG

WATER: 6-8 x 8 OZ.	FRUITS: 2-4	VEGGIES: 3-5	WHOLE GRAIN SERVINGS: 6-11	PROTEIN: 4-6 OZ.	LIMIT FAT?	ALCOHOLIC BEVERAGES?	LIMIT "EMPTY" CARBS?
☐☐☐☐ ☐☐☐☐	☐☐ ☐☐	☐☐☐ ☐☐	☐☐☐☐☐☐ ☐☐☐☐☐	☐☐☐ ☐☐☐	Y N	Y N	Y N

SUNDAY / Date:

Today's goal:

Training notes: _____

Distance: _____
Time: _____
Heart Rate: _____
i-Rate (1-10): _____
X-Training: _____
Sleep Hours: _____
Weight: _____
Mood: ☺ ☺ ☹ Other

WEATHER:
SUN WIND
RAIN CLOUDY
SNOW
TEMP: _____

FUEL LOG

WATER: 6-8 x 8 OZ.	FRUITS: 2-4	VEGGIES: 3-5	WHOLE GRAIN SERVINGS: 6-11	PROTEIN: 4-6 OZ.	LIMIT FAT?	ALCOHOLIC BEVERAGES?	LIMIT "EMPTY" CARBS?
☐☐☐☐ ☐☐☐☐	☐☐ ☐☐	☐☐☐ ☐☐	☐☐☐☐☐☐ ☐☐☐☐☐	☐☐☐ ☐☐☐	Y N	Y N	Y N

WEEK OF:

GOALS FOR WEEK:

WEEKLY TOTAL: _____

YEAR-TO-DATE TOTAL: _____

PENGUIN WORDS OF WISDOM

I'm not sure exactly when liking to run became longing to run, when wanting to run became needing to run. I only know that there are miles and moments and memories that only converge when the shoe strikes the ground.

MONDAY / Date:

Today's goal:

Training notes:

FUEL LOG

WATER: 6-8 x 8 OZ.	FRUITS: 2-4	VEGGIES: 3-5	WHOLE GRAIN SERVINGS: 6-11	PROTEIN: 4-6 OZ.	LIMIT FAT?	ALCOHOLIC BEVERAGES?	LIMIT "EMPTY" CARBS?
☐☐☐☐ ☐☐☐☐	☐☐ ☐☐	☐☐ ☐	☐☐☐☐ ☐☐☐ ☐	☐☐ ☐	Y N	Y N	Y N

WEATHER: SUN WIND RAIN CLOUDY SNOW TEMP:_____

Distance:
Time:
Heart Rate:
i-Rate (1-10)
X-Training:
Sleep Hours:
Weight:
Mood: ☺ ☺ ☹ Other

TUESDAY / Date:

Today's goal:

Training notes:

FUEL LOG

WATER: 6-8 x 8 OZ.	FRUITS: 2-4	VEGGIES: 3-5	WHOLE GRAIN SERVINGS: 6-11	PROTEIN: 4-6 OZ.	LIMIT FAT?	ALCOHOLIC BEVERAGES?	LIMIT "EMPTY" CARBS?
☐☐☐☐ ☐☐☐☐	☐☐ ☐☐	☐☐ ☐	☐☐☐☐ ☐☐☐ ☐	☐☐ ☐	Y N	Y N	Y N

WEATHER: SUN WIND RAIN CLOUDY SNOW TEMP:_____

Distance:
Time:
Heart Rate:
i-Rate (1-10)
X-Training:
Sleep Hours:
Weight:
Mood: ☺ ☺ ☹ Other

WEDNESDAY / Date:

Today's goal:

Training notes:

FUEL LOG

WATER: 6-8 x 8 OZ.	FRUITS: 2-4	VEGGIES: 3-5	WHOLE GRAIN SERVINGS: 6-11	PROTEIN: 4-6 OZ.	LIMIT FAT?	ALCOHOLIC BEVERAGES?	LIMIT "EMPTY" CARBS?
☐☐☐☐ ☐☐☐☐	☐☐ ☐☐	☐☐ ☐	☐☐☐☐ ☐☐☐ ☐	☐☐ ☐	Y N	Y N	Y N

WEATHER: SUN WIND RAIN CLOUDY SNOW TEMP:_____

Distance:
Time:
Heart Rate:
i-Rate (1-10)
X-Training:
Sleep Hours:
Weight:
Mood: ☺ ☺ ☹ Other

THURSDAY / Date:

Today's goal:

Training notes:

FUEL LOG

WATER: 6-8 x 8 OZ.	FRUITS: 2-4	VEGGIES: 3-5	WHOLE GRAIN SERVINGS: 6-11	PROTEIN: 4-6 OZ.	LIMIT FAT?	ALCOHOLIC BEVERAGES?	LIMIT "EMPTY" CARBS?
☐☐☐☐ ☐☐☐☐	☐☐ ☐☐	☐☐ ☐	☐☐☐☐ ☐☐☐ ☐	☐☐ ☐	Y N	Y N	Y N

WEATHER: SUN WIND RAIN CLOUDY SNOW TEMP:_____

Distance:
Time:
Heart Rate:
i-Rate (1-10)
X-Training:
Sleep Hours:
Weight:
Mood: ☺ ☺ ☹ Other

FRIDAY / Date:

Training notes:

Today's goal:

FUEL LOG

WATER: 6-8 × 8 OZ.	FRUITS: 2-4	VEGGIES: 3-5	WHOLE GRAIN SERVINGS: 6-11	PROTEIN: 4-6 OZ.	LIMIT FAT?	ALCOHOLIC BEVERAGES?	LIMIT "EMPTY" CARBS?
☐☐☐☐ ☐☐☐☐	☐☐ ☐☐	☐☐☐ ☐☐☐	☐☐☐☐☐☐ ☐☐☐☐☐☐	☐☐☐ ☐☐☐	Y N	Y N	Y N

WEATHER:
SUN WIND
RAIN CLOUDY
SNOW
TEMP: _____

Distance:
Time:
Heart Rate:
i-Rate (1-10)
X-Training:
Sleep Hours:
Weight:
Mood: ☺ ☺ ☹ Other

SATURDAY / Date:

Training notes:

Today's goal:

FUEL LOG

WATER: 6-8 × 8 OZ.	FRUITS: 2-4	VEGGIES: 3-5	WHOLE GRAIN SERVINGS: 6-11	PROTEIN: 4-6 OZ.	LIMIT FAT?	ALCOHOLIC BEVERAGES?	LIMIT "EMPTY" CARBS?
☐☐☐☐ ☐☐☐☐	☐☐ ☐☐	☐☐☐ ☐☐☐	☐☐☐☐☐☐ ☐☐☐☐☐☐	☐☐☐ ☐☐☐	Y N	Y N	Y N

WEATHER:
SUN WIND
RAIN CLOUDY
SNOW
TEMP: _____

Distance:
Time:
Heart Rate:
i-Rate (1-10)
X-Training:
Sleep Hours:
Weight:
Mood: ☺ ☺ ☹ Other

SUNDAY / Date:

Training notes:

Today's goal:

FUEL LOG

WATER: 6-8 × 8 OZ.	FRUITS: 2-4	VEGGIES: 3-5	WHOLE GRAIN SERVINGS: 6-11	PROTEIN: 4-6 OZ.	LIMIT FAT?	ALCOHOLIC BEVERAGES?	LIMIT "EMPTY" CARBS?
☐☐☐☐ ☐☐☐☐	☐☐ ☐☐	☐☐☐ ☐☐☐	☐☐☐☐☐☐ ☐☐☐☐☐☐	☐☐☐ ☐☐☐	Y N	Y N	Y N

WEATHER:
SUN WIND
RAIN CLOUDY
SNOW
TEMP: _____

Distance:
Time:
Heart Rate:
i-Rate (1-10)
X-Training:
Sleep Hours:
Weight:
Mood: ☺ ☺ ☹ Other

WEEK OF:

GOALS FOR WEEK:

WEEKLY TOTAL: _____

YEAR-TO-DATE TOTAL:

PENGUIN WORDS OF WISDOM

If you're waiting for the magic moment when you suddenly discover you're a runner, you'll probably be disappointed. There's no great cosmic announcement, no news flash. There's just a quiet accumulation of miles.

AUGUST

HOT SUMMER NIGHTS

I'd rather run in freezing temperatures than run in the heat of the summer. I'd rather layer up and put on gloves and a wool cap than step outside and start to sweat from the effort of tying my shoes. I'd rather chip icicles off my hair than be dripping wet five minutes into a run. But running in the heat is a fact of life for most of us and learning how to be safe and cool is an important skill.

The first factor in dealing with the heat is hydration. Your heart is going to send blood to your skin on a hot day to help cool you off. You are going to sweat away not only the fluids in your body but also important electrolytes like sodium and potassium. You don't have to be going on a long run to start to feel the effects of the loss of fluid and electrolytes.

Even a thirty-minute run can be long enough to get you in trouble.

Water alone will not keep you hydrated and protected during the hottest months. Water alone is fine for washing down energy bars and gels, but it won't replace the electrolytes that you are losing with every step. For that, you need a sports drink. We are fortunate to live in a time when there are a number of high quality sports drinks available. Find the one that works best for you, the one that you will drink more of, and carry it with you on your runs.

We're also lucky to live in an era where technical fabrics are available to all of us. Materials like Cool-Max and Drive Weave have made running in the heat tolerable, if not pleasant. These "wicking" materials transfer the perspiration off your skin and into the fabrics where your clothes can help your body cool itself down. These technical fabrics are designed to actually work with your system to provide maximum thermal protection and cooling effect.

A word here to the guys who insist on running with their shirts off. That may look cool (although to be fair, not everyone looks great without a shirt) but what you're really doing is providing a giant surface from which your perspiration will evaporate quickly. You'd be far better off with a light weight, loose fitting technical shirt.

And ladies . . . the summer months are not the time to wear your favorite oversized cotton t-shirt. You know the one. The one that you could use as a night shirt if you wanted. The one that covers you shoulder to knee cap. Wear that shirt to drive to your run, wear it on the way home, but for your sake, don't use it for running. With a little patience, you'll be able to find a flattering technical running top that suits your style and modesty needs.

MONDAY / Date:

Today's goal:

Training notes:

Distance:
Time:
Heart Rate:
i-Rate (1-10):
X-Training:
Sleep Hours:
Weight:
Mood: ☺ ☺ ☺ Other

FUEL LOG

WATER: 6-8 x 8 OZ.	FRUITS: 2-4	VEGGIES: 3-5	WHOLE GRAIN SERVINGS: 6-11	PROTEIN: 4-6 OZ.	LIMIT FAT? Y N	ALCOHOLIC BEVERAGES? Y N	LIMIT "EMPTY" CARBS? Y N
☐☐☐☐ ☐☐☐☐	☐☐ ☐☐	☐☐☐ ☐☐	☐☐☐☐ ☐☐☐ ☐	☐☐☐ ☐☐☐			

WEATHER: SUN WIND RAIN CLOUDY SNOW   TEMP:____

TUESDAY / Date:

Today's goal:

Training notes:

Distance:
Time:
Heart Rate:
i-Rate (1-10):
X-Training:
Sleep Hours:
Weight:
Mood: ☺ ☺ ☺ Other

FUEL LOG

WATER: 6-8 x 8 OZ.	FRUITS: 2-4	VEGGIES: 3-5	WHOLE GRAIN SERVINGS: 6-11	PROTEIN: 4-6 OZ.	LIMIT FAT? Y N	ALCOHOLIC BEVERAGES? Y N	LIMIT "EMPTY" CARBS? Y N
☐☐☐☐ ☐☐☐☐	☐☐ ☐☐	☐☐☐ ☐☐	☐☐☐☐ ☐☐☐ ☐	☐☐☐ ☐☐☐			

WEATHER: SUN WIND RAIN CLOUDY SNOW   TEMP:____

WEDNESDAY / Date:

Today's goal:

Training notes:

Distance:
Time:
Heart Rate:
i-Rate (1-10):
X-Training:
Sleep Hours:
Weight:
Mood: ☺ ☺ ☺ Other

FUEL LOG

WATER: 6-8 x 8 OZ.	FRUITS: 2-4	VEGGIES: 3-5	WHOLE GRAIN SERVINGS: 6-11	PROTEIN: 4-6 OZ.	LIMIT FAT? Y N	ALCOHOLIC BEVERAGES? Y N	LIMIT "EMPTY" CARBS? Y N
☐☐☐☐ ☐☐☐☐	☐☐ ☐☐	☐☐☐ ☐☐	☐☐☐☐ ☐☐☐ ☐	☐☐☐ ☐☐☐			

WEATHER: SUN WIND RAIN CLOUDY SNOW   TEMP:____

THURSDAY / Date:

Today's goal:

Training notes:

Distance:
Time:
Heart Rate:
i-Rate (1-10):
X-Training:
Sleep Hours:
Weight:
Mood: ☺ ☺ ☺ Other

FUEL LOG

WATER: 6-8 x 8 OZ.	FRUITS: 2-4	VEGGIES: 3-5	WHOLE GRAIN SERVINGS: 6-11	PROTEIN: 4-6 OZ.	LIMIT FAT? Y N	ALCOHOLIC BEVERAGES? Y N	LIMIT "EMPTY" CARBS? Y N
☐☐☐☐ ☐☐☐☐	☐☐ ☐☐	☐☐☐ ☐☐	☐☐☐☐ ☐☐☐ ☐	☐☐☐ ☐☐☐			

WEATHER: SUN WIND RAIN CLOUDY SNOW   TEMP:____

FRIDAY / Date:

Training notes: _____

Today's goal: _____

FUEL LOG

WATER: 6-8 x 8 OZ.	FRUITS: 2-4	VEGGIES: 3-5	WHOLE GRAIN SERVINGS: 6-11	PROTEIN: 4-6 OZ.	LIMIT FAT?	ALCOHOLIC BEVERAGES?	LIMIT "EMPTY" CARBS?
☐☐☐☐ ☐☐☐☐	☐☐ ☐☐	☐☐ ☐☐☐	☐☐☐☐☐ ☐☐☐☐☐ ☐	☐☐☐ ☐☐☐	Y N	Y N	Y N

WEATHER: SUN WIND RAIN CLOUDY SNOW TEMP: ____

Distance: _____
Time: _____
Heart Rate: _____
i-Rate (1-10): _____
X-Training: _____
Sleep Hours: _____
Weight: _____
Mood: ☺ ☺ ☹ Other

SATURDAY / Date:

Training notes: _____

Today's goal: _____

FUEL LOG

WATER: 6-8 x 8 OZ.	FRUITS: 2-4	VEGGIES: 3-5	WHOLE GRAIN SERVINGS: 6-11	PROTEIN: 4-6 OZ.	LIMIT FAT?	ALCOHOLIC BEVERAGES?	LIMIT "EMPTY" CARBS?
☐☐☐☐ ☐☐☐☐	☐☐ ☐☐	☐☐ ☐☐☐	☐☐☐☐☐ ☐☐☐☐☐ ☐	☐☐☐ ☐☐☐	Y N	Y N	Y N

WEATHER: SUN WIND RAIN CLOUDY SNOW TEMP: ____

Distance: _____
Time: _____
Heart Rate: _____
i-Rate (1-10): _____
X-Training: _____
Sleep Hours: _____
Weight: _____
Mood: ☺ ☺ ☹ Other

SUNDAY / Date:

Training notes: _____

Today's goal: _____

FUEL LOG

WATER: 6-8 x 8 OZ.	FRUITS: 2-4	VEGGIES: 3-5	WHOLE GRAIN SERVINGS: 6-11	PROTEIN: 4-6 OZ.	LIMIT FAT?	ALCOHOLIC BEVERAGES?	LIMIT "EMPTY" CARBS?
☐☐☐☐ ☐☐☐☐	☐☐ ☐☐	☐☐ ☐☐☐	☐☐☐☐☐ ☐☐☐☐☐ ☐	☐☐☐ ☐☐☐	Y N	Y N	Y N

WEATHER: SUN WIND RAIN CLOUDY SNOW TEMP: ____

Distance: _____
Time: _____
Heart Rate: _____
i-Rate (1-10): _____
X-Training: _____
Sleep Hours: _____
Weight: _____
Mood: ☺ ☺ ☹ Other

WEEK OF: _____

GOALS FOR WEEK: _____

WEEKLY TOTAL: _____

YEAR-TO-DATE TOTAL: _____

PENGUIN WORDS OF WISDOM

My running shoes are like soldiers in my war against the ravages of aging and a less than healthy previous lifestyle. And I am the general. I am the commanding officer over the brigade of shoes in my closet.

MONDAY / Date:

Today's goal:

Training notes:

FUEL LOG

WATER: 6-8 x 8 OZ.	FRUITS: 2-4	VEGGIES: 3-5	WHOLE GRAIN SERVINGS: 6-11	PROTEIN: 4-6 OZ.	LIMIT FAT?	ALCOHOLIC BEVERAGES?	LIMIT "EMPTY" CARBS?
☐☐☐☐ ☐☐☐☐	☐☐ ☐☐	☐☐☐ ☐☐	☐☐☐☐☐ ☐☐☐☐☐ ☐	☐☐☐ ☐☐☐	Y N	Y N	Y N

WEATHER: SUN WIND RAIN CLOUDY SNOW TEMP:____

Distance:
Time:
Heart Rate:
i-Rate (1-10)
X-Training:
Sleep Hours:
Weight:
Mood: ☺ ☺ ☹ Other

TUESDAY / Date:

Today's goal:

Training notes:

FUEL LOG

WATER: 6-8 x 8 OZ.	FRUITS: 2-4	VEGGIES: 3-5	WHOLE GRAIN SERVINGS: 6-11	PROTEIN: 4-6 OZ.	LIMIT FAT?	ALCOHOLIC BEVERAGES?	LIMIT "EMPTY" CARBS?
☐☐☐☐ ☐☐☐☐	☐☐ ☐☐	☐☐☐ ☐☐	☐☐☐☐☐ ☐☐☐☐☐ ☐	☐☐☐ ☐☐☐	Y N	Y N	Y N

WEATHER: SUN WIND RAIN CLOUDY SNOW TEMP:____

Distance:
Time:
Heart Rate:
i-Rate (1-10)
X-Training:
Sleep Hours:
Weight:
Mood: ☺ ☺ ☹ Other

WEDNESDAY / Date:

Today's goal:

Training notes:

FUEL LOG

WATER: 6-8 x 8 OZ.	FRUITS: 2-4	VEGGIES: 3-5	WHOLE GRAIN SERVINGS: 6-11	PROTEIN: 4-6 OZ.	LIMIT FAT?	ALCOHOLIC BEVERAGES?	LIMIT "EMPTY" CARBS?
☐☐☐☐ ☐☐☐☐	☐☐ ☐☐	☐☐☐ ☐☐	☐☐☐☐☐ ☐☐☐☐☐ ☐	☐☐☐ ☐☐☐	Y N	Y N	Y N

WEATHER: SUN WIND RAIN CLOUDY SNOW TEMP:____

Distance:
Time:
Heart Rate:
i-Rate (1-10)
X-Training:
Sleep Hours:
Weight:
Mood: ☺ ☺ ☹ Other

THURSDAY / Date:

Today's goal:

Training notes:

FUEL LOG

WATER: 6-8 x 8 OZ.	FRUITS: 2-4	VEGGIES: 3-5	WHOLE GRAIN SERVINGS: 6-11	PROTEIN: 4-6 OZ.	LIMIT FAT?	ALCOHOLIC BEVERAGES?	LIMIT "EMPTY" CARBS?
☐☐☐☐ ☐☐☐☐	☐☐ ☐☐	☐☐☐ ☐☐	☐☐☐☐☐ ☐☐☐☐☐ ☐	☐☐☐ ☐☐☐	Y N	Y N	Y N

WEATHER: SUN WIND RAIN CLOUDY SNOW TEMP:____

Distance:
Time:
Heart Rate:
i-Rate (1-10)
X-Training:
Sleep Hours:
Weight:
Mood: ☺ ☺ ☹ Other

FRIDAY / Date:

Today's goal:

Training notes:

Distance:
Time:
Heart Rate:
i-Rate (1-10)
X-Training:
Sleep Hours:
Weight:
Mood: ☺ ☺ ☺ Other

FUEL LOG

WATER: 6-8 x 8 OZ.	FRUITS: 2-4	VEGGIES: 3-5	WHOLE GRAIN SERVINGS: 6-11	PROTEIN: 4-6 OZ.	LIMIT FAT? Y N	ALCOHOLIC BEVERAGES? Y N	LIMIT "EMPTY" CARBS? Y N
☐☐☐☐ ☐☐☐☐	☐☐ ☐☐	☐☐ ☐	☐☐☐☐☐ ☐	☐☐☐ ☐☐			

WEATHER:
SUN WIND
RAIN CLOUDY
SNOW
TEMP: _____

SATURDAY / Date:

Today's goal:

Training notes:

Distance:
Time:
Heart Rate:
i-Rate (1-10)
X-Training:
Sleep Hours:
Weight:
Mood: ☺ ☺ ☺ Other

FUEL LOG

WATER: 6-8 x 8 OZ.	FRUITS: 2-4	VEGGIES: 3-5	WHOLE GRAIN SERVINGS: 6-11	PROTEIN: 4-6 OZ.	LIMIT FAT? Y N	ALCOHOLIC BEVERAGES? Y N	LIMIT "EMPTY" CARBS? Y N
☐☐☐☐ ☐☐☐☐	☐☐ ☐☐	☐☐ ☐	☐☐☐☐☐ ☐	☐☐☐ ☐☐			

WEATHER:
SUN WIND
RAIN CLOUDY
SNOW
TEMP: _____

SUNDAY / Date:

Today's goal:

Training notes:

Distance:
Time:
Heart Rate:
i-Rate (1-10)
X-Training:
Sleep Hours:
Weight:
Mood: ☺ ☺ ☺ Other

FUEL LOG

WATER: 6-8 x 8 OZ.	FRUITS: 2-4	VEGGIES: 3-5	WHOLE GRAIN SERVINGS: 6-11	PROTEIN: 4-6 OZ.	LIMIT FAT? Y N	ALCOHOLIC BEVERAGES? Y N	LIMIT "EMPTY" CARBS? Y N
☐☐☐☐ ☐☐☐☐	☐☐ ☐☐	☐☐ ☐	☐☐☐☐☐ ☐	☐☐☐ ☐☐			

WEATHER:
SUN WIND
RAIN CLOUDY
SNOW
TEMP: _____

WEEK OF:

GOALS FOR WEEK:

WEEKLY TOTAL: _____

YEAR-TO-DATE TOTAL:

PENGUIN WORDS OF WISDOM

This year try to stop looking back over your shoulder at the runner you were, and start squinting into the future to see the runner you're going to be.

MONDAY / Date:

Today's goal:

Training notes: _____

FUEL LOG

WATER: 6-8 × 8 OZ.	FRUITS: 2-4	VEGGIES: 3-5	WHOLE GRAIN SERVINGS: 6-11	PROTEIN: 4-6 OZ.	LIMIT FAT?	ALCOHOLIC BEVERAGES?	LIMIT "EMPTY" CARBS?
☐☐☐☐ ☐☐☐☐	☐☐ ☐☐	☐☐ ☐☐	☐☐☐☐☐ ☐	☐☐☐ ☐☐	Y N	Y N	Y N

WEATHER: SUN WIND RAIN CLOUDY SNOW TEMP: _____

Distance:
Time:
Heart Rate:
i-Rate (1-10)
X-Training:
Sleep Hours:
Weight:
Mood: ☺ ☺ ☹   Other

TUESDAY / Date:

Today's goal:

Training notes: _____

FUEL LOG

WATER: 6-8 × 8 OZ.	FRUITS: 2-4	VEGGIES: 3-5	WHOLE GRAIN SERVINGS: 6-11	PROTEIN: 4-6 OZ.	LIMIT FAT?	ALCOHOLIC BEVERAGES?	LIMIT "EMPTY" CARBS?
☐☐☐☐ ☐☐☐☐	☐☐ ☐☐	☐☐ ☐☐	☐☐☐☐☐ ☐	☐☐☐ ☐☐	Y N	Y N	Y N

WEATHER: SUN WIND RAIN CLOUDY SNOW TEMP: _____

Distance:
Time:
Heart Rate:
i-Rate (1-10)
X-Training:
Sleep Hours:
Weight:
Mood: ☺ ☺ ☹   Other

WEDNESDAY / Date:

Today's goal:

Training notes: _____

FUEL LOG

WATER: 6-8 × 8 OZ.	FRUITS: 2-4	VEGGIES: 3-5	WHOLE GRAIN SERVINGS: 6-11	PROTEIN: 4-6 OZ.	LIMIT FAT?	ALCOHOLIC BEVERAGES?	LIMIT "EMPTY" CARBS?
☐☐☐☐ ☐☐☐☐	☐☐ ☐☐	☐☐ ☐☐	☐☐☐☐☐ ☐	☐☐☐ ☐☐	Y N	Y N	Y N

WEATHER: SUN WIND RAIN CLOUDY SNOW TEMP: _____

Distance:
Time:
Heart Rate:
i-Rate (1-10)
X-Training:
Sleep Hours:
Weight:
Mood: ☺ ☺ ☹   Other

THURSDAY / Date:

Today's goal:

Training notes: _____

FUEL LOG

WATER: 6-8 × 8 OZ.	FRUITS: 2-4	VEGGIES: 3-5	WHOLE GRAIN SERVINGS: 6-11	PROTEIN: 4-6 OZ.	LIMIT FAT?	ALCOHOLIC BEVERAGES?	LIMIT "EMPTY" CARBS?
☐☐☐☐ ☐☐☐☐	☐☐ ☐☐	☐☐ ☐☐	☐☐☐☐☐ ☐	☐☐☐ ☐☐	Y N	Y N	Y N

WEATHER: SUN WIND RAIN CLOUDY SNOW TEMP: _____

Distance:
Time:
Heart Rate:
i-Rate (1-10)
X-Training:
Sleep Hours:
Weight:
Mood: ☺ ☺ ☹   Other

FRIDAY / Date:

Today's goal:

Training notes: _____

FUEL LOG

WATER: 6-8 x 8 OZ.	FRUITS: 2-4	VEGGIES: 3-5	WHOLE GRAIN SERVINGS: 6-11	PROTEIN: 4-6 OZ.	LIMIT FAT?	ALCOHOLIC BEVERAGES?	LIMIT "EMPTY" CARBS?
☐☐☐☐ ☐☐☐☐	☐☐ ☐☐	☐☐ ☐☐	☐☐☐☐☐ ☐☐☐☐☐☐	☐☐☐ ☐☐	Y N	Y N	Y N

WEATHER:
SUN WIND
RAIN CLOUDY
SNOW
TEMP: ____

Distance:
Time:
Heart Rate:
i-Rate (1-10)
X-Training:
Sleep Hours:
Weight:
Mood: ☺ ☺ ☹ ☹ Other

SATURDAY / Date:

Today's goal:

Training notes: _____

FUEL LOG

WATER: 6-8 x 8 OZ.	FRUITS: 2-4	VEGGIES: 3-5	WHOLE GRAIN SERVINGS: 6-11	PROTEIN: 4-6 OZ.	LIMIT FAT?	ALCOHOLIC BEVERAGES?	LIMIT "EMPTY" CARBS?
☐☐☐☐ ☐☐☐☐	☐☐ ☐☐	☐☐ ☐☐	☐☐☐☐☐ ☐☐☐☐☐☐	☐☐☐ ☐☐	Y N	Y N	Y N

WEATHER:
SUN WIND
RAIN CLOUDY
SNOW
TEMP: ____

Distance:
Time:
Heart Rate:
i-Rate (1-10)
X-Training:
Sleep Hours:
Weight:
Mood: ☺ ☺ ☹ ☹ Other

SUNDAY / Date:

Today's goal:

Training notes: _____

FUEL LOG

WATER: 6-8 x 8 OZ.	FRUITS: 2-4	VEGGIES: 3-5	WHOLE GRAIN SERVINGS: 6-11	PROTEIN: 4-6 OZ.	LIMIT FAT?	ALCOHOLIC BEVERAGES?	LIMIT "EMPTY" CARBS?
☐☐☐☐ ☐☐☐☐	☐☐ ☐☐	☐☐ ☐☐	☐☐☐☐☐ ☐☐☐☐☐☐	☐☐☐ ☐☐	Y N	Y N	Y N

WEATHER:
SUN WIND
RAIN CLOUDY
SNOW
TEMP: ____

Distance:
Time:
Heart Rate:
i-Rate (1-10)
X-Training:
Sleep Hours:
Weight:
Mood: ☺ ☺ ☹ ☹ Other

WEEK OF:

GOALS FOR WEEK:

WEEKLY TOTAL: _____

YEAR-TO-DATE TOTAL:

PENGUIN WORDS OF WISDOM

Part of the appeal of running is that it is, in its essence, an authentic undertaking. You either run or you don't. You run fast or you don't. You run far or you don't. Whatever kind of runner you are, that's the runner you are.

MONDAY / Date:

Today's goal:

Training notes:

FUEL LOG

WATER: 6-8 × 8 OZ.	FRUITS: 2-4	VEGGIES: 3-5	WHOLE GRAIN SERVINGS: 6-11	PROTEIN: 4-6 OZ.	LIMIT FAT?	ALCOHOLIC BEVERAGES?	LIMIT "EMPTY" CARBS?
☐☐☐☐ ☐☐☐☐	☐☐ ☐☐	☐☐ ☐	☐☐☐☐☐ ☐	☐☐☐ ☐	Y N	Y N	Y N

WEATHER: SUN WIND RAIN CLOUDY SNOW   TEMP: _____

Distance:
Time:
Heart Rate:
i-Rate (1-10)
X-Training:
Sleep Hours:
Weight:
Mood: ☺ ☺ ☹ ☹ Other

TUESDAY / Date:

Today's goal:

Training notes:

FUEL LOG

WATER: 6-8 × 8 OZ.	FRUITS: 2-4	VEGGIES: 3-5	WHOLE GRAIN SERVINGS: 6-11	PROTEIN: 4-6 OZ.	LIMIT FAT?	ALCOHOLIC BEVERAGES?	LIMIT "EMPTY" CARBS?
☐☐☐☐ ☐☐☐☐	☐☐ ☐☐	☐☐ ☐	☐☐☐☐☐ ☐	☐☐☐ ☐	Y N	Y N	Y N

WEATHER: SUN WIND RAIN CLOUDY SNOW   TEMP: _____

Distance:
Time:
Heart Rate:
i-Rate (1-10)
X-Training:
Sleep Hours:
Weight:
Mood: ☺ ☺ ☹ ☹ Other

WEDNESDAY / Date:

Today's goal:

Training notes:

FUEL LOG

WATER: 6-8 × 8 OZ.	FRUITS: 2-4	VEGGIES: 3-5	WHOLE GRAIN SERVINGS: 6-11	PROTEIN: 4-6 OZ.	LIMIT FAT?	ALCOHOLIC BEVERAGES?	LIMIT "EMPTY" CARBS?
☐☐☐☐ ☐☐☐☐	☐☐ ☐☐	☐☐ ☐	☐☐☐☐☐ ☐	☐☐☐ ☐	Y N	Y N	Y N

WEATHER: SUN WIND RAIN CLOUDY SNOW   TEMP: _____

Distance:
Time:
Heart Rate:
i-Rate (1-10)
X-Training:
Sleep Hours:
Weight:
Mood: ☺ ☺ ☹ ☹ Other

THURSDAY / Date:

Today's goal:

Training notes:

FUEL LOG

WATER: 6-8 × 8 OZ.	FRUITS: 2-4	VEGGIES: 3-5	WHOLE GRAIN SERVINGS: 6-11	PROTEIN: 4-6 OZ.	LIMIT FAT?	ALCOHOLIC BEVERAGES?	LIMIT "EMPTY" CARBS?
☐☐☐☐ ☐☐☐☐	☐☐ ☐☐	☐☐ ☐	☐☐☐☐☐ ☐	☐☐☐ ☐	Y N	Y N	Y N

WEATHER: SUN WIND RAIN CLOUDY SNOW   TEMP: _____

Distance:
Time:
Heart Rate:
i-Rate (1-10)
X-Training:
Sleep Hours:
Weight:
Mood: ☺ ☺ ☹ ☹ Other

FRIDAY / Date:

Training notes:

Today's goal:

Distance:
Time:
Heart Rate:
i-Rate (1-10)
X-Training:
Sleep Hours:
Weight:
Mood: ☺ ☺ ☹ Other

WEATHER: SUN WIND RAIN CLOUDY SNOW TEMP: _____

FUEL LOG

WATER: 6-8 x 8 OZ.	FRUITS: 2-4	VEGGIES: 3-5	WHOLE GRAIN SERVINGS: 6-11	PROTEIN: 4-6 OZ.	LIMIT FAT?	ALCOHOLIC BEVERAGES?	LIMIT "EMPTY" CARBS?
☐☐☐☐ ☐☐☐☐	☐☐ ☐☐	☐☐ ☐☐	☐☐☐☐☐ ☐☐☐☐☐ ☐	☐☐☐ ☐☐☐	Y N	Y N	Y N

SATURDAY / Date:

Training notes:

Today's goal:

Distance:
Time:
Heart Rate:
i-Rate (1-10)
X-Training:
Sleep Hours:
Weight:
Mood: ☺ ☺ ☹ Other

WEATHER: SUN WIND RAIN CLOUDY SNOW TEMP: _____

FUEL LOG

WATER: 6-8 x 8 OZ.	FRUITS: 2-4	VEGGIES: 3-5	WHOLE GRAIN SERVINGS: 6-11	PROTEIN: 4-6 OZ.	LIMIT FAT?	ALCOHOLIC BEVERAGES?	LIMIT "EMPTY" CARBS?
☐☐☐☐ ☐☐☐☐	☐☐ ☐☐	☐☐ ☐☐	☐☐☐☐☐ ☐☐☐☐☐ ☐	☐☐☐ ☐☐☐	Y N	Y N	Y N

SUNDAY / Date:

Training notes:

Today's goal:

Distance:
Time:
Heart Rate:
i-Rate (1-10)
X-Training:
Sleep Hours:
Weight:
Mood: ☺ ☺ ☹ Other

WEATHER: SUN WIND RAIN CLOUDY SNOW TEMP: _____

FUEL LOG

WATER: 6-8 x 8 OZ.	FRUITS: 2-4	VEGGIES: 3-5	WHOLE GRAIN SERVINGS: 6-11	PROTEIN: 4-6 OZ.	LIMIT FAT?	ALCOHOLIC BEVERAGES?	LIMIT "EMPTY" CARBS?
☐☐☐☐ ☐☐☐☐	☐☐ ☐☐	☐☐ ☐☐	☐☐☐☐☐ ☐☐☐☐☐ ☐	☐☐☐ ☐☐☐	Y N	Y N	Y N

WEEK OF:

GOALS FOR WEEK:

WEEKLY TOTAL: _____

YEAR-TO-DATE TOTAL:

PENGUIN WORDS OF WISDOM

What does it take to be an authentic runner? It doesn't take mega-mile weeks. It isn't about speed or method or style. It's about knowing that it doesn't matter how others define running. Running is a way by which we define ourselves.

SEPTEMBER

BACK TO SCHOOL

Even the great athletes have coaches. No matter what they've accomplished, all athletes need to spend time on a regular basis going back and reviewing the fundamentals. Running and walking alone won't insure that your form is good, that your technique is intact, and that you haven't managed to slip in some very bad habits. Every now and then we all need to go back to school.

Take the month of September to get back to basics. If you've been running for years, maybe it's time to find a local coach and take a few sessions. Pick a goal race and work with the coach to evaluate your current state of running and make out a training program that includes track workouts to improve your running economy and form drills to remind you of how it's supposed to look when you run.

If you're relatively new to running and walking, this is an even better time to find a coach who can help you avoid the most common mistakes like overtraining and ignoring your body and provide the structure and advice you need to take your running to the next level. Don't make the mistake of thinking that professional coaches only want to work with elite level athletes. Take it from me, often the coaches' greatest joy is in working with someone with more ambition than talent.

This is also a good time to review and evaluate your own running goals and objectives. Are you making the progress you thought you'd make" Why or why not? Are you meeting your mileage and pace goals? Have you set your goals too high? Or too low? Are you training well but racing poorly? Are you having as much fun as you'd like to have?

The biggest danger for athletes of all abilities and experience is to just keep doing what they're doing when they stop getting what they wanted. Banging on the same rock over and over only compounds the frustration, it doesn't break the rock. If you're hitting thresholds or plateaus in your running and walking, it's time to call in a professional.

If you don't like the idea of a personal coach, find a running camp or weekend workshop to attend. Join a training program that is led by coaches and that has a series of seminars about various aspects of running. At the very least, buy a book about running!

A little time spend every year going back to school on the running and walking basics can add up to a lifetime of pleasure and achievement.

MONDAY / Date:

Training notes: _____

Today's goal: _____

FUEL LOG

WATER: 6-8 x 8 OZ.	FRUITS: 2-4	VEGGIES: 3-5	WHOLE GRAIN SERVINGS: 6-11	PROTEIN: 4-6 OZ.	LIMIT FAT?	ALCOHOLIC BEVERAGES?	LIMIT "EMPTY" CARBS?
☐☐☐☐ ☐☐☐☐	☐☐ ☐☐	☐☐ ☐☐	☐☐☐☐ ☐☐☐	☐☐☐ ☐☐☐	Y N	Y N	Y N

WEATHER: SUN WIND RAIN CLOUDY SNOW TEMP:_____

Distance: _____
Time: _____
Heart Rate: _____
i-Rate (1-10) _____
X-Training: _____
Sleep Hours: _____
Weight: _____
Mood: ☺ ☺ ☹ ☹ Other

TUESDAY / Date:

Training notes: _____

Today's goal: _____

FUEL LOG

WATER: 6-8 x 8 OZ.	FRUITS: 2-4	VEGGIES: 3-5	WHOLE GRAIN SERVINGS: 6-11	PROTEIN: 4-6 OZ.	LIMIT FAT?	ALCOHOLIC BEVERAGES?	LIMIT "EMPTY" CARBS?
☐☐☐☐ ☐☐☐☐	☐☐ ☐☐	☐☐ ☐☐	☐☐☐☐ ☐☐☐	☐☐☐ ☐☐☐	Y N	Y N	Y N

WEATHER: SUN WIND RAIN CLOUDY SNOW TEMP:_____

Distance: _____
Time: _____
Heart Rate: _____
i-Rate (1-10) _____
X-Training: _____
Sleep Hours: _____
Weight: _____
Mood: ☺ ☺ ☹ ☹ Other

WEDNESDAY / Date:

Training notes: _____

Today's goal: _____

FUEL LOG

WATER: 6-8 x 8 OZ.	FRUITS: 2-4	VEGGIES: 3-5	WHOLE GRAIN SERVINGS: 6-11	PROTEIN: 4-6 OZ.	LIMIT FAT?	ALCOHOLIC BEVERAGES?	LIMIT "EMPTY" CARBS?
☐☐☐☐ ☐☐☐☐	☐☐ ☐☐	☐☐ ☐☐	☐☐☐☐ ☐☐☐	☐☐☐ ☐☐☐	Y N	Y N	Y N

WEATHER: SUN WIND RAIN CLOUDY SNOW TEMP:_____

Distance: _____
Time: _____
Heart Rate: _____
i-Rate (1-10) _____
X-Training: _____
Sleep Hours: _____
Weight: _____
Mood: ☺ ☺ ☹ ☹ Other

THURSDAY / Date:

Training notes: _____

Today's goal: _____

FUEL LOG

WATER: 6-8 x 8 OZ.	FRUITS: 2-4	VEGGIES: 3-5	WHOLE GRAIN SERVINGS: 6-11	PROTEIN: 4-6 OZ.	LIMIT FAT?	ALCOHOLIC BEVERAGES?	LIMIT "EMPTY" CARBS?
☐☐☐☐ ☐☐☐☐	☐☐ ☐☐	☐☐ ☐☐	☐☐☐☐ ☐☐☐	☐☐☐ ☐☐☐	Y N	Y N	Y N

WEATHER: SUN WIND RAIN CLOUDY SNOW TEMP:_____

Distance: _____
Time: _____
Heart Rate: _____
i-Rate (1-10) _____
X-Training: _____
Sleep Hours: _____
Weight: _____
Mood: ☺ ☺ ☹ ☹ Other

FRIDAY / Date:

Today's goal:

Training notes:

Distance:
Time:
Heart Rate:
i-Rate (1-10)
X-Training:
Sleep Hours:
Weight:
Mood: ☺ 😐 ☹ Other

WEATHER:
SUN WIND
RAIN CLOUDY
SNOW
TEMP:____

FUEL LOG

WATER: 6-8 x 8 OZ.	FRUITS: 2-4	VEGGIES: 3-5	WHOLE GRAIN SERVINGS: 6-11	PROTEIN: 4-6 OZ.	LIMIT FAT?	ALCOHOLIC BEVERAGES?	LIMIT "EMPTY" CARBS?
☐☐☐☐ ☐☐☐☐	☐☐ ☐☐	☐☐ ☐	☐☐☐☐ ☐☐☐☐ ☐☐☐	☐☐☐ ☐☐	Y N	Y N	Y N

SATURDAY / Date:

Today's goal:

Training notes:

Distance:
Time:
Heart Rate:
i-Rate (1-10)
X-Training:
Sleep Hours:
Weight:
Mood: ☺ 😐 ☹ Other

WEATHER:
SUN WIND
RAIN CLOUDY
SNOW
TEMP:____

FUEL LOG

WATER: 6-8 x 8 OZ.	FRUITS: 2-4	VEGGIES: 3-5	WHOLE GRAIN SERVINGS: 6-11	PROTEIN: 4-6 OZ.	LIMIT FAT?	ALCOHOLIC BEVERAGES?	LIMIT "EMPTY" CARBS?
☐☐☐☐ ☐☐☐☐	☐☐ ☐☐	☐☐ ☐	☐☐☐☐ ☐☐☐☐ ☐☐☐	☐☐☐ ☐☐	Y N	Y N	Y N

SUNDAY / Date:

Today's goal:

Training notes:

Distance:
Time:
Heart Rate:
i-Rate (1-10)
X-Training:
Sleep Hours:
Weight:
Mood: ☺ 😐 ☹ Other

WEATHER:
SUN WIND
RAIN CLOUDY
SNOW
TEMP:____

FUEL LOG

WATER: 6-8 x 8 OZ.	FRUITS: 2-4	VEGGIES: 3-5	WHOLE GRAIN SERVINGS: 6-11	PROTEIN: 4-6 OZ.	LIMIT FAT?	ALCOHOLIC BEVERAGES?	LIMIT "EMPTY" CARBS?
☐☐☐☐ ☐☐☐☐	☐☐ ☐☐	☐☐ ☐	☐☐☐☐ ☐☐☐☐ ☐☐☐	☐☐☐ ☐☐	Y N	Y N	Y N

WEEK OF:

GOALS FOR WEEK:

WEEKLY TOTAL:____

YEAR-TO-DATE TOTAL:

PENGUIN WORDS OF WISDOM

When I began running, the act of moving was more important than stride length and foot strikes. The movement of my body reflected the movement of my spirit and that's what mattered most. More than speed or distance it was the movement that I craved.

MONDAY / Date:

Today's goal:

Training notes:

FUEL LOG

WATER: 6-8 x 8 OZ.	FRUITS: 2-4	VEGGIES: 3-5	WHOLE GRAIN SERVINGS: 6-11	PROTEIN: 4-6 OZ.	LIMIT FAT?	ALCOHOLIC BEVERAGES?	LIMIT "EMPTY" CARBS?
☐☐☐☐ / ☐☐☐☐	☐☐ / ☐☐	☐☐ / ☐☐	☐☐☐ / ☐☐☐☐ / ☐☐	☐☐☐ / ☐☐☐	Y N	Y N	Y N

WEATHER: SUN WIND RAIN CLOUDY SNOW TEMP: _____

Distance:
Time:
Heart Rate:
i-Rate (1-10)
X-Training:
Sleep Hours:
Weight:
Mood: ☺ ☺ ☺ ☹ Other

TUESDAY / Date:

Today's goal:

Training notes:

FUEL LOG

WATER: 6-8 x 8 OZ.	FRUITS: 2-4	VEGGIES: 3-5	WHOLE GRAIN SERVINGS: 6-11	PROTEIN: 4-6 OZ.	LIMIT FAT?	ALCOHOLIC BEVERAGES?	LIMIT "EMPTY" CARBS?
☐☐☐☐ / ☐☐☐☐	☐☐ / ☐☐	☐☐ / ☐☐	☐☐☐ / ☐☐☐☐ / ☐☐	☐☐☐ / ☐☐☐	Y N	Y N	Y N

WEATHER: SUN WIND RAIN CLOUDY SNOW TEMP: _____

Distance:
Time:
Heart Rate:
i-Rate (1-10)
X-Training:
Sleep Hours:
Weight:
Mood: ☺ ☺ ☺ ☹ Other

WEDNESDAY / Date:

Today's goal:

Training notes:

FUEL LOG

WATER: 6-8 x 8 OZ.	FRUITS: 2-4	VEGGIES: 3-5	WHOLE GRAIN SERVINGS: 6-11	PROTEIN: 4-6 OZ.	LIMIT FAT?	ALCOHOLIC BEVERAGES?	LIMIT "EMPTY" CARBS?
☐☐☐☐ / ☐☐☐☐	☐☐ / ☐☐	☐☐ / ☐☐	☐☐☐ / ☐☐☐☐ / ☐☐	☐☐☐ / ☐☐☐	Y N	Y N	Y N

WEATHER: SUN WIND RAIN CLOUDY SNOW TEMP: _____

Distance:
Time:
Heart Rate:
i-Rate (1-10)
X-Training:
Sleep Hours:
Weight:
Mood: ☺ ☺ ☺ ☹ Other

THURSDAY / Date:

Today's goal:

Training notes:

FUEL LOG

WATER: 6-8 x 8 OZ.	FRUITS: 2-4	VEGGIES: 3-5	WHOLE GRAIN SERVINGS: 6-11	PROTEIN: 4-6 OZ.	LIMIT FAT?	ALCOHOLIC BEVERAGES?	LIMIT "EMPTY" CARBS?
☐☐☐☐ / ☐☐☐☐	☐☐ / ☐☐	☐☐ / ☐☐	☐☐☐ / ☐☐☐☐ / ☐☐	☐☐☐ / ☐☐☐	Y N	Y N	Y N

WEATHER: SUN WIND RAIN CLOUDY SNOW TEMP: _____

Distance:
Time:
Heart Rate:
i-Rate (1-10)
X-Training:
Sleep Hours:
Weight:
Mood: ☺ ☺ ☺ ☹ Other

FRIDAY / Date:

Training notes:

Today's goal:

FUEL LOG

WATER: 6-8 x 8 OZ.	FRUITS: 2-4	VEGGIES: 3-5	WHOLE GRAIN SERVINGS: 6-11	PROTEIN: 4-6 OZ.	LIMIT FAT?	ALCOHOLIC BEVERAGES?	LIMIT "EMPTY" CARBS?
☐☐☐☐ ☐☐☐☐	☐☐ ☐☐	☐☐ ☐☐	☐☐☐☐ ☐☐☐☐ ☐☐☐	☐☐☐ ☐☐☐	Y N	Y N	Y N

WEATHER: SUN WIND RAIN CLOUDY SNOW TEMP: _____

Distance:
Time:
Heart Rate:
i-Rate (1-10)
X-Training:
Sleep Hours:
Weight:
Mood: ☺ ☺ ☹ Other

SATURDAY / Date:

Training notes:

Today's goal:

FUEL LOG

WATER: 6-8 x 8 OZ.	FRUITS: 2-4	VEGGIES: 3-5	WHOLE GRAIN SERVINGS: 6-11	PROTEIN: 4-6 OZ.	LIMIT FAT?	ALCOHOLIC BEVERAGES?	LIMIT "EMPTY" CARBS?
☐☐☐☐ ☐☐☐☐	☐☐ ☐☐	☐☐ ☐☐	☐☐☐☐ ☐☐☐☐ ☐☐☐	☐☐☐ ☐☐☐	Y N	Y N	Y N

WEATHER: SUN WIND RAIN CLOUDY SNOW TEMP: _____

Distance:
Time:
Heart Rate:
i-Rate (1-10)
X-Training:
Sleep Hours:
Weight:
Mood: ☺ ☺ ☹ Other

SUNDAY / Date:

Training notes:

Today's goal:

FUEL LOG

WATER: 6-8 x 8 OZ.	FRUITS: 2-4	VEGGIES: 3-5	WHOLE GRAIN SERVINGS: 6-11	PROTEIN: 4-6 OZ.	LIMIT FAT?	ALCOHOLIC BEVERAGES?	LIMIT "EMPTY" CARBS?
☐☐☐☐ ☐☐☐☐	☐☐ ☐☐	☐☐ ☐☐	☐☐☐☐ ☐☐☐☐ ☐☐☐	☐☐☐ ☐☐☐	Y N	Y N	Y N

WEATHER: SUN WIND RAIN CLOUDY SNOW TEMP: _____

Distance:
Time:
Heart Rate:
i-Rate (1-10)
X-Training:
Sleep Hours:
Weight:
Mood: ☺ ☺ ☹ Other

WEEK OF:

GOALS FOR WEEK:

WEEKLY TOTAL: _____

YEAR-TO-DATE TOTAL:

PENGUIN WORDS OF WISDOM

Some new runners misunderstand the difficulties they encounter at first. They attribute their fatigue and soreness, or even injury, to the running. They're missing the point. The fatigue is from all the years of not running.

MONDAY / Date: _____ Training notes: _____

Today's goal: _____

FUEL LOG

WATER: 6-8 × 8 OZ.	FRUITS: 2-4	VEGGIES: 3-5	WHOLE GRAIN SERVINGS: 6-11	PROTEIN: 4-6 OZ.	LIMIT FAT?	ALCOHOLIC BEVERAGES?	LIMIT "EMPTY" CARBS?
☐☐☐☐ ☐☐☐☐	☐☐ ☐☐	☐☐ ☐☐	☐☐☐☐ ☐☐☐☐ ☐☐☐	☐☐☐ ☐☐☐	Y N	Y N	Y N

WEATHER: SUN WIND RAIN CLOUDY SNOW   TEMP: ____

Distance:
Time:
Heart Rate:
i-Rate (1-10)
X-Training:
Sleep Hours:
Weight:
Mood: ☺ ☺ ☹ ☹ Other

TUESDAY / Date: _____ Training notes: _____

Today's goal: _____

FUEL LOG

WATER: 6-8 × 8 OZ.	FRUITS: 2-4	VEGGIES: 3-5	WHOLE GRAIN SERVINGS: 6-11	PROTEIN: 4-6 OZ.	LIMIT FAT?	ALCOHOLIC BEVERAGES?	LIMIT "EMPTY" CARBS?
☐☐☐☐ ☐☐☐☐	☐☐ ☐☐	☐☐ ☐☐	☐☐☐☐ ☐☐☐☐ ☐☐☐	☐☐☐ ☐☐☐	Y N	Y N	Y N

WEATHER: SUN WIND RAIN CLOUDY SNOW   TEMP: ____

Distance:
Time:
Heart Rate:
i-Rate (1-10)
X-Training:
Sleep Hours:
Weight:
Mood: ☺ ☺ ☹ ☹ Other

WEDNESDAY / Date: _____ Training notes: _____

Today's goal: _____

FUEL LOG

WATER: 6-8 × 8 OZ.	FRUITS: 2-4	VEGGIES: 3-5	WHOLE GRAIN SERVINGS: 6-11	PROTEIN: 4-6 OZ.	LIMIT FAT?	ALCOHOLIC BEVERAGES?	LIMIT "EMPTY" CARBS?
☐☐☐☐ ☐☐☐☐	☐☐ ☐☐	☐☐ ☐☐	☐☐☐☐ ☐☐☐☐ ☐☐☐	☐☐☐ ☐☐☐	Y N	Y N	Y N

WEATHER: SUN WIND RAIN CLOUDY SNOW   TEMP: ____

Distance:
Time:
Heart Rate:
i-Rate (1-10)
X-Training:
Sleep Hours:
Weight:
Mood: ☺ ☺ ☹ ☹ Other

THURSDAY / Date: _____ Training notes: _____

Today's goal: _____

FUEL LOG

WATER: 6-8 × 8 OZ.	FRUITS: 2-4	VEGGIES: 3-5	WHOLE GRAIN SERVINGS: 6-11	PROTEIN: 4-6 OZ.	LIMIT FAT?	ALCOHOLIC BEVERAGES?	LIMIT "EMPTY" CARBS?
☐☐☐☐ ☐☐☐☐	☐☐ ☐☐	☐☐ ☐☐	☐☐☐☐ ☐☐☐☐ ☐☐☐	☐☐☐ ☐☐☐	Y N	Y N	Y N

WEATHER: SUN WIND RAIN CLOUDY SNOW   TEMP: ____

Distance:
Time:
Heart Rate:
i-Rate (1-10)
X-Training:
Sleep Hours:
Weight:
Mood: ☺ ☺ ☹ ☹ Other

FRIDAY / Date:

Training notes:

Today's goal:

FUEL LOG

WATER: 6-8 x 8 oz.	FRUITS: 2-4	VEGGIES: 3-5	WHOLE GRAIN SERVINGS: 6-11	PROTEIN: 4-6 oz.	LIMIT FAT?	ALCOHOLIC BEVERAGES?	LIMIT "EMPTY" CARBS?
☐☐☐☐ ☐☐☐☐	☐☐ ☐☐	☐☐ ☐☐	☐☐☐☐ ☐☐☐☐	☐☐☐ ☐☐☐	Y N	Y N	Y N

WEATHER: SUN WIND RAIN CLOUDY SNOW TEMP:_____

Distance:
Time:
Heart Rate:
i-Rate (1-10)
X-Training:
Sleep Hours:
Weight:
Mood: ☺ ☺ ☹ Other

SATURDAY / Date:

Training notes:

Today's goal:

FUEL LOG

WATER: 6-8 x 8 oz.	FRUITS: 2-4	VEGGIES: 3-5	WHOLE GRAIN SERVINGS: 6-11	PROTEIN: 4-6 oz.	LIMIT FAT?	ALCOHOLIC BEVERAGES?	LIMIT "EMPTY" CARBS?
☐☐☐☐ ☐☐☐☐	☐☐ ☐☐	☐☐ ☐☐	☐☐☐☐ ☐☐☐☐	☐☐☐ ☐☐☐	Y N	Y N	Y N

WEATHER: SUN WIND RAIN CLOUDY SNOW TEMP:_____

Distance:
Time:
Heart Rate:
i-Rate (1-10)
X-Training:
Sleep Hours:
Weight:
Mood: ☺ ☺ ☹ Other

SUNDAY / Date:

Training notes:

Today's goal:

FUEL LOG

WATER: 6-8 x 8 oz.	FRUITS: 2-4	VEGGIES: 3-5	WHOLE GRAIN SERVINGS: 6-11	PROTEIN: 4-6 oz.	LIMIT FAT?	ALCOHOLIC BEVERAGES?	LIMIT "EMPTY" CARBS?
☐☐☐☐ ☐☐☐☐	☐☐ ☐☐	☐☐ ☐☐	☐☐☐☐ ☐☐☐☐	☐☐☐ ☐☐☐	Y N	Y N	Y N

WEATHER: SUN WIND RAIN CLOUDY SNOW TEMP:_____

Distance:
Time:
Heart Rate:
i-Rate (1-10)
X-Training:
Sleep Hours:
Weight:
Mood: ☺ ☺ ☹ Other

WEEK OF:

GOALS FOR WEEK:

WEEKLY TOTAL: _____

YEAR-TO-DATE TOTAL:

PENGUIN WORDS OF WISDOM

It's only when movement becomes the most natural state in our lives that we can finally begin to enjoy the motion. It is only when running, in and for itself, becomes the one part of lives that we can't do with-out that we can experience the joy of becoming ourselves.

MONDAY / Date:

Today's goal: _____

Training notes: _____
_____
_____

Distance: _____
Time: _____
Heart Rate: _____
i-Rate (1-10): _____
X-Training: _____
Sleep Hours: _____
Weight: _____
Mood: ☺ ☺ ☺ ☹ ☹ Other

FUEL LOG

WATER: 6-8 x 8 OZ.	FRUITS: 2-4	VEGGIES: 3-5	WHOLE GRAIN SERVINGS: 6-11	PROTEIN: 4-6 OZ.	LIMIT FAT?	ALCOHOLIC BEVERAGES?	LIMIT "EMPTY" CARBS?
☐☐☐☐ ☐☐☐☐	☐☐ ☐☐	☐☐ ☐	☐☐☐☐☐ ☐	☐☐☐ ☐☐ ☐	Y N	Y N	Y N

WEATHER: SUN WIND RAIN CLOUDY SNOW TEMP:____

TUESDAY / Date:

Today's goal: _____

Training notes: _____
_____
_____

Distance: _____
Time: _____
Heart Rate: _____
i-Rate (1-10): _____
X-Training: _____
Sleep Hours: _____
Weight: _____
Mood: ☺ ☺ ☺ ☹ ☹ Other

FUEL LOG

WATER: 6-8 x 8 OZ.	FRUITS: 2-4	VEGGIES: 3-5	WHOLE GRAIN SERVINGS: 6-11	PROTEIN: 4-6 OZ.	LIMIT FAT?	ALCOHOLIC BEVERAGES?	LIMIT "EMPTY" CARBS?
☐☐☐☐ ☐☐☐☐	☐☐ ☐☐	☐☐ ☐	☐☐☐☐☐ ☐	☐☐☐ ☐☐ ☐	Y N	Y N	Y N

WEATHER: SUN WIND RAIN CLOUDY SNOW TEMP:____

WEDNESDAY / Date:

Today's goal: _____

Training notes: _____
_____
_____

Distance: _____
Time: _____
Heart Rate: _____
i-Rate (1-10): _____
X-Training: _____
Sleep Hours: _____
Weight: _____
Mood: ☺ ☺ ☺ ☹ ☹ Other

FUEL LOG

WATER: 6-8 x 8 OZ.	FRUITS: 2-4	VEGGIES: 3-5	WHOLE GRAIN SERVINGS: 6-11	PROTEIN: 4-6 OZ.	LIMIT FAT?	ALCOHOLIC BEVERAGES?	LIMIT "EMPTY" CARBS?
☐☐☐☐ ☐☐☐☐	☐☐ ☐☐	☐☐ ☐	☐☐☐☐☐ ☐	☐☐☐ ☐☐ ☐	Y N	Y N	Y N

WEATHER: SUN WIND RAIN CLOUDY SNOW TEMP:____

THURSDAY / Date:

Today's goal: _____

Training notes: _____
_____
_____

Distance: _____
Time: _____
Heart Rate: _____
i-Rate (1-10): _____
X-Training: _____
Sleep Hours: _____
Weight: _____
Mood: ☺ ☺ ☺ ☹ ☹ Other

FUEL LOG

WATER: 6-8 x 8 OZ.	FRUITS: 2-4	VEGGIES: 3-5	WHOLE GRAIN SERVINGS: 6-11	PROTEIN: 4-6 OZ.	LIMIT FAT?	ALCOHOLIC BEVERAGES?	LIMIT "EMPTY" CARBS?
☐☐☐☐ ☐☐☐☐	☐☐ ☐☐	☐☐ ☐	☐☐☐☐☐ ☐	☐☐☐ ☐☐ ☐	Y N	Y N	Y N

WEATHER: SUN WIND RAIN CLOUDY SNOW TEMP:____

FRIDAY / Date: _____ Training notes: _____

Today's goal: _____

Distance: _____
Time: _____
Heart Rate: _____
i-Rate (1-10): _____
X-Training: _____
Sleep Hours: _____
Weight: _____
Mood: ☺ 😐 ☹ Other

FUEL LOG

WATER: 6-8 x 8 OZ.	FRUITS: 2-4	VEGGIES: 3-5	WHOLE GRAIN SERVINGS: 6-11	PROTEIN: 4-6 OZ.	LIMIT FAT?	ALCOHOLIC BEVERAGES?	LIMIT "EMPTY" CARBS?	WEATHER:
☐☐☐☐ ☐☐☐☐	☐☐ ☐☐	☐☐☐ ☐☐	☐☐☐☐☐☐ ☐☐☐☐☐☐	☐☐☐ ☐☐☐	Y N	Y N	Y N	SUN WIND RAIN CLOUDY SNOW TEMP:____

SATURDAY / Date: _____ Training notes: _____

Today's goal: _____

Distance: _____
Time: _____
Heart Rate: _____
i-Rate (1-10): _____
X-Training: _____
Sleep Hours: _____
Weight: _____
Mood: ☺ 😐 ☹ Other

FUEL LOG

WATER: 6-8 x 8 OZ.	FRUITS: 2-4	VEGGIES: 3-5	WHOLE GRAIN SERVINGS: 6-11	PROTEIN: 4-6 OZ.	LIMIT FAT?	ALCOHOLIC BEVERAGES?	LIMIT "EMPTY" CARBS?	WEATHER:
☐☐☐☐ ☐☐☐☐	☐☐ ☐☐	☐☐☐ ☐☐	☐☐☐☐☐☐ ☐☐☐☐☐☐	☐☐☐ ☐☐☐	Y N	Y N	Y N	SUN WIND RAIN CLOUDY SNOW TEMP:____

SUNDAY / Date: _____ Training notes: _____

Today's goal: _____

Distance: _____
Time: _____
Heart Rate: _____
i-Rate (1-10): _____
X-Training: _____
Sleep Hours: _____
Weight: _____
Mood: ☺ 😐 ☹ Other

FUEL LOG

WATER: 6-8 x 8 OZ.	FRUITS: 2-4	VEGGIES: 3-5	WHOLE GRAIN SERVINGS: 6-11	PROTEIN: 4-6 OZ.	LIMIT FAT?	ALCOHOLIC BEVERAGES?	LIMIT "EMPTY" CARBS?	WEATHER:
☐☐☐☐ ☐☐☐☐	☐☐ ☐☐	☐☐☐ ☐☐	☐☐☐☐☐☐ ☐☐☐☐☐☐	☐☐☐ ☐☐☐	Y N	Y N	Y N	SUN WIND RAIN CLOUDY SNOW TEMP:____

WEEK OF: _____

GOALS FOR WEEK: _____

WEEKLY TOTAL: _____

YEAR-TO-DATE TOTAL: _____

PENGUIN WORDS OF WISDOM

We all have them. Runs when what we want and what we get are so different that we can't hold it together. Runs when nothing goes right, nothing feels good, and there isn't a thing we can do about it.

MONDAY / Date:

Training notes: _____

Distance: _____
Time: _____
Heart Rate: _____
i-Rate (1-10) _____
X-Training: _____
Sleep Hours: _____
Weight: _____
Mood: ☺ ☺ ☺ Other

WEATHER:
SUN WIND
RAIN CLOUDY
SNOW
TEMP: _____

FUEL LOG

WATER: 6-8 × 8 oz.	FRUITS: 2-4	VEGGIES: 3-5	WHOLE GRAIN SERVINGS: 6-11	PROTEIN: 4-6 oz.	LIMIT FAT?	ALCOHOLIC BEVERAGES?	LIMIT "EMPTY" CARBS?
☐☐☐☐ ☐☐☐☐	☐☐ ☐☐	☐☐ ☐☐	☐☐☐ ☐☐☐ ☐	☐☐☐ ☐☐☐	Y N	Y N	Y N

TUESDAY / Date:

Today's goal: _____

Training notes: _____

Distance: _____
Time: _____
Heart Rate: _____
i-Rate (1-10) _____
X-Training: _____
Sleep Hours: _____
Weight: _____
Mood: ☺ ☺ ☺ Other

WEATHER:
SUN WIND
RAIN CLOUDY
SNOW
TEMP: _____

FUEL LOG

WATER: 6-8 × 8 oz.	FRUITS: 2-4	VEGGIES: 3-5	WHOLE GRAIN SERVINGS: 6-11	PROTEIN: 4-6 oz.	LIMIT FAT?	ALCOHOLIC BEVERAGES?	LIMIT "EMPTY" CARBS?
☐☐☐☐ ☐☐☐☐	☐☐ ☐☐	☐☐ ☐☐	☐☐☐ ☐☐☐ ☐	☐☐☐ ☐☐☐	Y N	Y N	Y N

WEDNESDAY / Date:

Today's goal: _____

Training notes: _____

Distance: _____
Time: _____
Heart Rate: _____
i-Rate (1-10) _____
X-Training: _____
Sleep Hours: _____
Weight: _____
Mood: ☺ ☺ ☺ Other

WEATHER:
SUN WIND
RAIN CLOUDY
SNOW
TEMP: _____

FUEL LOG

WATER: 6-8 × 8 oz.	FRUITS: 2-4	VEGGIES: 3-5	WHOLE GRAIN SERVINGS: 6-11	PROTEIN: 4-6 oz.	LIMIT FAT?	ALCOHOLIC BEVERAGES?	LIMIT "EMPTY" CARBS?
☐☐☐☐ ☐☐☐☐	☐☐ ☐☐	☐☐ ☐☐	☐☐☐ ☐☐☐ ☐	☐☐☐ ☐☐☐	Y N	Y N	Y N

THURSDAY / Date:

Today's goal: _____

Training notes: _____

Distance: _____
Time: _____
Heart Rate: _____
i-Rate (1-10) _____
X-Training: _____
Sleep Hours: _____
Weight: _____
Mood: ☺ ☺ ☺ Other

WEATHER:
SUN WIND
RAIN CLOUDY
SNOW
TEMP: _____

FUEL LOG

WATER: 6-8 × 8 oz.	FRUITS: 2-4	VEGGIES: 3-5	WHOLE GRAIN SERVINGS: 6-11	PROTEIN: 4-6 oz.	LIMIT FAT?	ALCOHOLIC BEVERAGES?	LIMIT "EMPTY" CARBS?
☐☐☐☐ ☐☐☐☐	☐☐ ☐☐	☐☐ ☐☐	☐☐☐ ☐☐☐ ☐	☐☐☐ ☐☐☐	Y N	Y N	Y N

FRIDAY / Date:

Today's goal:

Training notes:

Distance:
Time:
Heart Rate:
i-Rate (1-10):
X-Training:
Sleep Hours:
Weight:
Mood: ☺ ☺ ☹ Other

FUEL LOG

WATER: 6-8 × 8 OZ.	FRUITS: 2-4	VEGGIES: 3-5	WHOLE GRAIN SERVINGS: 6-11	PROTEIN: 4-6 OZ.	LIMIT FAT?	ALCOHOLIC BEVERAGES?	LIMIT "EMPTY" CARBS?
☐☐☐☐ ☐☐☐☐	☐☐ ☐☐	☐☐☐ ☐☐	☐☐☐☐☐ ☐☐☐☐☐ ☐	☐☐☐ ☐☐☐	Y N	Y N	Y N

WEATHER:
SUN WIND
RAIN CLOUDY
SNOW
TEMP: _____

SATURDAY / Date:

Today's goal:

Training notes:

Distance:
Time:
Heart Rate:
i-Rate (1-10):
X-Training:
Sleep Hours:
Weight:
Mood: ☺ ☺ ☹ Other

FUEL LOG

WATER: 6-8 × 8 OZ.	FRUITS: 2-4	VEGGIES: 3-5	WHOLE GRAIN SERVINGS: 6-11	PROTEIN: 4-6 OZ.	LIMIT FAT?	ALCOHOLIC BEVERAGES?	LIMIT "EMPTY" CARBS?
☐☐☐☐ ☐☐☐☐	☐☐ ☐☐	☐☐☐ ☐☐	☐☐☐☐☐ ☐☐☐☐☐ ☐	☐☐☐ ☐☐☐	Y N	Y N	Y N

WEATHER:
SUN WIND
RAIN CLOUDY
SNOW
TEMP: _____

SUNDAY / Date:

Today's goal:

Training notes:

Distance:
Time:
Heart Rate:
i-Rate (1-10):
X-Training:
Sleep Hours:
Weight:
Mood: ☺ ☺ ☹ Other

FUEL LOG

WATER: 6-8 × 8 OZ.	FRUITS: 2-4	VEGGIES: 3-5	WHOLE GRAIN SERVINGS: 6-11	PROTEIN: 4-6 OZ.	LIMIT FAT?	ALCOHOLIC BEVERAGES?	LIMIT "EMPTY" CARBS?
☐☐☐☐ ☐☐☐☐	☐☐ ☐☐	☐☐☐ ☐☐	☐☐☐☐☐ ☐☐☐☐☐ ☐	☐☐☐ ☐☐☐	Y N	Y N	Y N

WEATHER:
SUN WIND
RAIN CLOUDY
SNOW
TEMP: _____

WEEK OF:

GOALS FOR WEEK:

WEEKLY TOTAL: _____

YEAR-TO-DATE TOTAL:

PENGUIN WORDS OF WISDOM

For all the time we spend running with others, it's still easy for us to isolate ourselves. Running is a solitary activity, but it needn't be an activity of solitude. We may all run alone, but we need never run lonely.

OCTOBER

TRICK OR TREAT

The biggest difference between the elite athletes and folks like me is that the elites seem to know exactly what they are capable of on any given day. And I have no idea whether, on any given day, my run will be an absolute treat, or an evil trick. Even when I've been training well, planning well, and being consistent in my workouts, there is always that chance that the running gods are going to bless me with the run of a lifetime, or curse me to my very core.

For the longest time I thought this meant that there was something wrong with me. I suffered from the illusion that once I had enough experience, once I had run enough miles, covered enough ground, been through enough variables, I'd be able to know exactly how I was going to feel before I walked out the door. I was sure that there would come a time when actually doing the run would only confirm what I already knew. Good or bad, I thought that the run itself was a given.

Like so much else, I was wrong. I can assure you that tomorrow's run will be a mystery to me. As I get out my clothes, thoughts about the run will start to overcome me. I'll be aware of how I feel, aware of where I am in my training sequence, aware of the weather, and aware of my goals for that workout. As I tie my shoes I'll be imagining how it will feel to get those first tentative steps out of the way and ease into the rhythm of my run. As I walk out the door I'll start to imagine the run that awaits me.

All this is fine until I actually start to run. Then it's as if my body and brain have been taken over by alien forces. Rather than confirm my speculation about how I was feeling, my body seems determined to assert it's own view of my current state of fitness. How else do you explain how one day fast feels easy and then next day slow feels hard and that the exact opposite could just as easily be true. The total disconnect between what my head thinks and my body does is shocking.

Within minutes my best laid plans have gone out the window and I am literally along for the ride. My body knows what it needs today. My body knows, far better than my imagination, what it can do, what it will do, and what it will *not* do—no matter what. I used to argue with my body, but that only frustrated me. I was never going to win the battle. Like it or not, it's my body that decides on what each run will be.

Over time, though, I have learned to live with the situation. I realize now that my body is doing my head a favor by letting it ride along. I've learned to enjoy the run my body is taking, regardless of what I thought it would be.

MONDAY / Date:

Today's goal:

Training notes:

FUEL LOG

WATER: 6-8 x 8 oz.	FRUITS: 2-4	VEGGIES: 3-5	WHOLE GRAIN SERVINGS: 6-11	PROTEIN: 4-6 oz.	LIMIT FAT?	ALCOHOLIC BEVERAGES?	LIMIT "EMPTY" CARBS?
☐☐☐☐ ☐☐☐☐	☐☐ ☐☐	☐☐ ☐☐	☐☐☐☐☐ ☐☐☐☐☐	☐☐☐ ☐☐☐	Y N	Y N	Y N

WEATHER: SUN WIND RAIN CLOUDY SNOW TEMP:___

Distance:
Time:
Heart Rate:
i-Rate (1-10)
X-Training:
Sleep Hours:
Weight:
Mood: ☺ ☺ ☹ Other

TUESDAY / Date:

Today's goal:

Training notes:

FUEL LOG

WATER: 6-8 x 8 oz.	FRUITS: 2-4	VEGGIES: 3-5	WHOLE GRAIN SERVINGS: 6-11	PROTEIN: 4-6 oz.	LIMIT FAT?	ALCOHOLIC BEVERAGES?	LIMIT "EMPTY" CARBS?
☐☐☐☐ ☐☐☐☐	☐☐ ☐☐	☐☐ ☐☐	☐☐☐☐☐ ☐☐☐☐☐	☐☐☐ ☐☐☐	Y N	Y N	Y N

WEATHER: SUN WIND RAIN CLOUDY SNOW TEMP:___

Distance:
Time:
Heart Rate:
i-Rate (1-10)
X-Training:
Sleep Hours:
Weight:
Mood: ☺ ☺ ☹ Other

WEDNESDAY / Date:

Today's goal:

Training notes:

FUEL LOG

WATER: 6-8 x 8 oz.	FRUITS: 2-4	VEGGIES: 3-5	WHOLE GRAIN SERVINGS: 6-11	PROTEIN: 4-6 oz.	LIMIT FAT?	ALCOHOLIC BEVERAGES?	LIMIT "EMPTY" CARBS?
☐☐☐☐ ☐☐☐☐	☐☐ ☐☐	☐☐ ☐☐	☐☐☐☐☐ ☐☐☐☐☐	☐☐☐ ☐☐☐	Y N	Y N	Y N

WEATHER: SUN WIND RAIN CLOUDY SNOW TEMP:___

Distance:
Time:
Heart Rate:
i-Rate (1-10)
X-Training:
Sleep Hours:
Weight:
Mood: ☺ ☺ ☹ Other

THURSDAY / Date:

Today's goal:

Training notes:

FUEL LOG

WATER: 6-8 x 8 oz.	FRUITS: 2-4	VEGGIES: 3-5	WHOLE GRAIN SERVINGS: 6-11	PROTEIN: 4-6 oz.	LIMIT FAT?	ALCOHOLIC BEVERAGES?	LIMIT "EMPTY" CARBS?
☐☐☐☐ ☐☐☐☐	☐☐ ☐☐	☐☐ ☐☐	☐☐☐☐☐ ☐☐☐☐☐	☐☐☐ ☐☐☐	Y N	Y N	Y N

WEATHER: SUN WIND RAIN CLOUDY SNOW TEMP:___

Distance:
Time:
Heart Rate:
i-Rate (1-10)
X-Training:
Sleep Hours:
Weight:
Mood: ☺ ☺ ☹ Other

FRIDAY / Date: _____   Training notes: _____

Today's goal: _____

FUEL LOG

WATER: 6-8 × 8 OZ.	FRUITS: 2-4	VEGGIES: 3-5	WHOLE GRAIN SERVINGS: 6-11	PROTEIN: 4-6 OZ.	LIMIT FAT?	ALCOHOLIC BEVERAGES?	LIMIT "EMPTY" CARBS?
☐☐☐☐ ☐☐☐☐	☐☐ ☐☐	☐☐ ☐☐	☐☐☐☐☐ ☐☐☐☐☐ ☐	☐☐☐ ☐☐☐ ☐☐	Y N	Y N	Y N

WEATHER: SUN WIND RAIN CLOUDY SNOW   TEMP: ____

Distance: _____
Time: _____
Heart Rate: _____
i-Rate (1-10): _____
X-Training: _____
Sleep Hours: _____
Weight: _____
Mood: ☺ 😐 ☹ Other

SATURDAY / Date: _____   Training notes: _____

Today's goal: _____

FUEL LOG

WATER: 6-8 × 8 OZ.	FRUITS: 2-4	VEGGIES: 3-5	WHOLE GRAIN SERVINGS: 6-11	PROTEIN: 4-6 OZ.	LIMIT FAT?	ALCOHOLIC BEVERAGES?	LIMIT "EMPTY" CARBS?
☐☐☐☐ ☐☐☐☐	☐☐ ☐☐	☐☐ ☐☐	☐☐☐☐☐ ☐☐☐☐☐ ☐	☐☐☐ ☐☐☐ ☐☐	Y N	Y N	Y N

WEATHER: SUN WIND RAIN CLOUDY SNOW   TEMP: ____

Distance: _____
Time: _____
Heart Rate: _____
i-Rate (1-10): _____
X-Training: _____
Sleep Hours: _____
Weight: _____
Mood: ☺ 😐 ☹ Other

SUNDAY / Date: _____   Training notes: _____

Today's goal: _____

FUEL LOG

WATER: 6-8 × 8 OZ.	FRUITS: 2-4	VEGGIES: 3-5	WHOLE GRAIN SERVINGS: 6-11	PROTEIN: 4-6 OZ.	LIMIT FAT?	ALCOHOLIC BEVERAGES?	LIMIT "EMPTY" CARBS?
☐☐☐☐ ☐☐☐☐	☐☐ ☐☐	☐☐ ☐☐	☐☐☐☐☐ ☐☐☐☐☐ ☐	☐☐☐ ☐☐☐ ☐☐	Y N	Y N	Y N

WEATHER: SUN WIND RAIN CLOUDY SNOW   TEMP: ____

Distance: _____
Time: _____
Heart Rate: _____
i-Rate (1-10): _____
X-Training: _____
Sleep Hours: _____
Weight: _____
Mood: ☺ 😐 ☹ Other

WEEK OF: _____

GOALS FOR WEEK: _____

WEEKLY TOTAL: _____

YEAR-TO-DATE TOTAL: _____

PENGUIN WORDS OF WISDOM

Many of us think that running is a matter of devising a plan, laying out goals and strategies, marking a course to reach our goal, and then sitting back and watching our dreams come true. It isn't. We have to create our course every day.

MONDAY / Date:

Training notes:

Today's goal:

FUEL LOG

WATER: 6-8 × 8 OZ.	FRUITS: 2-4	VEGGIES: 3-5	WHOLE GRAIN SERVINGS: 6-11	PROTEIN: 4-6 OZ.	LIMIT FAT?	ALCOHOLIC BEVERAGES?	LIMIT "EMPTY" CARBS?
☐☐☐☐ ☐☐☐☐	☐☐ ☐☐	☐☐☐	☐☐☐☐☐☐ ☐☐☐☐☐	☐☐☐ ☐☐☐	Y N	Y N	Y N

WEATHER:
SUN WIND
RAIN CLOUDY
SNOW
TEMP:_____

Distance:
Time:
Heart Rate:
i-Rate (1-10)
X-Training:
Sleep Hours:
Weight:
Mood: ☺ ☺ ☹ Other

TUESDAY / Date:

Training notes:

Today's goal:

FUEL LOG

WATER: 6-8 × 8 OZ.	FRUITS: 2-4	VEGGIES: 3-5	WHOLE GRAIN SERVINGS: 6-11	PROTEIN: 4-6 OZ.	LIMIT FAT?	ALCOHOLIC BEVERAGES?	LIMIT "EMPTY" CARBS?
☐☐☐☐ ☐☐☐☐	☐☐ ☐☐	☐☐☐	☐☐☐☐☐☐ ☐☐☐☐☐	☐☐☐ ☐☐☐	Y N	Y N	Y N

WEATHER:
SUN WIND
RAIN CLOUDY
SNOW
TEMP:_____

Distance:
Time:
Heart Rate:
i-Rate (1-10)
X-Training:
Sleep Hours:
Weight:
Mood: ☺ ☺ ☹ Other

WEDNESDAY / Date:

Training notes:

Today's goal:

FUEL LOG

WATER: 6-8 × 8 OZ.	FRUITS: 2-4	VEGGIES: 3-5	WHOLE GRAIN SERVINGS: 6-11	PROTEIN: 4-6 OZ.	LIMIT FAT?	ALCOHOLIC BEVERAGES?	LIMIT "EMPTY" CARBS?
☐☐☐☐ ☐☐☐☐	☐☐ ☐☐	☐☐☐	☐☐☐☐☐☐ ☐☐☐☐☐	☐☐☐ ☐☐☐	Y N	Y N	Y N

WEATHER:
SUN WIND
RAIN CLOUDY
SNOW
TEMP:_____

Distance:
Time:
Heart Rate:
i-Rate (1-10)
X-Training:
Sleep Hours:
Weight:
Mood: ☺ ☺ ☹ Other

THURSDAY / Date:

Training notes:

Today's goal:

FUEL LOG

WATER: 6-8 × 8 OZ.	FRUITS: 2-4	VEGGIES: 3-5	WHOLE GRAIN SERVINGS: 6-11	PROTEIN: 4-6 OZ.	LIMIT FAT?	ALCOHOLIC BEVERAGES?	LIMIT "EMPTY" CARBS?
☐☐☐☐ ☐☐☐☐	☐☐ ☐☐	☐☐☐	☐☐☐☐☐☐ ☐☐☐☐☐	☐☐☐ ☐☐☐	Y N	Y N	Y N

WEATHER:
SUN WIND
RAIN CLOUDY
SNOW
TEMP:_____

Distance:
Time:
Heart Rate:
i-Rate (1-10)
X-Training:
Sleep Hours:
Weight:
Mood: ☺ ☺ ☹ Other

FRIDAY / Date:

Today's goal:

Training notes: _____

FUEL LOG

WATER: 6-8 x 8 OZ.	FRUITS: 2-4	VEGGIES: 3-5	WHOLE GRAIN SERVINGS: 6-11	PROTEIN: 4-6 OZ.	LIMIT FAT?	ALCOHOLIC BEVERAGES?	LIMIT "EMPTY" CARBS?
☐☐☐☐ ☐☐☐☐	☐☐ ☐☐	☐☐☐ ☐☐	☐☐☐☐☐☐ ☐☐☐☐☐	☐☐☐ ☐☐☐	Y N	Y N	Y N

WEATHER: SUN WIND RAIN CLOUDY SNOW TEMP: _____

Distance:
Time:
Heart Rate:
i-Rate (1-10):
X-Training:
Sleep Hours:
Weight:
Mood: ☺ ☺ ☹ Other

SATURDAY / Date:

Today's goal:

Training notes: _____

FUEL LOG

WATER: 6-8 x 8 OZ.	FRUITS: 2-4	VEGGIES: 3-5	WHOLE GRAIN SERVINGS: 6-11	PROTEIN: 4-6 OZ.	LIMIT FAT?	ALCOHOLIC BEVERAGES?	LIMIT "EMPTY" CARBS?
☐☐☐☐ ☐☐☐☐	☐☐ ☐☐	☐☐☐ ☐☐	☐☐☐☐☐☐ ☐☐☐☐☐	☐☐☐ ☐☐☐	Y N	Y N	Y N

WEATHER: SUN WIND RAIN CLOUDY SNOW TEMP: _____

Distance:
Time:
Heart Rate:
i-Rate (1-10):
X-Training:
Sleep Hours:
Weight:
Mood: ☺ ☺ ☹ Other

SUNDAY / Date:

Today's goal:

Training notes: _____

FUEL LOG

WATER: 6-8 x 8 OZ.	FRUITS: 2-4	VEGGIES: 3-5	WHOLE GRAIN SERVINGS: 6-11	PROTEIN: 4-6 OZ.	LIMIT FAT?	ALCOHOLIC BEVERAGES?	LIMIT "EMPTY" CARBS?
☐☐☐☐ ☐☐☐☐	☐☐ ☐☐	☐☐☐ ☐☐	☐☐☐☐☐☐ ☐☐☐☐☐	☐☐☐ ☐☐☐	Y N	Y N	Y N

WEATHER: SUN WIND RAIN CLOUDY SNOW TEMP: _____

Distance:
Time:
Heart Rate:
i-Rate (1-10):
X-Training:
Sleep Hours:
Weight:
Mood: ☺ ☺ ☹ Other

WEEK OF:

GOALS FOR WEEK:

WEEKLY TOTAL: _____

YEAR-TO-DATE TOTAL:

PENGUIN WORDS OF WISDOM

It's important to have goals, but it's more important to be honest about what it takes to achieve them. It's important to assess yourself, to observe and even be critical of yourself.

MONDAY / Date:

Today's goal:

Training notes:

FUEL LOG

WATER: 6-8 x 8 OZ.	FRUITS: 2-4	VEGGIES: 3-5	WHOLE GRAIN SERVINGS: 6-11	PROTEIN: 4-6 OZ.	LIMIT FAT?	ALCOHOLIC BEVERAGES?	LIMIT "EMPTY" CARBS?
☐☐☐☐ ☐☐☐☐	☐☐ ☐☐	☐☐ ☐☐	☐☐☐☐☐ ☐☐☐☐☐☐	☐☐☐ ☐☐☐	Y N	Y N	Y N

WEATHER:
SUN   WIND
RAIN CLOUDY
SNOW
TEMP:_____

Distance:
Time:
Heart Rate:
i-Rate (1-10)
X-Training:
Sleep Hours:
Weight:
Mood: ☺ ☺ ☹

TUESDAY / Date:

Today's goal:

Training notes:

FUEL LOG

WATER: 6-8 x 8 OZ.	FRUITS: 2-4	VEGGIES: 3-5	WHOLE GRAIN SERVINGS: 6-11	PROTEIN: 4-6 OZ.	LIMIT FAT?	ALCOHOLIC BEVERAGES?	LIMIT "EMPTY" CARBS?
☐☐☐☐ ☐☐☐☐	☐☐ ☐☐	☐☐ ☐☐	☐☐☐☐☐ ☐☐☐☐☐☐	☐☐☐ ☐☐☐	Y N	Y N	Y N

WEATHER:
SUN   WIND
RAIN CLOUDY
SNOW
TEMP:_____

Distance:
Time:
Heart Rate:
i-Rate (1-10)
X-Training:
Sleep Hours:
Weight:
Mood: ☺ ☺ ☹

WEDNESDAY / Date:

Today's goal:

Training notes:

FUEL LOG

WATER: 6-8 x 8 OZ.	FRUITS: 2-4	VEGGIES: 3-5	WHOLE GRAIN SERVINGS: 6-11	PROTEIN: 4-6 OZ.	LIMIT FAT?	ALCOHOLIC BEVERAGES?	LIMIT "EMPTY" CARBS?
☐☐☐☐ ☐☐☐☐	☐☐ ☐☐	☐☐ ☐☐	☐☐☐☐☐ ☐☐☐☐☐☐	☐☐☐ ☐☐☐	Y N	Y N	Y N

WEATHER:
SUN   WIND
RAIN CLOUDY
SNOW
TEMP:_____

Distance:
Time:
Heart Rate:
i-Rate (1-10)
X-Training:
Sleep Hours:
Weight:
Mood: ☺ ☺ ☹

THURSDAY / Date:

Today's goal:

Training notes:

FUEL LOG

WATER: 6-8 x 8 OZ.	FRUITS: 2-4	VEGGIES: 3-5	WHOLE GRAIN SERVINGS: 6-11	PROTEIN: 4-6 OZ.	LIMIT FAT?	ALCOHOLIC BEVERAGES?	LIMIT "EMPTY" CARBS?
☐☐☐☐ ☐☐☐☐	☐☐ ☐☐	☐☐ ☐☐	☐☐☐☐☐ ☐☐☐☐☐☐	☐☐☐ ☐☐☐	Y N	Y N	Y N

WEATHER:
SUN   WIND
RAIN CLOUDY
SNOW
TEMP:_____

Distance:
Time:
Heart Rate:
i-Rate (1-10)
X-Training:
Sleep Hours:
Weight:
Mood: ☺ ☺ ☹ Other

FRIDAY / Date:

Training notes: _____

Today's goal: _____

FUEL LOG

WATER: 6-8 x 8 oz.	FRUITS: 2-4	VEGGIES: 3-5	WHOLE GRAIN SERVINGS: 6-11	PROTEIN: 4-6 oz.	LIMIT FAT?	ALCOHOLIC BEVERAGES?	LIMIT "EMPTY" CARBS?
☐☐☐☐ ☐☐☐☐	☐☐ ☐☐	☐☐☐ ☐☐	☐☐☐☐☐ ☐☐☐☐☐☐	☐☐☐ ☐☐☐	Y N	Y N	Y N

WEATHER: SUN WIND RAIN CLOUDY SNOW TEMP: _____

Distance: _____
Time: _____
Heart Rate: _____
i-Rate (1-10) _____
X-Training: _____
Sleep Hours: _____
Weight: _____
Mood: ☺ ☺ ☹ Other

SATURDAY / Date:

Training notes: _____

Today's goal: _____

FUEL LOG

WATER: 6-8 x 8 oz.	FRUITS: 2-4	VEGGIES: 3-5	WHOLE GRAIN SERVINGS: 6-11	PROTEIN: 4-6 oz.	LIMIT FAT?	ALCOHOLIC BEVERAGES?	LIMIT "EMPTY" CARBS?
☐☐☐☐ ☐☐☐☐	☐☐ ☐☐	☐☐☐ ☐☐	☐☐☐☐☐ ☐☐☐☐☐☐	☐☐☐ ☐☐☐	Y N	Y N	Y N

WEATHER: SUN WIND RAIN CLOUDY SNOW TEMP: _____

Distance: _____
Time: _____
Heart Rate: _____
i-Rate (1-10) _____
X-Training: _____
Sleep Hours: _____
Weight: _____
Mood: ☺ ☺ ☹ Other

SUNDAY / Date:

Training notes: _____

Today's goal: _____

FUEL LOG

WATER: 6-8 x 8 oz.	FRUITS: 2-4	VEGGIES: 3-5	WHOLE GRAIN SERVINGS: 6-11	PROTEIN: 4-6 oz.	LIMIT FAT?	ALCOHOLIC BEVERAGES?	LIMIT "EMPTY" CARBS?
☐☐☐☐ ☐☐☐☐	☐☐ ☐☐	☐☐☐ ☐☐	☐☐☐☐☐ ☐☐☐☐☐☐	☐☐☐ ☐☐☐	Y N	Y N	Y N

WEATHER: SUN WIND RAIN CLOUDY SNOW TEMP: _____

Distance: _____
Time: _____
Heart Rate: _____
i-Rate (1-10) _____
X-Training: _____
Sleep Hours: _____
Weight: _____
Mood: ☺ ☺ ☹ Other

WEEK OF:

GOALS FOR WEEK:

WEEKLY TOTAL: _____

YEAR-TO-DATE TOTAL: _____

PENGUIN WORDS OF WISDOM

Deciding to be a runner is only the first step. Actually being a runner is a daily commitment. It's running when you should and not running when you shouldn't.

MONDAY / Date:

Today's goal:

Training notes:

Distance:
Time:
Heart Rate:
i-Rate (1-10)
X-Training:
Sleep Hours:
Weight:
Mood: ☺ ☺ ☹ Other

WEATHER:
SUN WIND
RAIN CLOUDY
SNOW
TEMP:_____

FUEL LOG

WATER: 6-8 × 8 OZ.	FRUITS: 2-4	VEGGIES: 3-5	WHOLE GRAIN SERVINGS: 6-11	PROTEIN: 4-6 OZ.	LIMIT FAT?	ALCOHOLIC BEVERAGES?	LIMIT "EMPTY" CARBS?
☐☐☐☐ ☐☐☐☐	☐☐ ☐☐	☐☐☐ ☐☐	☐☐☐☐ ☐☐☐	☐☐☐ ☐☐	Y N	Y N	Y N

TUESDAY / Date:

Today's goal:

Training notes:

Distance:
Time:
Heart Rate:
i-Rate (1-10)
X-Training:
Sleep Hours:
Weight:
Mood: ☺ ☺ ☹ Other

WEATHER:
SUN WIND
RAIN CLOUDY
SNOW
TEMP:_____

FUEL LOG

WATER: 6-8 × 8 OZ.	FRUITS: 2-4	VEGGIES: 3-5	WHOLE GRAIN SERVINGS: 6-11	PROTEIN: 4-6 OZ.	LIMIT FAT?	ALCOHOLIC BEVERAGES?	LIMIT "EMPTY" CARBS?
☐☐☐☐ ☐☐☐☐	☐☐ ☐☐	☐☐☐ ☐☐	☐☐☐☐ ☐☐☐	☐☐☐ ☐☐	Y N	Y N	Y N

WEDNESDAY / Date:

Today's goal:

Training notes:

Distance:
Time:
Heart Rate:
i-Rate (1-10)
X-Training:
Sleep Hours:
Weight:
Mood: ☺ ☺ ☹ Other

WEATHER:
SUN WIND
RAIN CLOUDY
SNOW
TEMP:_____

FUEL LOG

WATER: 6-8 × 8 OZ.	FRUITS: 2-4	VEGGIES: 3-5	WHOLE GRAIN SERVINGS: 6-11	PROTEIN: 4-6 OZ.	LIMIT FAT?	ALCOHOLIC BEVERAGES?	LIMIT "EMPTY" CARBS?
☐☐☐☐ ☐☐☐☐	☐☐ ☐☐	☐☐☐ ☐☐	☐☐☐☐ ☐☐☐	☐☐☐ ☐☐	Y N	Y N	Y N

THURSDAY / Date:

Today's goal:

Training notes:

Distance:
Time:
Heart Rate:
i-Rate (1-10)
X-Training:
Sleep Hours:
Weight:
Mood: ☺ ☺ ☹ Other

WEATHER:
SUN WIND
RAIN CLOUDY
SNOW
TEMP:_____

FUEL LOG

WATER: 6-8 × 8 OZ.	FRUITS: 2-4	VEGGIES: 3-5	WHOLE GRAIN SERVINGS: 6-11	PROTEIN: 4-6 OZ.	LIMIT FAT?	ALCOHOLIC BEVERAGES?	LIMIT "EMPTY" CARBS?
☐☐☐☐ ☐☐☐☐	☐☐ ☐☐	☐☐☐ ☐☐	☐☐☐☐ ☐☐☐	☐☐☐ ☐☐	Y N	Y N	Y N

FRIDAY / Date:

Training notes:

Distance:
Time:
Heart Rate:
i-Rate (1-10)
X-Training:
Sleep Hours:
Weight:
Mood: ☺ 😐 ☹ Other

WEATHER:
SUN WIND
RAIN CLOUDY
SNOW
TEMP:

FUEL LOG

WATER: 6-8 x 8 OZ.	FRUITS: 2-4	VEGGIES: 3-5	WHOLE GRAIN SERVINGS: 6-11	PROTEIN: 4-6 OZ.	LIMIT FAT?	ALCOHOLIC BEVERAGES?	LIMIT "EMPTY" CARBS?
☐☐☐☐ ☐☐☐☐	☐☐ ☐☐	☐☐☐ ☐☐	☐☐☐☐☐ ☐☐☐☐☐☐	☐☐☐ ☐☐☐	Y N	Y N	Y N

SATURDAY / Date:

Training notes:

Distance:
Time:
Heart Rate:
i-Rate (1-10)
X-Training:
Sleep Hours:
Weight:
Mood: ☺ 😐 ☹ Other

WEATHER:
SUN WIND
RAIN CLOUDY
SNOW
TEMP:

FUEL LOG

WATER: 6-8 x 8 OZ.	FRUITS: 2-4	VEGGIES: 3-5	WHOLE GRAIN SERVINGS: 6-11	PROTEIN: 4-6 OZ.	LIMIT FAT?	ALCOHOLIC BEVERAGES?	LIMIT "EMPTY" CARBS?
☐☐☐☐ ☐☐☐☐	☐☐ ☐☐	☐☐☐ ☐☐	☐☐☐☐☐ ☐☐☐☐☐	☐☐☐ ☐☐☐	Y N	Y N	Y N

SUNDAY / Date:

Training notes:

Distance:
Time:
Heart Rate:
i-Rate (1-10)
X-Training:
Sleep Hours:
Weight:
Mood: ☺ 😐 ☹ Other

WEATHER:
SUN WIND
RAIN CLOUDY
SNOW
TEMP:

FUEL LOG

WATER: 6-8 x 8 OZ.	FRUITS: 2-4	VEGGIES: 3-5	WHOLE GRAIN SERVINGS: 6-11	PROTEIN: 4-6 OZ.	LIMIT FAT?	ALCOHOLIC BEVERAGES?	LIMIT "EMPTY" CARBS?
☐☐☐☐ ☐☐☐☐	☐☐ ☐☐	☐☐☐ ☐☐	☐☐☐☐☐ ☐☐☐☐☐	☐☐☐ ☐☐☐	Y N	Y N	Y N

WEEK OF:

GOALS FOR WEEK:

WEEKLY TOTAL:

YEAR-TO-DATE TOTAL:

PENGUIN WORDS OF WISDOM

I am still astounded by what my body will allow me to do. I am still in awe that the heart and lungs that I took for granted can work together to permit me to run distances that I used to think were far to drive.

NOVEMBER

GIVING THANKS

One of the saddest moments I've ever seen is when someone finishing a race and then immediately beginning to criticize themselves and complain about their time. Unfortunately it happens all the time. You've seen it. A person crosses the finish line of a local 5K in 16 minutes and then explodes as they go through the chutes. They start screaming at the top of their lungs about how awful their race was, how terrible the run went, and how much harder they are going to have to work. Maybe if they saw how silly they look they wouldn't do it, but I doubt it.

Somehow it has escaped those runners that we are all, from the first to the last, very lucky to have the health and opportunity to get out and walk or run. Those complainers have completely missed the point that at any distance, at any pace, at any age, we—the active adults—are among a very select minority of the population. And, dare I say it, even the modestly talented like me are elites when compared to the average man or woman on the street. We should congratulate ourselves for our accomplishments, where ever they fall on the continuum of fast to slow.

We should also give thanks for our continued ability to train our fragile bodies, to clear our cloudy minds, and to reach for, find, and exceed our limits. We should never, not for one minute of one run, take for granted the privilege we have been granted. We should never come to believe that we are somehow entitled to fast or far. We are not. Every run, every step is a gift.

For one month, find some way of giving thanks for each and every run. It doesn't have to be an elaborate plan. It might be as simple as committing to donating a dollar to your favorite charity for every run you have, or deciding to donate your running shoes to a homeless shelter at the end of the month. It doesn't matter. Commit to something outside of yourself, outside of your running, and let running be the medium for being thankful.

My guess is that by the end of the month running will have become a greater joy for you than you could ever have imagined.

MONDAY / Date:

Today's goal:

Training notes:

Distance:
Time:
Heart Rate:
i-Rate (1-10)
X-Training:
Sleep Hours:
Weight:
Mood: ☺ ☺ ☹ Other

FUEL LOG

WATER: 6-8 x 8 OZ.	FRUITS: 2-4	VEGGIES: 3-5	WHOLE GRAIN SERVINGS: 6-11	PROTEIN: 4-6 OZ.	LIMIT FAT?	ALCOHOLIC BEVERAGES?	LIMIT "EMPTY" CARBS?
☐☐☐☐ ☐☐☐☐	☐☐ ☐☐	☐☐ ☐☐	☐☐☐ ☐☐☐ ☐☐	☐☐☐ ☐☐☐	Y N	Y N	Y N

WEATHER:
SUN WIND
RAIN CLOUDY
SNOW
TEMP: _____

TUESDAY / Date:

Today's goal:

Training notes:

Distance:
Time:
Heart Rate:
i-Rate (1-10)
X-Training:
Sleep Hours:
Weight:
Mood: ☺ ☺ ☹ Other

FUEL LOG

WATER: 6-8 x 8 OZ.	FRUITS: 2-4	VEGGIES: 3-5	WHOLE GRAIN SERVINGS: 6-11	PROTEIN: 4-6 OZ.	LIMIT FAT?	ALCOHOLIC BEVERAGES?	LIMIT "EMPTY" CARBS?
☐☐☐☐ ☐☐☐☐	☐☐ ☐☐	☐☐ ☐☐	☐☐☐ ☐☐☐ ☐☐	☐☐☐ ☐☐☐	Y N	Y N	Y N

WEATHER:
SUN WIND
RAIN CLOUDY
SNOW
TEMP: _____

WEDNESDAY / Date:

Today's goal:

Training notes:

Distance:
Time:
Heart Rate:
i-Rate (1-10)
X-Training:
Sleep Hours:
Weight:
Mood: ☺ ☺ ☹ Other

FUEL LOG

WATER: 6-8 x 8 OZ.	FRUITS: 2-4	VEGGIES: 3-5	WHOLE GRAIN SERVINGS: 6-11	PROTEIN: 4-6 OZ.	LIMIT FAT?	ALCOHOLIC BEVERAGES?	LIMIT "EMPTY" CARBS?
☐☐☐☐ ☐☐☐☐	☐☐ ☐☐	☐☐ ☐☐	☐☐☐ ☐☐☐ ☐☐	☐☐☐ ☐☐☐	Y N	Y N	Y N

WEATHER:
SUN WIND
RAIN CLOUDY
SNOW
TEMP: _____

THURSDAY / Date:

Today's goal:

Training notes:

Distance:
Time:
Heart Rate:
i-Rate (1-10)
X-Training:
Sleep Hours:
Weight:
Mood: ☺ ☺ ☹ Other

FUEL LOG

WATER: 6-8 x 8 OZ.	FRUITS: 2-4	VEGGIES: 3-5	WHOLE GRAIN SERVINGS: 6-11	PROTEIN: 4-6 OZ.	LIMIT FAT?	ALCOHOLIC BEVERAGES?	LIMIT "EMPTY" CARBS?
☐☐☐☐ ☐☐☐☐	☐☐ ☐☐	☐☐ ☐☐	☐☐☐ ☐☐☐ ☐☐	☐☐☐ ☐☐☐	Y N	Y N	Y N

WEATHER:
SUN WIND
RAIN CLOUDY
SNOW
TEMP: _____

FRIDAY / Date:

Today's goal:

Training notes:

FUEL LOG

WATER: 6-8 x 8 OZ.	FRUITS: 2-4	VEGGIES: 3-5	WHOLE GRAIN SERVINGS: 6-11	PROTEIN: 4-6 OZ.	LIMIT FAT?	ALCOHOLIC BEVERAGES?	LIMIT "EMPTY" CARBS?
☐☐☐☐ ☐☐☐☐	☐☐ ☐☐	☐☐☐ ☐☐	☐☐☐☐☐☐ ☐☐☐☐☐	☐☐☐ ☐☐☐	Y N	Y N	Y N

WEATHER: SUN   WIND   RAIN   CLOUDY   SNOW   TEMP: _____

Distance:
Time:
Heart Rate:
i-Rate (1-10)
X-Training:
Sleep Hours:
Weight:
Mood: ☺ ☺ ☹ ☹ Other

SATURDAY / Date:

Today's goal:

Training notes:

FUEL LOG

WATER: 6-8 x 8 OZ.	FRUITS: 2-4	VEGGIES: 3-5	WHOLE GRAIN SERVINGS: 6-11	PROTEIN: 4-6 OZ.	LIMIT FAT?	ALCOHOLIC BEVERAGES?	LIMIT "EMPTY" CARBS?
☐☐☐☐ ☐☐☐☐	☐☐ ☐☐	☐☐☐ ☐☐	☐☐☐☐☐☐ ☐☐☐☐☐	☐☐☐ ☐☐☐	Y N	Y N	Y N

WEATHER: SUN   WIND   RAIN   CLOUDY   SNOW   TEMP: _____

Distance:
Time:
Heart Rate:
i-Rate (1-10)
X-Training:
Sleep Hours:
Weight:
Mood: ☺ ☺ ☹ ☹ Other

SUNDAY / Date:

Today's goal:

Training notes:

FUEL LOG

WATER: 6-8 x 8 OZ.	FRUITS: 2-4	VEGGIES: 3-5	WHOLE GRAIN SERVINGS: 6-11	PROTEIN: 4-6 OZ.	LIMIT FAT?	ALCOHOLIC BEVERAGES?	LIMIT "EMPTY" CARBS?
☐☐☐☐ ☐☐☐☐	☐☐ ☐☐	☐☐☐ ☐☐	☐☐☐☐☐☐ ☐☐☐☐☐	☐☐☐ ☐☐☐	Y N	Y N	Y N

WEATHER: SUN   WIND   RAIN   CLOUDY   SNOW   TEMP: _____

Distance:
Time:
Heart Rate:
i-Rate (1-10)
X-Training:
Sleep Hours:
Weight:
Mood: ☺ ☺ ☹ ☹ Other

WEEK OF:

GOALS FOR WEEK:

WEEKLY TOTAL: _____

YEAR-TO-DATE TOTAL:

PENGUIN WORDS OF WISDOM

Letting go of the past and not worrying about the future seems a small price to pay for all the happiness of the present.

MONDAY / Date:

Today's goal:

Training notes:

Distance:
Time:
Heart Rate:
i-Rate (1-10)
X-Training:
Sleep Hours:
Weight:
Mood: ☺ ☺ ☹ ☹ Other

WEATHER:
SUN WIND
RAIN CLOUDY
SNOW
TEMP: _____

FUEL LOG

WATER: 6-8 x 8 OZ.	FRUITS: 2-4	VEGGIES: 3-5	WHOLE GRAIN SERVINGS: 6-11	PROTEIN: 4-6 OZ.	LIMIT FAT?	ALCOHOLIC BEVERAGES?	LIMIT "EMPTY" CARBS?
☐☐☐☐ ☐☐☐☐	☐☐ ☐☐	☐☐☐ ☐☐	☐☐☐☐ ☐☐☐☐☐	☐☐☐ ☐☐☐	Y N	Y N	Y N

TUESDAY / Date:

Today's goal:

Training notes:

Distance:
Time:
Heart Rate:
i-Rate (1-10)
X-Training:
Sleep Hours:
Weight:
Mood: ☺ ☺ ☹ ☹ Other

WEATHER:
SUN WIND
RAIN CLOUDY
SNOW
TEMP: _____

FUEL LOG

WATER: 6-8 x 8 OZ.	FRUITS: 2-4	VEGGIES: 3-5	WHOLE GRAIN SERVINGS: 6-11	PROTEIN: 4-6 OZ.	LIMIT FAT?	ALCOHOLIC BEVERAGES?	LIMIT "EMPTY" CARBS?
☐☐☐☐ ☐☐☐☐	☐☐ ☐☐	☐☐☐ ☐☐	☐☐☐☐ ☐☐☐☐☐	☐☐☐ ☐☐☐	Y N	Y N	Y N

WEDNESDAY / Date:

Today's goal:

Training notes:

Distance:
Time:
Heart Rate:
i-Rate (1-10)
X-Training:
Sleep Hours:
Weight:
Mood: ☺ ☺ ☹ ☹ Other

WEATHER:
SUN WIND
RAIN CLOUDY
SNOW
TEMP: _____

FUEL LOG

WATER: 6-8 x 8 OZ.	FRUITS: 2-4	VEGGIES: 3-5	WHOLE GRAIN SERVINGS: 6-11	PROTEIN: 4-6 OZ.	LIMIT FAT?	ALCOHOLIC BEVERAGES?	LIMIT "EMPTY" CARBS?
☐☐☐☐ ☐☐☐☐	☐☐ ☐☐	☐☐☐ ☐☐	☐☐☐☐ ☐☐☐☐☐	☐☐☐ ☐☐☐	Y N	Y N	Y N

THURSDAY / Date:

Today's goal:

Training notes:

Distance:
Time:
Heart Rate:
i-Rate (1-10)
X-Training:
Sleep Hours:
Weight:
Mood: ☺ ☺ ☹ ☹ Other

WEATHER:
SUN WIND
RAIN CLOUDY
SNOW
TEMP: _____

FUEL LOG

WATER: 6-8 x 8 OZ.	FRUITS: 2-4	VEGGIES: 3-5	WHOLE GRAIN SERVINGS: 6-11	PROTEIN: 4-6 OZ.	LIMIT FAT?	ALCOHOLIC BEVERAGES?	LIMIT "EMPTY" CARBS?
☐☐☐☐ ☐☐☐☐	☐☐ ☐☐	☐☐☐ ☐☐	☐☐☐☐ ☐☐☐☐☐	☐☐☐ ☐☐☐	Y N	Y N	Y N

FRIDAY / Date:

Today's goal:

Training notes:

FUEL LOG

WATER: 6-8 × 8 OZ.	FRUITS: 2-4	VEGGIES: 3-5	WHOLE GRAIN SERVINGS: 6-11	PROTEIN: 4-6 OZ.	LIMIT FAT?	ALCOHOLIC BEVERAGES?	LIMIT "EMPTY" CARBS?
☐☐☐ ☐☐☐	☐☐ ☐☐	☐☐ ☐	☐☐☐☐ ☐☐☐	☐☐☐ ☐☐	Y N	Y N	Y N

WEATHER:
SUN WIND
RAIN CLOUDY
SNOW
TEMP: ___

Distance:
Time:
Heart Rate:
i-Rate (1-10)
X-Training:
Sleep Hours:
Weight:
Mood: ☺ ☺ ☹ Other

SATURDAY / Date:

Today's goal:

Training notes:

FUEL LOG

WATER: 6-8 × 8 OZ.	FRUITS: 2-4	VEGGIES: 3-5	WHOLE GRAIN SERVINGS: 6-11	PROTEIN: 4-6 OZ.	LIMIT FAT?	ALCOHOLIC BEVERAGES?	LIMIT "EMPTY" CARBS?
☐☐☐ ☐☐☐	☐☐ ☐☐	☐☐ ☐	☐☐☐☐ ☐☐☐	☐☐☐ ☐☐	Y N	Y N	Y N

WEATHER:
SUN WIND
RAIN CLOUDY
SNOW
TEMP: ___

Distance:
Time:
Heart Rate:
i-Rate (1-10)
X-Training:
Sleep Hours:
Weight:
Mood: ☺ ☺ ☹ Other

SUNDAY / Date:

Today's goal:

Training notes:

FUEL LOG

WATER: 6-8 × 8 OZ.	FRUITS: 2-4	VEGGIES: 3-5	WHOLE GRAIN SERVINGS: 6-11	PROTEIN: 4-6 OZ.	LIMIT FAT?	ALCOHOLIC BEVERAGES?	LIMIT "EMPTY" CARBS?
☐☐☐ ☐☐☐	☐☐ ☐☐	☐☐ ☐	☐☐☐☐ ☐☐☐	☐☐☐ ☐☐	Y N	Y N	Y N

WEATHER:
SUN WIND
RAIN CLOUDY
SNOW
TEMP: ___

Distance:
Time:
Heart Rate:
i-Rate (1-10)
X-Training:
Sleep Hours:
Weight:
Mood: ☺ ☺ ☹ Other

WEEK OF:

GOALS FOR WEEK:

WEEKLY TOTAL: _____

YEAR-TO-DATE TOTAL:

PENGUIN WORDS OF WISDOM

All of us who pin on a number understand that there will be times when we get a little too close to the flame. The passion that drives us to start can sometimes push us to continue even when we shouldn't.

MONDAY / Date:

Training notes:

Today's goal:

FUEL LOG

WATER: 6-8 x 8 OZ.	FRUITS: 2-4	VEGGIES: 3-5	WHOLE GRAIN SERVINGS: 6-11	PROTEIN: 4-6 OZ.	LIMIT FAT?	ALCOHOLIC BEVERAGES?	LIMIT "EMPTY" CARBS?
☐☐☐☐ ☐☐☐☐	☐☐ ☐☐	☐☐ ☐☐	☐☐☐☐☐☐ ☐	☐☐☐ ☐☐	Y N	Y N	Y N

WEATHER:
SUN WIND
RAIN CLOUDY
SNOW
TEMP:_____

Distance:
Time:
Heart Rate:
i-Rate (1-10)
X-Training:
Sleep Hours:
Weight:
Mood: ☺ ☺ ☹ ☹ Other

TUESDAY / Date:

Training notes:

Today's goal:

FUEL LOG

WATER: 6-8 x 8 OZ.	FRUITS: 2-4	VEGGIES: 3-5	WHOLE GRAIN SERVINGS: 6-11	PROTEIN: 4-6 OZ.	LIMIT FAT?	ALCOHOLIC BEVERAGES?	LIMIT "EMPTY" CARBS?
☐☐☐☐ ☐☐☐☐	☐☐ ☐☐	☐☐ ☐☐	☐☐☐ ☐☐☐ ☐	☐☐☐ ☐☐	Y N	Y N	Y N

WEATHER:
SUN WIND
RAIN CLOUDY
SNOW
TEMP:_____

Distance:
Time:
Heart Rate:
i-Rate (1-10)
X-Training:
Sleep Hours:
Weight:
Mood: ☺ ☺ ☹ ☹ Other

WEDNESDAY / Date:

Training notes:

Today's goal:

FUEL LOG

WATER: 6-8 x 8 OZ.	FRUITS: 2-4	VEGGIES: 3-5	WHOLE GRAIN SERVINGS: 6-11	PROTEIN: 4-6 OZ.	LIMIT FAT?	ALCOHOLIC BEVERAGES?	LIMIT "EMPTY" CARBS?
☐☐☐☐ ☐☐☐☐	☐☐ ☐☐	☐☐ ☐☐	☐☐☐ ☐☐☐ ☐	☐☐☐ ☐☐	Y N	Y N	Y N

WEATHER:
SUN WIND
RAIN CLOUDY
SNOW
TEMP:_____

Distance:
Time:
Heart Rate:
i-Rate (1-10)
X-Training:
Sleep Hours:
Weight:
Mood: ☺ ☺ ☹ ☹ Other

THURSDAY / Date:

Today's goal:

Training notes:

FUEL LOG

WATER: 6-8 x 8 OZ.	FRUITS: 2-4	VEGGIES: 3-5	WHOLE GRAIN SERVINGS: 6-11	PROTEIN: 4-6 OZ.	LIMIT FAT?	ALCOHOLIC BEVERAGES?	LIMIT "EMPTY" CARBS?
☐☐☐☐ ☐☐☐☐	☐☐ ☐☐	☐☐ ☐☐	☐☐☐ ☐☐☐ ☐	☐☐☐ ☐☐	Y N	Y N	Y N

WEATHER:
SUN WIND
RAIN CLOUDY
SNOW
TEMP:_____

Distance:
Time:
Heart Rate:
i-Rate (1-10)
X-Training:
Sleep Hours:
Weight:
Mood: ☺ ☺ ☹ ☹ Other

FRIDAY / Date:

Today's goal:

Training notes:

FUEL LOG

WATER: 6-8 × 8 OZ.	FRUITS: 2-4	VEGGIES: 3-5	WHOLE GRAIN SERVINGS: 6-11	PROTEIN: 4-6 OZ.	LIMIT FAT?	ALCOHOLIC BEVERAGES?	LIMIT "EMPTY" CARBS?
☐☐☐☐ ☐☐☐☐	☐☐ ☐☐	☐☐ ☐☐	☐☐☐☐ ☐☐☐☐ ☐☐☐	☐☐☐ ☐☐☐	Y N	Y N	Y N

WEATHER: SUN WIND RAIN CLOUDY SNOW   TEMP: ____

Distance:
Time:
Heart Rate:
i-Rate (1-10):
X-Training:
Sleep Hours:
Weight:
Mood: ☺ ☺ ☹ Other

SATURDAY / Date:

Today's goal:

Training notes:

FUEL LOG

WATER: 6-8 × 8 OZ.	FRUITS: 2-4	VEGGIES: 3-5	WHOLE GRAIN SERVINGS: 6-11	PROTEIN: 4-6 OZ.	LIMIT FAT?	ALCOHOLIC BEVERAGES?	LIMIT "EMPTY" CARBS?
☐☐☐☐ ☐☐☐☐	☐☐ ☐☐	☐☐ ☐☐	☐☐☐☐ ☐☐☐☐ ☐☐☐	☐☐☐ ☐☐☐	Y N	Y N	Y N

WEATHER: SUN WIND RAIN CLOUDY SNOW   TEMP: ____

Distance:
Time:
Heart Rate:
i-Rate (1-10):
X-Training:
Sleep Hours:
Weight:
Mood: ☺ ☺ ☹ Other

SUNDAY / Date:

Today's goal:

Training notes:

FUEL LOG

WATER: 6-8 × 8 OZ.	FRUITS: 2-4	VEGGIES: 3-5	WHOLE GRAIN SERVINGS: 6-11	PROTEIN: 4-6 OZ.	LIMIT FAT?	ALCOHOLIC BEVERAGES?	LIMIT "EMPTY" CARBS?
☐☐☐☐ ☐☐☐☐	☐☐ ☐☐	☐☐ ☐☐	☐☐☐☐ ☐☐☐☐ ☐☐☐	☐☐☐ ☐☐☐	Y N	Y N	Y N

WEATHER: SUN WIND RAIN CLOUDY SNOW   TEMP: ____

Distance:
Time:
Heart Rate:
i-Rate (1-10):
X-Training:
Sleep Hours:
Weight:
Mood: ☺ ☺ ☹ Other

WEEK OF:

GOALS FOR WEEK:

WEEKLY TOTAL: _____

YEAR-TO-DATE TOTAL:

PENGUIN WORDS OF WISDOM

We must search for the limits of our body and demand that our spirit not give up on us. We've got to take what we've got and make the most out of it. We make ourselves athletes one workout at a time.

MONDAY / Date:

Training notes: _____

Today's goal: _____

Distance: _____
Time: _____
Heart Rate: _____
i-Rate (1-10) _____
X-Training: _____
Sleep Hours: _____
Weight: _____
Mood: ☺ ☺ ☹ ☹ Other

FUEL LOG

WATER: 6-8 × 8 OZ.	FRUITS: 2-4	VEGGIES: 3-5	WHOLE GRAIN SERVINGS: 6-11	PROTEIN: 4-6 OZ.	LIMIT FAT?	ALCOHOLIC BEVERAGES?	LIMIT "EMPTY" CARBS?	WEATHER:
☐☐☐ ☐☐☐ ☐☐	☐☐ ☐☐	☐☐ ☐☐	☐☐☐ ☐☐☐ ☐☐	☐☐ ☐☐	Y N	Y N	Y N	SUN WIND RAIN CLOUDY SNOW TEMP:___

TUESDAY / Date:

Training notes: _____

Today's goal: _____

Distance: _____
Time: _____
Heart Rate: _____
i-Rate (1-10) _____
X-Training: _____
Sleep Hours: _____
Weight: _____
Mood: ☺ ☺ ☹ ☹ Other

FUEL LOG

WATER: 6-8 × 8 OZ.	FRUITS: 2-4	VEGGIES: 3-5	WHOLE GRAIN SERVINGS: 6-11	PROTEIN: 4-6 OZ.	LIMIT FAT?	ALCOHOLIC BEVERAGES?	LIMIT "EMPTY" CARBS?	WEATHER:
☐☐☐ ☐☐☐ ☐☐	☐☐ ☐☐	☐☐ ☐☐	☐☐☐ ☐☐☐ ☐☐	☐☐ ☐☐	Y N	Y N	Y N	SUN WIND RAIN CLOUDY SNOW TEMP:___

WEDNESDAY / Date:

Training notes: _____

Today's goal: _____

Distance: _____
Time: _____
Heart Rate: _____
i-Rate (1-10) _____
X-Training: _____
Sleep Hours: _____
Weight: _____
Mood: ☺ ☺ ☹ ☹ Other

FUEL LOG

WATER: 6-8 × 8 OZ.	FRUITS: 2-4	VEGGIES: 3-5	WHOLE GRAIN SERVINGS: 6-11	PROTEIN: 4-6 OZ.	LIMIT FAT?	ALCOHOLIC BEVERAGES?	LIMIT "EMPTY" CARBS?	WEATHER:
☐☐☐ ☐☐☐ ☐☐	☐☐ ☐☐	☐☐ ☐☐	☐☐☐ ☐☐☐ ☐☐	☐☐ ☐☐	Y N	Y N	Y N	SUN WIND RAIN CLOUDY SNOW TEMP:___

THURSDAY / Date:

Training notes: _____

Today's goal: _____

Distance: _____
Time: _____
Heart Rate: _____
i-Rate (1-10) _____
X-Training: _____
Sleep Hours: _____
Weight: _____
Mood: ☺ ☺ ☹ ☹ Other

FUEL LOG

WATER: 6-8 × 8 OZ.	FRUITS: 2-4	VEGGIES: 3-5	WHOLE GRAIN SERVINGS: 6-11	PROTEIN: 4-6 OZ.	LIMIT FAT?	ALCOHOLIC BEVERAGES?	LIMIT "EMPTY" CARBS?	WEATHER:
☐☐☐ ☐☐☐ ☐☐	☐☐ ☐☐	☐☐ ☐☐	☐☐☐ ☐☐☐ ☐☐	☐☐ ☐☐	Y N	Y N	Y N	SUN WIND RAIN CLOUDY SNOW TEMP:___

FRIDAY / Date:

Today's goal:

Training notes:

FUEL LOG

WATER: 6-8 x 8 oz.	FRUITS: 2-4	VEGGIES: 3-5	WHOLE GRAIN SERVINGS: 6-11	PROTEIN: 4-6 oz.	LIMIT FAT?	ALCOHOLIC BEVERAGES?	LIMIT "EMPTY" CARBS?
☐☐☐☐ ☐☐☐☐	☐☐ ☐☐	☐☐ ☐	☐☐☐☐ ☐☐☐☐ ☐☐☐	☐☐☐ ☐☐	Y N	Y N	Y N

Distance:
Time:
Heart Rate:
i-Rate (1-10):
X-Training:
Sleep Hours:
Weight:
Mood: ☺ ☺ ☹ Other

WEATHER:
SUN WIND
RAIN CLOUDY
SNOW
TEMP:

SATURDAY / Date:

Today's goal:

Training notes:

FUEL LOG

WATER: 6-8 x 8 oz.	FRUITS: 2-4	VEGGIES: 3-5	WHOLE GRAIN SERVINGS: 6-11	PROTEIN: 4-6 oz.	LIMIT FAT?	ALCOHOLIC BEVERAGES?	LIMIT "EMPTY" CARBS?
☐☐☐☐ ☐☐☐☐	☐☐ ☐☐	☐☐ ☐	☐☐☐☐ ☐☐☐☐ ☐☐☐	☐☐☐ ☐☐	Y N	Y N	Y N

Distance:
Time:
Heart Rate:
i-Rate (1-10):
X-Training:
Sleep Hours:
Weight:
Mood: ☺ ☺ ☹ Other

WEATHER:
SUN WIND
RAIN CLOUDY
SNOW
TEMP:

SUNDAY / Date:

Today's goal:

Training notes:

FUEL LOG

WATER: 6-8 x 8 oz.	FRUITS: 2-4	VEGGIES: 3-5	WHOLE GRAIN SERVINGS: 6-11	PROTEIN: 4-6 oz.	LIMIT FAT?	ALCOHOLIC BEVERAGES?	LIMIT "EMPTY" CARBS?
☐☐☐☐ ☐☐☐☐	☐☐ ☐☐	☐☐ ☐	☐☐☐☐ ☐☐☐☐ ☐☐☐	☐☐☐ ☐☐	Y N	Y N	Y N

Distance:
Time:
Heart Rate:
i-Rate (1-10):
X-Training:
Sleep Hours:
Weight:
Mood: ☺ ☺ ☹ Other

WEATHER:
SUN WIND
RAIN CLOUDY
SNOW
TEMP:

WEEK OF:

GOALS FOR WEEK:

WEEKLY TOTAL:

YEAR-TO-DATE TOTAL:

PENGUIN WORDS OF WISDOM

In every race there is a defining moment. Nonrunners tend to think of that moment as being at the finish. More often, though, that moment occurs miles before the finish.

DECEMBER

HOLIDAY CHEER

Folks who know me well know that December is my favorite month of the year. In part, to be honest, it's because my birthday is in December. In fact, it's on December 13th if you want to mark it in your logbook so that you'll remember to send me a card! But December is special to me for more than just selfish reasons. December, for me, is a month of hope.

The shortest day of the calendar year is December 21, but I don't focus on the shortness of that day, I think about how great it is that December 22nd will be longer than the 21st. Every day brings just a little more light, a little more hope that the world is spinning and that the universe is in place and okay.

In Chicago, where I live, December nearly always means snow. It means that there will be days when the ground is white and, well, pure as the driven snow. On those days the world will glisten, at least for a little while. There will be days of bitter cold, but there will also be that occasional December day when, for no reason at all, the sun shines and the temperature rises to spring-like levels. Those days are more precious in December than in March because you know they won't last very long.

December is also a time when the cycle of life seems the clearest to me. I know, most people think it's Spring when the buds are on the trees and the flowers are just beginning to bloom. That's a part of the cycle, to be sure, but it's the most obvious. In December, as the frozen ground shelters the seeds of spring, the very earth seems to have hope. More than hope, the seeds have faith that there will be another spring.

As the rest of the world works through this period of hibernation I look to it as a time of renewal. I embrace the cold as the surest sign that I am alive. I can see my breath, I can see the sweat freezing on my shoulders, and I can hear the ground crunch under my feet.

In December I can bring the year to closure. I can look at what I've accomplished and know that it is whatever it is. Most likely I will not have accomplished all that I had hoped to twelve months earlier. I will not have run as fast as I wanted. I will not have run as far. I will not have always listened as carefully to my body as I would have liked. I will have had success and failures and joys and frustrations. In my running and in my life.

But as I pass by December 13th one more time, I know that I still have time left to get it right.

Waddle on, friends.

MONDAY / Date:

Today's goal: _____

Training notes: _____

_____

_____

FUEL LOG

WATER: 6-8 × 8 OZ.	FRUITS: 2-4	VEGGIES: 3-5	WHOLE GRAIN SERVINGS: 6-11	PROTEIN: 4-6 OZ.	LIMIT FAT?	ALCOHOLIC BEVERAGES?	LIMIT "EMPTY" CARBS?
☐☐☐☐ ☐☐☐☐	☐☐ ☐☐	☐☐☐ ☐☐	☐☐☐ ☐☐☐ ☐☐	☐☐ ☐☐ ☐☐	Y N	Y N	Y N

WEATHER: SUN WIND RAIN CLOUDY SNOW TEMP: ____

Distance: _____
Time: _____
Heart Rate: _____
i-Rate (1-10) _____
X-Training: _____
Sleep Hours: _____
Weight: _____
Mood: ☺ ☺ ☹ ☹ Other

TUESDAY / Date:

Today's goal: _____

Training notes: _____

_____

_____

FUEL LOG

WATER: 6-8 × 8 OZ.	FRUITS: 2-4	VEGGIES: 3-5	WHOLE GRAIN SERVINGS: 6-11	PROTEIN: 4-6 OZ.	LIMIT FAT?	ALCOHOLIC BEVERAGES?	LIMIT "EMPTY" CARBS?
☐☐☐☐ ☐☐☐☐	☐☐ ☐☐	☐☐☐ ☐☐	☐☐☐ ☐☐☐ ☐☐	☐☐ ☐☐ ☐☐	Y N	Y N	Y N

WEATHER: SUN WIND RAIN CLOUDY SNOW TEMP: ____

Distance: _____
Time: _____
Heart Rate: _____
i-Rate (1-10) _____
X-Training: _____
Sleep Hours: _____
Weight: _____
Mood: ☺ ☺ ☹ ☹ Other

WEDNESDAY / Date:

Today's goal: _____

Training notes: _____

_____

_____

FUEL LOG

WATER: 6-8 × 8 OZ.	FRUITS: 2-4	VEGGIES: 3-5	WHOLE GRAIN SERVINGS: 6-11	PROTEIN: 4-6 OZ.	LIMIT FAT?	ALCOHOLIC BEVERAGES?	LIMIT "EMPTY" CARBS?
☐☐☐☐ ☐☐☐☐	☐☐ ☐☐	☐☐☐ ☐☐	☐☐☐ ☐☐☐ ☐☐	☐☐ ☐☐ ☐☐	Y N	Y N	Y N

WEATHER: SUN WIND RAIN CLOUDY SNOW TEMP: ____

Distance: _____
Time: _____
Heart Rate: _____
i-Rate (1-10) _____
X-Training: _____
Sleep Hours: _____
Weight: _____
Mood: ☺ ☺ ☹ ☹ Other

THURSDAY / Date:

Today's goal: _____

Training notes: _____

_____

_____

FUEL LOG

WATER: 6-8 × 8 OZ.	FRUITS: 2-4	VEGGIES: 3-5	WHOLE GRAIN SERVINGS: 6-11	PROTEIN: 4-6 OZ.	LIMIT FAT?	ALCOHOLIC BEVERAGES?	LIMIT "EMPTY" CARBS?
☐☐☐☐ ☐☐☐☐	☐☐ ☐☐	☐☐☐ ☐☐	☐☐☐ ☐☐☐ ☐☐	☐☐ ☐☐ ☐☐	Y N	Y N	Y N

WEATHER: SUN WIND RAIN CLOUDY SNOW TEMP: ____

Distance: _____
Time: _____
Heart Rate: _____
i-Rate (1-10) _____
X-Training: _____
Sleep Hours: _____
Weight: _____
Mood: ☺ ☺ ☹ ☹ Other

FRIDAY / Date:

Training notes:

Today's goal:

FUEL LOG

WATER: 6-8 × 8 OZ.	FRUITS: 2-4	VEGGIES: 3-5	WHOLE GRAIN SERVINGS: 6-11	PROTEIN: 4-6 OZ.	LIMIT FAT?	ALCOHOLIC BEVERAGES?	LIMIT "EMPTY" CARBS?
☐☐☐☐ ☐☐☐☐	☐☐ ☐☐	☐☐ ☐	☐☐☐☐☐ ☐☐☐☐☐ ☐	☐☐☐ ☐☐	Y N	Y N	Y N

WEATHER:
SUN WIND
RAIN CLOUDY
SNOW
TEMP:_____

Distance:
Time:
Heart Rate:
i-Rate (1-10)
X-Training:
Sleep Hours:
Weight:
Mood: ☺ ☺ ☹ Other

SATURDAY / Date:

Training notes:

Today's goal:

FUEL LOG

WATER: 6-8 × 8 OZ.	FRUITS: 2-4	VEGGIES: 3-5	WHOLE GRAIN SERVINGS: 6-11	PROTEIN: 4-6 OZ.	LIMIT FAT?	ALCOHOLIC BEVERAGES?	LIMIT "EMPTY" CARBS?
☐☐☐☐ ☐☐☐☐	☐☐ ☐☐	☐☐ ☐	☐☐☐☐☐ ☐☐☐☐☐ ☐	☐☐☐ ☐☐	Y N	Y N	Y N

WEATHER:
SUN WIND
RAIN CLOUDY
SNOW
TEMP:_____

Distance:
Time:
Heart Rate:
i-Rate (1-10)
X-Training:
Sleep Hours:
Weight:
Mood: ☺ ☺ ☹ Other

SUNDAY / Date:

Training notes:

Today's goal:

FUEL LOG

WATER: 6-8 × 8 OZ.	FRUITS: 2-4	VEGGIES: 3-5	WHOLE GRAIN SERVINGS: 6-11	PROTEIN: 4-6 OZ.	LIMIT FAT?	ALCOHOLIC BEVERAGES?	LIMIT "EMPTY" CARBS?
☐☐☐☐ ☐☐☐☐	☐☐ ☐☐	☐☐ ☐	☐☐☐☐☐ ☐☐☐☐☐ ☐	☐☐☐ ☐☐	Y N	Y N	Y N

WEATHER:
SUN WIND
RAIN CLOUDY
SNOW
TEMP:_____

Distance:
Time:
Heart Rate:
i-Rate (1-10)
X-Training:
Sleep Hours:
Weight:
Mood: ☺ ☺ ☹ Other

WEEK OF:

GOALS FOR WEEK:

WEEKLY TOTAL: _____

YEAR-TO-DATE TOTAL:

PENGUIN WORDS OF WISDOM

What makes running a great sport is the untold acts of kindness performed by uncountable numbers of people, from race directors to sponsors to volunteers to the spectators.

MONDAY / Date:

Today's goal:

Training notes: _____

FUEL LOG

WATER: 6-8 × 8 OZ.	FRUITS: 2-4	VEGGIES: 3-5	WHOLE GRAIN SERVINGS: 6-11	PROTEIN: 4-6 OZ.	LIMIT FAT?	ALCOHOLIC BEVERAGES?	LIMIT "EMPTY" CARBS?
☐☐☐☐ ☐☐☐☐	☐☐ ☐☐	☐☐☐ ☐☐	☐☐☐☐☐ ☐	☐☐☐ ☐☐☐	Y N	Y N	Y N

WEATHER:
SUN WIND
RAIN CLOUDY
SNOW
TEMP: _____

Distance:
Time:
Heart Rate:
i-Rate (1-10)
X-Training:
Sleep Hours:
Weight:
Mood: ☺ ☺ ☹ Other____

TUESDAY / Date:

Today's goal:

Training notes: _____

FUEL LOG

WATER: 6-8 × 8 OZ.	FRUITS: 2-4	VEGGIES: 3-5	WHOLE GRAIN SERVINGS: 6-11	PROTEIN: 4-6 OZ.	LIMIT FAT?	ALCOHOLIC BEVERAGES?	LIMIT "EMPTY" CARBS?
☐☐☐☐ ☐☐☐☐	☐☐ ☐☐	☐☐☐ ☐☐	☐☐☐☐☐ ☐	☐☐☐ ☐☐☐	Y N	Y N	Y N

WEATHER:
SUN WIND
RAIN CLOUDY
SNOW
TEMP: _____

Distance:
Time:
Heart Rate:
i-Rate (1-10)
X-Training:
Sleep Hours:
Weight:
Mood: ☺ ☺ ☹ Other____

WEDNESDAY / Date:

Today's goal:

Training notes: _____

FUEL LOG

WATER: 6-8 × 8 OZ.	FRUITS: 2-4	VEGGIES: 3-5	WHOLE GRAIN SERVINGS: 6-11	PROTEIN: 4-6 OZ.	LIMIT FAT?	ALCOHOLIC BEVERAGES?	LIMIT "EMPTY" CARBS?
☐☐☐☐ ☐☐☐☐	☐☐ ☐☐	☐☐☐ ☐☐	☐☐☐☐☐ ☐	☐☐☐ ☐☐☐	Y N	Y N	Y N

WEATHER:
SUN WIND
RAIN CLOUDY
SNOW
TEMP: _____

Distance:
Time:
Heart Rate:
i-Rate (1-10)
X-Training:
Sleep Hours:
Weight:
Mood: ☺ ☺ ☹ Other____

THURSDAY / Date:

Today's goal:

Training notes: _____

FUEL LOG

WATER: 6-8 × 8 OZ.	FRUITS: 2-4	VEGGIES: 3-5	WHOLE GRAIN SERVINGS: 6-11	PROTEIN: 4-6 OZ.	LIMIT FAT?	ALCOHOLIC BEVERAGES?	LIMIT "EMPTY" CARBS?
☐☐☐☐ ☐☐☐☐	☐☐ ☐☐	☐☐☐ ☐☐	☐☐☐☐☐ ☐	☐☐☐ ☐☐☐	Y N	Y N	Y N

WEATHER:
SUN WIND
RAIN CLOUDY
SNOW
TEMP: _____

Distance:
Time:
Heart Rate:
i-Rate (1-10)
X-Training:
Sleep Hours:
Weight:
Mood: ☺ ☺ ☹ Other____

FRIDAY / Date:

Training notes: _____

Today's goal: _____

FUEL LOG

WATER: 6-8 x 8 OZ.	FRUITS: 2-4	VEGGIES: 3-5	WHOLE GRAIN SERVINGS: 6-11	PROTEIN: 4-6 OZ.	LIMIT FAT?	ALCOHOLIC BEVERAGES?	LIMIT "EMPTY" CARBS?
☐☐☐☐ ☐☐☐☐	☐☐ ☐☐	☐☐ ☐☐	☐☐☐☐☐ ☐☐☐☐☐ ☐	☐☐☐ ☐☐☐	Y N	Y N	Y N

WEATHER: SUN WIND RAIN CLOUDY SNOW TEMP: _____

- Distance:
- Time:
- Heart Rate:
- i-Rate (1-10):
- X-Training:
- Sleep Hours:
- Weight:
- Mood: ☺ ☺ ☹ ☹ Other

SATURDAY / Date:

Training notes: _____

Today's goal: _____

FUEL LOG

WATER: 6-8 x 8 OZ.	FRUITS: 2-4	VEGGIES: 3-5	WHOLE GRAIN SERVINGS: 6-11	PROTEIN: 4-6 OZ.	LIMIT FAT?	ALCOHOLIC BEVERAGES?	LIMIT "EMPTY" CARBS?
☐☐☐☐ ☐☐☐☐	☐☐ ☐☐	☐☐ ☐☐	☐☐☐☐☐ ☐☐☐☐☐ ☐	☐☐☐ ☐☐☐	Y N	Y N	Y N

WEATHER: SUN WIND RAIN CLOUDY SNOW TEMP: _____

- Distance:
- Time:
- Heart Rate:
- i-Rate (1-10):
- X-Training:
- Sleep Hours:
- Weight:
- Mood: ☺ ☺ ☹ ☹ Other

SUNDAY / Date:

Training notes: _____

Today's goal: _____

FUEL LOG

WATER: 6-8 x 8 OZ.	FRUITS: 2-4	VEGGIES: 3-5	WHOLE GRAIN SERVINGS: 6-11	PROTEIN: 4-6 OZ.	LIMIT FAT?	ALCOHOLIC BEVERAGES?	LIMIT "EMPTY" CARBS?
☐☐☐☐ ☐☐☐☐	☐☐ ☐☐	☐☐ ☐☐	☐☐☐☐☐ ☐☐☐☐☐ ☐	☐☐☐ ☐☐☐	Y N	Y N	Y N

WEATHER: SUN WIND RAIN CLOUDY SNOW TEMP: _____

- Distance:
- Time:
- Heart Rate:
- i-Rate (1-10):
- X-Training:
- Sleep Hours:
- Weight:
- Mood: ☺ ☺ ☹ ☹ Other

WEEK OF:

GOALS FOR WEEK:

PENGUIN WORDS OF WISDOM

It isn't the socks, the shoes, the clothes, or even the speed that makes me a runner. *It's the running.*

WEEKLY TOTAL: _____

YEAR-TO-DATE TOTAL:

MONDAY / Date: _____

Today's goal: _____

Training notes: _____

Distance: _____
Time: _____
Heart Rate: _____
i-Rate (1-10): _____
X-Training: _____
Sleep Hours: _____
Weight: _____
Mood: ☺ ☺ ☹ Other

FUEL LOG

WATER: 6-8 x 8 oz.	FRUITS: 2-4	VEGGIES: 3-5	WHOLE GRAIN SERVINGS: 6-11	PROTEIN: 4-6 oz.	LIMIT FAT?	ALCOHOLIC BEVERAGES?	LIMIT "EMPTY" CARBS?
☐☐☐☐ ☐☐☐☐	☐☐ ☐☐	☐☐☐ ☐☐	☐☐☐☐☐☐ ☐☐☐☐☐	☐☐☐ ☐☐☐	Y N	Y N	Y N

WEATHER:
SUN WIND
RAIN CLOUDY
SNOW
TEMP: _____

TUESDAY / Date: _____

Today's goal: _____

Training notes: _____

Distance: _____
Time: _____
Heart Rate: _____
i-Rate (1-10): _____
X-Training: _____
Sleep Hours: _____
Weight: _____
Mood: ☺ ☺ ☹ Other

FUEL LOG

WATER: 6-8 x 8 oz.	FRUITS: 2-4	VEGGIES: 3-5	WHOLE GRAIN SERVINGS: 6-11	PROTEIN: 4-6 oz.	LIMIT FAT?	ALCOHOLIC BEVERAGES?	LIMIT "EMPTY" CARBS?
☐☐☐☐ ☐☐☐☐	☐☐ ☐☐	☐☐☐ ☐☐	☐☐☐☐☐☐ ☐☐☐☐☐	☐☐☐ ☐☐☐	Y N	Y N	Y N

WEATHER:
SUN WIND
RAIN CLOUDY
SNOW
TEMP: _____

WEDNESDAY / Date: _____

Today's goal: _____

Training notes: _____

Distance: _____
Time: _____
Heart Rate: _____
i-Rate (1-10): _____
X-Training: _____
Sleep Hours: _____
Weight: _____
Mood: ☺ ☺ ☹ Other

FUEL LOG

WATER: 6-8 x 8 oz.	FRUITS: 2-4	VEGGIES: 3-5	WHOLE GRAIN SERVINGS: 6-11	PROTEIN: 4-6 oz.	LIMIT FAT?	ALCOHOLIC BEVERAGES?	LIMIT "EMPTY" CARBS?
☐☐☐☐ ☐☐☐☐	☐☐ ☐☐	☐☐☐ ☐☐	☐☐☐☐☐☐ ☐☐☐☐☐	☐☐☐ ☐☐☐	Y N	Y N	Y N

WEATHER:
SUN WIND
RAIN CLOUDY
SNOW
TEMP: _____

THURSDAY / Date: _____

Today's goal: _____

Training notes: _____

Distance: _____
Time: _____
Heart Rate: _____
i-Rate (1-10): _____
X-Training: _____
Sleep Hours: _____
Weight: _____
Mood: ☺ ☺ ☹ Other

FUEL LOG

WATER: 6-8 x 8 oz.	FRUITS: 2-4	VEGGIES: 3-5	WHOLE GRAIN SERVINGS: 6-11	PROTEIN: 4-6 oz.	LIMIT FAT?	ALCOHOLIC BEVERAGES?	LIMIT "EMPTY" CARBS?
☐☐☐☐ ☐☐☐☐	☐☐ ☐☐	☐☐☐ ☐☐	☐☐☐☐☐☐ ☐☐☐☐☐	☐☐☐ ☐☐☐	Y N	Y N	Y N

WEATHER:
SUN WIND
RAIN CLOUDY
SNOW
TEMP: _____

FRIDAY / Date:

Today's goal: _____

Training notes: _____

Distance: _____
Time: _____
Heart Rate: _____
i-Rate (1-10) _____
X-Training: _____
Sleep Hours: _____
Weight: _____
Mood: ☺ ☺ ☹ ☹ Other

FUEL LOG

WATER: 6-8 × 8 OZ.	FRUITS: 2-4	VEGGIES: 3-5	WHOLE GRAIN SERVINGS: 6-11	PROTEIN: 4-6 OZ.	LIMIT FAT?	ALCOHOLIC BEVERAGES?	LIMIT "EMPTY" CARBS?
☐☐☐☐ ☐☐☐☐	☐☐ ☐☐	☐☐☐ ☐☐	☐☐☐☐☐ ☐☐☐☐☐	☐☐☐ ☐☐☐	Y N	Y N	Y N

WEATHER: SUN WIND RAIN CLOUDY SNOW TEMP: _____

SATURDAY / Date:

Today's goal: _____

Training notes: _____

Distance: _____
Time: _____
Heart Rate: _____
i-Rate (1-10) _____
X-Training: _____
Sleep Hours: _____
Weight: _____
Mood: ☺ ☺ ☹ ☹ Other

FUEL LOG

WATER: 6-8 × 8 OZ.	FRUITS: 2-4	VEGGIES: 3-5	WHOLE GRAIN SERVINGS: 6-11	PROTEIN: 4-6 OZ.	LIMIT FAT?	ALCOHOLIC BEVERAGES?	LIMIT "EMPTY" CARBS?
☐☐☐☐ ☐☐☐☐	☐☐ ☐☐	☐☐☐ ☐☐	☐☐☐ ☐☐☐ ☐☐	☐☐☐ ☐☐☐	Y N	Y N	Y N

WEATHER: SUN WIND RAIN CLOUDY SNOW TEMP: _____

SUNDAY / Date:

Today's goal: _____

Training notes: _____

Distance: _____
Time: _____
Heart Rate: _____
i-Rate (1-10) _____
X-Training: _____
Sleep Hours: _____
Weight: _____
Mood: ☺ ☺ ☹ ☹ Other

FUEL LOG

WATER: 6-8 × 8 OZ.	FRUITS: 2-4	VEGGIES: 3-5	WHOLE GRAIN SERVINGS: 6-11	PROTEIN: 4-6 OZ.	LIMIT FAT?	ALCOHOLIC BEVERAGES?	LIMIT "EMPTY" CARBS?
☐☐☐☐ ☐☐☐☐	☐☐ ☐☐	☐☐☐ ☐☐	☐☐☐ ☐☐☐ ☐☐	☐☐☐ ☐☐☐	Y N	Y N	Y N

WEATHER: SUN WIND RAIN CLOUDY SNOW TEMP: _____

WEEK OF:

GOALS FOR WEEK:

WEEKLY TOTAL: _____

YEAR-TO-DATE TOTAL: _____

PENGUIN WORDS OF WISDOM

Some of us started running because nothing else eased the pain of living.

MONDAY / Date:

Today's goal:

Training notes:

FUEL LOG

WATER: 6-8 × 8 OZ.	FRUITS: 2-4	VEGGIES: 3-5	WHOLE GRAIN SERVINGS: 6-11	PROTEIN: 4-6 OZ.	LIMIT FAT?	ALCOHOLIC BEVERAGES?	LIMIT "EMPTY" CARBS?
☐☐☐☐ ☐☐☐☐	☐☐ ☐☐	☐☐ ☐	☐☐☐☐ ☐☐☐☐ ☐☐☐	☐☐☐ ☐☐☐	Y N	Y N	Y N

WEATHER: SUN WIND RAIN CLOUDY SNOW TEMP:___

Distance:
Time:
Heart Rate:
i-Rate (1-10)
X-Training:
Sleep Hours:
Weight:
Mood: ☺ ☺ ☹ Other

TUESDAY / Date:

Today's goal:

Training notes:

FUEL LOG

WATER: 6-8 × 8 OZ.	FRUITS: 2-4	VEGGIES: 3-5	WHOLE GRAIN SERVINGS: 6-11	PROTEIN: 4-6 OZ.	LIMIT FAT?	ALCOHOLIC BEVERAGES?	LIMIT "EMPTY" CARBS?
☐☐☐☐ ☐☐☐☐	☐☐ ☐☐	☐☐ ☐	☐☐☐☐ ☐☐☐☐ ☐☐☐	☐☐☐ ☐☐☐	Y N	Y N	Y N

WEATHER: SUN WIND RAIN CLOUDY SNOW TEMP:___

Distance:
Time:
Heart Rate:
i-Rate (1-10)
X-Training:
Sleep Hours:
Weight:
Mood: ☺ ☺ ☹ Other

WEDNESDAY / Date:

Today's goal:

Training notes:

FUEL LOG

WATER: 6-8 × 8 OZ.	FRUITS: 2-4	VEGGIES: 3-5	WHOLE GRAIN SERVINGS: 6-11	PROTEIN: 4-6 OZ.	LIMIT FAT?	ALCOHOLIC BEVERAGES?	LIMIT "EMPTY" CARBS?
☐☐☐☐ ☐☐☐☐	☐☐ ☐☐	☐☐ ☐	☐☐☐☐ ☐☐☐☐ ☐☐☐	☐☐☐ ☐☐☐	Y N	Y N	Y N

WEATHER: SUN WIND RAIN CLOUDY SNOW TEMP:___

Distance:
Time:
Heart Rate:
i-Rate (1-10)
X-Training:
Sleep Hours:
Weight:
Mood: ☺ ☺ ☹ Other

THURSDAY / Date:

Today's goal:

Training notes:

FUEL LOG

WATER: 6-8 × 8 OZ.	FRUITS: 2-4	VEGGIES: 3-5	WHOLE GRAIN SERVINGS: 6-11	PROTEIN: 4-6 OZ.	LIMIT FAT?	ALCOHOLIC BEVERAGES?	LIMIT "EMPTY" CARBS?
☐☐☐☐ ☐☐☐☐	☐☐ ☐☐	☐☐ ☐	☐☐☐☐ ☐☐☐☐ ☐☐☐	☐☐☐ ☐☐☐	Y N	Y N	Y N

WEATHER: SUN WIND RAIN CLOUDY SNOW TEMP:___

Distance:
Time:
Heart Rate:
i-Rate (1-10)
X-Training:
Sleep Hours:
Weight:
Mood: ☺ ☺ ☹ Other

FRIDAY / Date:

Today's goal:

Training notes:

Distance:
Time:
Heart Rate:
i-Rate (1-10)
X-Training:
Sleep Hours:
Weight:
Mood: ☺ ☺ ☺ ☹ Other

FUEL LOG

WATER: 6-8 × 8 OZ.	FRUITS: 2-4	VEGGIES: 3-5	WHOLE GRAIN SERVINGS: 6-11	PROTEIN: 4-6 OZ.	LIMIT FAT?	ALCOHOLIC BEVERAGES?	LIMIT "EMPTY" CARBS?
☐☐☐☐ ☐☐☐☐	☐☐ ☐☐	☐☐ ☐☐	☐☐☐☐☐ ☐☐☐☐	☐☐☐ ☐☐☐	Y N	Y N	Y N

WEATHER:
SUN WIND
RAIN CLOUDY
SNOW
TEMP:

SATURDAY / Date:

Today's goal:

Training notes:

Distance:
Time:
Heart Rate:
i-Rate (1-10)
X-Training:
Sleep Hours:
Weight:
Mood: ☺ ☺ ☺ ☹ Other

FUEL LOG

WATER: 6-8 × 8 OZ.	FRUITS: 2-4	VEGGIES: 3-5	WHOLE GRAIN SERVINGS: 6-11	PROTEIN: 4-6 OZ.	LIMIT FAT?	ALCOHOLIC BEVERAGES?	LIMIT "EMPTY" CARBS?
☐☐☐☐ ☐☐☐☐	☐☐ ☐☐	☐☐ ☐☐	☐☐☐☐☐ ☐☐☐☐	☐☐☐ ☐☐☐	Y N	Y N	Y N

WEATHER:
SUN WIND
RAIN CLOUDY
SNOW
TEMP:

SUNDAY / Date:

Today's goal:

Training notes:

Distance:
Time:
Heart Rate:
i-Rate (1-10)
X-Training:
Sleep Hours:
Weight:
Mood: ☺ ☺ ☺ ☹ Other

FUEL LOG

WATER: 6-8 × 8 OZ.	FRUITS: 2-4	VEGGIES: 3-5	WHOLE GRAIN SERVINGS: 6-11	PROTEIN: 4-6 OZ.	LIMIT FAT?	ALCOHOLIC BEVERAGES?	LIMIT "EMPTY" CARBS?
☐☐☐☐ ☐☐☐☐	☐☐ ☐☐	☐☐ ☐☐	☐☐☐☐☐ ☐☐☐☐	☐☐☐ ☐☐☐	Y N	Y N	Y N

WEATHER:
SUN WIND
RAIN CLOUDY
SNOW
TEMP:

WEEK OF:

GOALS FOR WEEK:

WEEKLY TOTAL:

YEAR-TO-DATE TOTAL:

PENGUIN WORDS OF WISDOM

In the absence of talent, there is no substitute for preparation.

MONDAY / Date:

Today's goal:

Training notes:

| Distance: |
| Time: |
| Heart Rate: |
| i-Rate (1-10) |
| X-Training: |
| Sleep Hours: |
| Weight: |
| Mood: ☺ ☺ ☹ Other |

FUEL LOG

WATER: 6-8 x 8 OZ.	FRUITS: 2-4	VEGGIES: 3-5	WHOLE GRAIN SERVINGS: 6-11	PROTEIN: 4-6 OZ.	LIMIT FAT?	ALCOHOLIC BEVERAGES?	LIMIT "EMPTY" CARBS?
☐☐☐☐ ☐☐☐☐	☐☐ ☐☐	☐☐☐ ☐☐	☐☐☐☐☐ ☐	☐☐☐ ☐☐☐	Y N	Y N	Y N

WEATHER: SUN WIND RAIN CLOUDY SNOW TEMP:_____

TUESDAY / Date:

Today's goal:

Training notes:

| Distance: |
| Time: |
| Heart Rate: |
| i-Rate (1-10) |
| X-Training: |
| Sleep Hours: |
| Weight: |
| Mood: ☺ ☺ ☹ Other |

FUEL LOG

WATER: 6-8 x 8 OZ.	FRUITS: 2-4	VEGGIES: 3-5	WHOLE GRAIN SERVINGS: 6-11	PROTEIN: 4-6 OZ.	LIMIT FAT?	ALCOHOLIC BEVERAGES?	LIMIT "EMPTY" CARBS?
☐☐☐☐ ☐☐☐☐	☐☐ ☐☐	☐☐☐ ☐☐	☐☐☐☐☐ ☐	☐☐☐ ☐☐☐	Y N	Y N	Y N

WEATHER: SUN WIND RAIN CLOUDY SNOW TEMP:_____

WEDNESDAY / Date:

Today's goal:

Training notes:

| Distance: |
| Time: |
| Heart Rate: |
| i-Rate (1-10) |
| X-Training: |
| Sleep Hours: |
| Weight: |
| Mood: ☺ ☺ ☹ Other |

FUEL LOG

WATER: 6-8 x 8 OZ.	FRUITS: 2-4	VEGGIES: 3-5	WHOLE GRAIN SERVINGS: 6-11	PROTEIN: 4-6 OZ.	LIMIT FAT?	ALCOHOLIC BEVERAGES?	LIMIT "EMPTY" CARBS?
☐☐☐☐ ☐☐☐☐	☐☐ ☐☐	☐☐☐ ☐☐	☐☐☐☐☐ ☐	☐☐☐ ☐☐☐	Y N	Y N	Y N

WEATHER: SUN WIND RAIN CLOUDY SNOW TEMP:_____

THURSDAY / Date:

Today's goal:

Training notes:

| Distance: |
| Time: |
| Heart Rate: |
| i-Rate (1-10) |
| X-Training: |
| Sleep Hours: |
| Weight: |
| Mood: ☺ ☺ ☹ Other |

FUEL LOG

WATER: 6-8 x 8 OZ.	FRUITS: 2-4	VEGGIES: 3-5	WHOLE GRAIN SERVINGS: 6-11	PROTEIN: 4-6 OZ.	LIMIT FAT?	ALCOHOLIC BEVERAGES?	LIMIT "EMPTY" CARBS?
☐☐☐☐ ☐☐☐☐	☐☐ ☐☐	☐☐☐ ☐☐	☐☐☐☐☐ ☐	☐☐☐ ☐☐☐	Y N	Y N	Y N

WEATHER: SUN WIND RAIN CLOUDY SNOW TEMP:_____

FRIDAY / Date:

Training notes: _____

Today's goal: _____

FUEL LOG

WATER: 6-8 × 8 OZ.	FRUITS: 2-4	VEGGIES: 3-5	WHOLE GRAIN SERVINGS: 6-11	PROTEIN: 4-6 OZ.	LIMIT FAT?	ALCOHOLIC BEVERAGES?	LIMIT "EMPTY" CARBS?
☐☐☐☐ ☐☐☐☐	☐☐ ☐☐	☐☐☐ ☐☐	☐☐☐☐☐ ☐☐☐☐☐☐	☐☐☐ ☐☐☐	Y N	Y N	Y N

Distance: _____
Time: _____
Heart Rate: _____
i-Rate (1-10) _____
X-Training: _____
Sleep Hours: _____
Weight: _____
Mood: ☺ ☺ ☺ ☹ Other

WEATHER:
SUN WIND
RAIN CLOUDY
SNOW
TEMP: ____

SATURDAY / Date:

Training notes: _____

Today's goal: _____

FUEL LOG

WATER: 6-8 × 8 OZ.	FRUITS: 2-4	VEGGIES: 3-5	WHOLE GRAIN SERVINGS: 6-11	PROTEIN: 4-6 OZ.	LIMIT FAT?	ALCOHOLIC BEVERAGES?	LIMIT "EMPTY" CARBS?
☐☐☐☐ ☐☐☐☐	☐☐ ☐☐	☐☐☐ ☐☐	☐☐☐☐☐ ☐☐☐☐☐☐	☐☐☐ ☐☐☐	Y N	Y N	Y N

Distance: _____
Time: _____
Heart Rate: _____
i-Rate (1-10) _____
X-Training: _____
Sleep Hours: _____
Weight: _____
Mood: ☺ ☺ ☺ ☹ Other

WEATHER:
SUN WIND
RAIN CLOUDY
SNOW
TEMP: ____

SUNDAY / Date:

Training notes: _____

Today's goal: _____

FUEL LOG

WATER: 6-8 × 8 OZ.	FRUITS: 2-4	VEGGIES: 3-5	WHOLE GRAIN SERVINGS: 6-11	PROTEIN: 4-6 OZ.	LIMIT FAT?	ALCOHOLIC BEVERAGES?	LIMIT "EMPTY" CARBS?
☐☐☐☐ ☐☐☐☐	☐☐ ☐☐	☐☐☐ ☐☐	☐☐☐☐☐ ☐☐☐☐☐☐	☐☐☐ ☐☐☐	Y N	Y N	Y N

Distance: _____
Time: _____
Heart Rate: _____
i-Rate (1-10) _____
X-Training: _____
Sleep Hours: _____
Weight: _____
Mood: ☺ ☺ ☺ ☹ Other

WEATHER:
SUN WIND
RAIN CLOUDY
SNOW
TEMP: ____

WEEK OF:

GOALS FOR WEEK:

WEEKLY TOTAL: _____

YEAR-TO-DATE TOTAL:

PENGUIN WORDS OF WISDOM

Postponing the joy of the journey until you reach your destination is the WORST possible plan. Waiting to celebrate until you've gotten to where you think you want to go means missing all the wonderful places that you pass on the way.

NOTES, GOALS, TRENDS

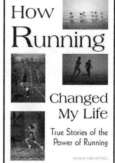

John "The Penguin" Bingham

He's been called the Pied Piper of the second running boom-and for good reason. Since his column, "The Chronicles," started in *Runner's World* magazine in 1996, John "The Penguin" Bingham has become one of the running community's most popular and recognized personalities.

Through his books and his *RW* column, now published in every English-language edition of *RW*, Bingham has inspired a generation of new runners to find joy in walking, running, and racing. His transformation from a life of "sedentary confinement" to marathoner has become a model for people of all ages and abilities.

Once an overweight couch potato, he looked midlife in the face—and got moving. Since then, he has participated in several dozen marathons and hundreds of 5K and 10K races.

Bingham says, "Through running, I create myself as I have always wanted to be. Nothing in my experience was as powerful as crossing the finish line of my first race. With that single step, I overcame a lifetime of unkept promises to myself." In a self-effacing and humorous manner, Bingham delivers his message of hope and inspiration to people who've been running for a week or a lifetime.

Coach Jenny Hadfield

Jenny Hadfield is a fitness expert, coach, and co-owner of Chicago Endurance Sports. She is best known for empowering people to move outside their self-perceived limits and reach for higher ground. More than just a coach, Jenny has become a trusted guide, mentor, and good friend on the journey to the finish line. She is known for her personal and comprehensive approach to training. Jenny has been coaching for over 10 years, is a Boston-qualified marathon runner and three-time Eco-Challenge competitor (the world's toughest endurance race). Jenny is the co-author of *Marathoning for Mortals: A Regular Person's Guide to the Joy of Walk and Running a Half and Full Marathon.*